S0-BZE-310

HATING
WOMEN

Also by Shmuley Boteach

Dreams

The Wolf Shall Lie with the Lamb

Wrestling with the Divine

Wisdom, Understanding, and Knowledge

Moses of Oxford, Volumes I and II

Kosher Sex

Dating Secrets of the Ten Commandments

Kosher Emotions

The Rabbi and the Psychic

Why Can't I Fall in Love

Judaism for Everyone

The Private Adam

Kosher Adultery

Face Your Fear

10 Conversations You Need to Have with Your Children

HATING WOMEN

AMERICA'S HOSTILE CAMPAIGN
AGAINST THE FAIRER SEX

SHMULEY BOTEACH

HARPER

NEW YORK · LONDON · TORONTO · SYDNEY

HARPER

A hardcover edition of this book was published in 2005 by HarperCollins Publishers.

HATING WOMEN. Copyright © 2005 by Shmuley Boteach. All rights reserved. Printed in the United States of America. No part of this book may be used or reproduced in any manner whatsoever without written permission except in the case of brief quotations embodied in critical articles and reviews. For information address HarperCollins Publishers, 10 East 53rd Street, New York, NY 10022.

HarperCollins books may be purchased for educational, business, or sales promotional use. For information please write: Special Markets Department, HarperCollins Publishers, 10 East 53rd Street, New York, NY 10022.

FIRST PAPERBACK EDITION PUBLISHED 2006.

Designed by Publications Development Company of Texas

The Library of Congress has cataloged the hardcover edition as follows:

Boteach, Shmuel.
  Hating women : America's hostile campaign against the
fairer sex / Shmuley Boteach.
1st ed.
New York : Regan Books, 2005—
ix, 326 p. ; 24 cm.
006078122X
HQ1421.B68 2005

2005046591

ISBN : 978-0-06-083415-9 (pbk.)

  12 13 14 15 RRD 10 9 8 7 6

To my five daughters
Chaya Mushka
Chana
Shterna Sarah
Shaina Brocha
Rochel Leah (Baba)
In the hope that we adults will bequeath to you
a world that values and feels enriched by women

CONTENTS

∽

PART ONE

**THE SHOCKING ASSAULT ON
THE AMERICAN WOMAN**

1 Fall of the Feminist Dream   3

2 Waking Up from the Misogynistic Nightmare   15

3 In a World without Ladies, There Cannot
Be Gentlemen   29

PART TWO

**THE NOBILITY ACCORDED
WOMEN IN AGES PAST**

4 Veneration for Women in Times Gone By   41

5 Disrespecting Women Is the Principal
Cause of the World's Devolution   51

6 The Line and the Circle: The Masculine and
Feminine Energies   61

PART THREE

**FORTY YEARS OF FEMINISM
ERASED IN A SINGLE DECADE**

7 An Unequal Equality   79

8 The Fall of Eve   87

9 Women Behaving Like Men   95

10 The Portrayal of Women as the Walking
Male Orgasm   99

11 Gentlemen Prefer Bimbos   105

12 The Musical "Axis of Evil"   109

13 Becoming Famous by Becoming Naked   121

14 The Wide World of Sports   133

15 A World of Veiled Women—Islam   137

16 Women as Nature's System of Checks
   and Balances   147

PART FOUR
THE TYRANNY OF THE BEAUTIFUL

17 The Assault on Ugly and Fat Women   153

18 A Crisis in Manhood   171

19 Husbands Have Lost Awe and Reverence
   for Their Wives   177

20 Turning Your Wife into the Cleaner   181

21 Fat Wives Have Their Husbands to Blame   191

22 Four Foul Archetypes of Women—Four
   Vulgar Archetypes of Men   197

23 Becoming Lesbians to Get Away from Men   207

24 Rise of the Platonic Lesbian   213

25 The New Manly Woman   217

26 Women as Healers   229

27 Losing the Healing Force   235

28 Gay Men as the World's Last Nurturers   239

29 Chivalry: An Acknowledgment of the
   Sanctity of Woman   243

PART FIVE
RESTORING WOMEN TO AN HONORED PLACE

30 Broadening the Pedestal: Learning to Be Successful
   without Being Ruthless   251

31 A Casual Sex Freeze-Out   257

32 The Twenty-first Century Lady: A Full
Brain versus a Well-Poised Cranium   263

33 Where Is Dad?   269

34 Education Edification—Taking the Sex Out
of Schooling   275

35 A More Mysterious Society   279

36 Can Men Respect Women in the Office if
They Are Conditioned to Be Perverts
Outside It?   283

37 Young Girls Should Have Healthier Outlets
than Shopping   287

38 Marriage Is Not "Sex on Tap" or
Legalized Prostitution   293

39 Younger Women Should Refrain from
Dating Much Older Men   303

40 Women Should Frown On Shallow Exhibitionists—
Not Defend Them   305

Acknowledgments   311

Index   313

PART
ONE

THE SHOCKING ASSAULT ON THE AMERICAN WOMAN

1

∽

FALL OF THE FEMINIST DREAM

As I watched President Bush deliver the 2005 State of the Union address, I experienced a redemptive sense of vindication. For years I had been hammering away, on radio, television, and in print, at the crisis of American manhood, manifested specifically in the growing male tendency to disrespect women. I was shocked at how the principal portrayal of women as empty, shallow, and sleazy vessels who just want men's cash, and who do anything for fame and publicity, including sleeping with complete strangers and taking their clothes off for celebrity, gradually became mainstream. I was likewise astonished at how no one seemed to care how this brutal portrayal was adversely affecting the respect men had for women. Then, smack in the middle of the most important political speech of the year, along with such pressing international priorities as holding Iran accountable for its desire to build nuclear weapons, President Bush suddenly announced that he had appointed his wife, Laura, to head a national effort to raise a new generation of American men who know how to respect women.

Now, with the country beginning to recognize the depth of the women-hating crisis among men, I want to welcome you to my world. I am the father of five young daughters, and I am deeply troubled by the world they are growing up to inhabit as women. It is a world that values a woman's bust over her brains, her body over her moral fiber, and her sexual nature over her soul and spirit. It is a world that increasingly diminishes a woman into the sum total of her bodily parts. It is a world where men routinely use the word *bitch*, and where women are portrayed as complacent playthings to lecherous men.

I have been stunned to see the growing misogyny in our culture, and I am even more shocked to see how little women seem to care about their degradation. Indeed, it is difficult to gauge what is more shocking: the rampant exploitation of women or the near complete silence and lack of protest about this alarming trend. And it is all happening so fast. Before one degrading TV show about women like *Joe Millionaire* or *For Love or Money* has run its course, ten even more degrading shows have sprung up to take its place.

This devolution in the portrayal of women in our culture is happening at warp speed, and there is no telling where it will end. As a young boy growing up in a religious home, I was raised to revere and respect women. I was taught that they were the fairer sex, more naturally dignified and gentler than men. Indeed, it took a woman to domesticate and ennoble a man, and in the thought of my Jewish tradition, this was why a wife was such a blessing to her husband. In the yeshivas where I studied to be a rabbi, I was taught that a woman is a reflection of the divine countenance, a more authentic reflection of the divine image than men. Part of my religious instruction was to recite King Solomon's "Ode to a Woman of Valor," the final chapter in Proverbs, which is sung to one's wife on the Sabbath, the holiest of days.

Even in the mainstream culture, women used to be portrayed as models of dignity and refinement, deserving of men's respect and veneration. The great movie actresses of Hollywood's Golden Age included such memorable ladies of the silver screen as Grace Kelly, Lauren Bacall, and Katharine Hepburn. The image of a woman was one of refinement and grace, intelligence and elegance, spirituality and strength. But all that is gone today, replaced by vulgar icons of bad taste and crude morals such as Britney Spears and Paris Hilton, arguably the two most famous female cultural icons in contemporary America.

As a father of five daughters, shocked and appalled by the sweeping change in female role models and our treatment of women in this culture, I have had a personal stake in understanding how and why this evolution has occurred. In truth, it does not take a rocket scientist or philosopher to see the influences that have helped create these mores that malign women. Instead of cultivating the image of woman as nurturer, helpmate, role model, and intellectual equal, we as a society have stooped to looking at women as objects to be used and abused. Women are depicted as pieces of meat to be devoured by the hungry eyes of licentious men. This is the essential picture of woman in the popular culture, and it is having a grave effect on how women are treated by men.

In fact, the bulk of reality TV shows depict women as creatures whose highest calling is to fulfill the erotic and sexual needs of men. From television to the Internet, women are portrayed as stupid, shallow, parasitical bimbos who will do anything for money and fame—*anything*, from dating men solely for their money, to having sex with horses, to lifting up their shirts and flashing their breasts in exchange for a T-shirt in the *Girls Gone Wild* videos.

In a song from his 1975 album, *Shaved Fish*, John Lennon famously said, "Woman is the nigger of the world." Little did he realize that his words were prophetic. Did Lennon somehow foresee that two decades after his death the principal depiction of women in the popular culture would be as mindless nymphomaniacs, money-grubbing gold diggers, promiscuous prostitutes prepared to do anything to get on TV—catty witches who fight one another for a boyfriend? Women today have become the fashionable group to subject to relentless and horrendous defamation.

Where and how this defamation will end, nobody actually knows. What we do know is that, historically, the unremitting degradation and scorn of any group of people is often the prelude to their oppression. Jean-Jacques Rousseau's famous pronouncement, "Man is born free, but everywhere he is in chains," would seem far more aptly applied to women than to men. Here we are, forty years after the women's liberation movement; women *think* they are freer than ever, when in reality the past few decades have produced a monolithic and degrading depiction of women as the carnal manifestations of male fantasy. How free are women when, even as they become doctors, lawyers, and diplomats, they continue to be judged first and mostly by their appearance? How free are women when in their place of work they are subjected to continual sexual harassment, brought about by the incessant male exposure to women as sexual rather than thinking creatures? How free are women in a culture dominated by a $15 billion-a-year porn industry that is available at the touch of a button to every man in almost every office and home in the United States? And how free are women when, even as they go to colleges to receive an education, they are surrounded by young men who are encouraged to have sex with as many of them as possible to squeeze the fullest sexual experimentation out of their college years? Indeed, how free are women when men, tragically conditioned to view women as the walking gratification of their sexual needs, are coercing more and more of them into sex? A report by the Alan Guttmacher Institute maintains that 70 percent of all sexually active fourteen-year-old girls have had sexual intercourse against their wills, while the FBI estimates that one out of three American women will be raped in their lifetime.

Moreover, we must ask ourselves what this onslaught of disrespect toward women says about the very fabric of our society, its cultural mores, and most important, how it affects men's treatment of women.

It is often said that one of the most accurate measures of a society's moral state is how it treats its most vulnerable members—its women and children. Do they oppress and exploit them, or do they cherish and honor them? There are many means of female degradation in the world, ranging from oppression in the East to deprecation in the West. *Time* magazine captured this well in an article (November 10, 2003) about Vida Samadzai, the first Miss Afghanistan to appear in a beauty pageant in thirty-one years. As part of the competition, she appeared in a bikini and was promptly condemned to Hell by the Afghan Supreme Court, who called her behavior "totally un-Islamic." The *Time* piece concluded, "Ah, if only all Afghan women enjoyed the dignity Western women are afforded: to be judged not by the hem of their burkas but by the size of their breasts."

Oppression in the East, Degradation in the West

Although Western society, compared with the full-scale abuse of women's rights in Islamic society, might seem far less guilty, it is nonetheless necessary to look with a more critical eye at the harm our society is inflicting.

Western society *is* at the forefront of creating an increasingly misogynistic civilization in which the deprecation of women is not only acceptable, but serves as the primary engine for many cultural and commercial outlets, from television to film, and from the Internet to advertising. Naked women are no longer found only in the pages of *Playboy* and *Penthouse*. Rather, they are absolutely everywhere, from roadside billboards to the Super Bowl. No sooner did the Enron scandal break than *Playboy* magazine featured a cover story called "Women of Enron," with female employees of the company posing naked. A great many people question whether the sexual depiction of women is even degrading. A lot of women even claim that it is liberating, as if the primary depiction of women capable of giving a man an erection is a flattering portrayal of the full panoply of female potential.

But imagine for a moment that there was a television show that took thirty Jews to a castle in France, and told them that they had the opportunity of befriending a megamillionaire. The twist in the program is that the millionaire is really a New Jersey construction worker. The objective of the show is to see if the Jews, *who everyone assumes love money above all else*, will terminate the friendship on discovering that their new buddy is broke. And imagine also that this show is so wildly successful that fully 50 million people watch its finale, and that a new international version is quickly readied for release during the fall ratings sweep.

You would be justified in thinking that the show's creator is Joseph Goebbels and that the intended audience is Nazi Germany.

But that is essentially the theme of the trendsetting show, *Joe Millionaire* (produced a few years ago by the Fox Television Network), which spawned so many even worse imitations. The only difference is that the Jews are now a group of leggy women, and they meet and compete for a suitor who is supposedly a multimillionaire. The suspense builds as the audience waits to see if the winning contestant will dump him when she discovers that he is, in fact, penniless. Incredible! A whole TV show perpetuating the stereotype of women as greedy gold diggers for whom love and romance are worthless compared with credit cards and cash. And even though the last contestant ends up staying with her pauper of a prince, the point is still abundantly clear: With rare exceptions, women are prepared to prostitute themselves for cash and marry for money.

And yet, the show's revolting premise wasn't met with angry protests by the viewers. No feminist organization made a significant stink about it. Nope, there was no feminist picket line outside Fox studios. Instead, women watched the show by the millions and loved it.

ABC's short-lived reality TV show *Are You Hot?* literally put women on the block to have each feature of their bodies evaluated, as if they were sex slaves about to be sold on the market. As I watched this particularly nefarious piece of trash, I expected the sleazy male judges to walk over to each woman to check her teeth and gums, the way purchasers used to examine slaves. This was not harmless fun. The premise of this show literally defined women as if they were sexual objects. They were paraded on stage as pieces of meat to be carved up by men. "Next up we have Susan," the announcer would say, "Is Susan hot?" And then the judges would launch in with things along the lines of, "Well, her legs are nice and long, but her breasts are too small. And they're too pear shaped. They should be rounder. Susan, smile for us now, I want to see your teeth." Amazingly, Susan would comply with the indignity, smiling throughout her public humiliation. How far we have come—or fallen—when women happily giggle as they are reduced to a couple of "inadequate" body parts?

The portrayal of woman as prostitute is so pervasive in American culture that there is no escaping it. Even after CBS and the National Football League (NFL) were fined and rebuked for Janet Jackson's portrayal of her breast as a football that needed to be thrown out onto the gridiron in front of millions of American kids, ABC came back less than a year later with their disgusting intro to Monday Night Football, in which *Desperate Housewives*' Nicolette Sheridan dropped her towel and begged Terrell Owens for casual sex. And this is a football game, for goodness sake. But then, is this radically different from having women jump up and down, in what looks like their underwear, at professional football games every time a man scores a touchdown? I never did figure out the point behind cheerleading, always believing it was an anachronism that feminism would eventually kill. And yet it, along with the breasts of the cheerleaders, is bigger than ever.

Sixty years after the advent of feminism, women must now ask themselves a sobering question: Is this what they fought for? For women to devolve into men's sex slaves? And if not, why are they silent when this has become the most rampant stereotype in American popular culture?

To be sure, some will say that *Are You Hot?* degraded both men and women, since both genders appeared as contestants. And while that may be true, men are not as naturally vulnerable as women, and thus cannot be sexually exploited in the same way. Men are not rendered powerless when they are ogled by women. Since men lack the natural refinement and dignity of women (indeed, they mostly learn it from women), when they appear in a show like *Are You Hot?* they treat it as nothing more than a fraternity prank, to be laughed off over a couple of beers. Their essential dignity is not compromised when they are judged by their biceps. Not to mention, the very inclusion of men on a show like *Are You Hot?* was essentially a farcical stab at equality. The dissection of the female form was the very point of the show. If the women had not been on, the ratings would have looked very different.

Encountering negative propaganda against women often makes me want to shout, "How can women allow this? Does no one see just how offensive this is? Where are the protests?" Many of the women I ask are puzzled by the question. "Where are *what* protests?" they ask me. "Why would we protest? This stuff is not that offensive. It's just harmless fun."

But this trend is neither harmless nor fun. Amazingly, almost every reality television show is premised on the image of women as brainless bimbos. Many women say that it is just innocuous entertainment, but do they really believe that these depictions don't have enormous influence over how men view women, and how women view themselves?

Contrast this laid-back attitude for a moment with a story in the *Wall Street Journal* about the NFL. In August 2003, ESPN, the sports television network, released a new drama series called *Playmakers*. Among the many negative stereotypes about professional football players, it showed a football player at a crack house, a team doctor giving a shot to a player who clearly should not be going back on the field, and two players who, when pulled over by police, quickly hide cocaine in the glove compartment. In other episodes, a drug-addicted running back steals morphine from a sick child he visits in the hospital, and a football player is arrested for assaulting his wife.

What was the reaction to this single TV series with its negative depiction of football players? Harmless fun? The NFL sure didn't see it that way. Paul Tagliabue, the NFL commissioner, called Michael Eisner, chairman of the Disney Corporation, which owns ESPN, to complain about the "negative impact the show could have on the league." Tagliabue and the league would not take no for an answer. ESPN decided to stop running promotions for *Playmakers* during NFL games. And although they said they made the decision on their own, the fact is that they were in the sixth year of an eight-year, $4.8 billion deal to air NFL games and nobody wanted to rock the boat. Pat Bowlen, owner of the Denver Broncos and head of the committee that negotiates NFL television contracts, called the show "horrible" and said he could not understand why ESPN, which has profited from its relationship with pro football, would "go out and crap all over the product." Jeff Lurie, owner of the Philadelphia Eagles, called a press conference to voice his outrage with ESPN, saying he wondered how Disney would like it if "Minnie Mouse were portrayed as Pablo Escobar and the Magic Kingdom as a drug cartel."

To be sure, the NFL did not have a complete victory insofar as the series was not dropped completely (until the ratings eventually killed off the sorry drivel). But the protest was instrumental in hastening the show's decline. And all this resulted from a *single* TV show depicting NFL players as unsavory wife-beaters. This is a tiny exposure compared with the daily trampling women receive through scores of television shows, advertisements, websites, and other media—all depicting women as sleazy airheads with boobs and genitalia and nothing else to offer.

Cyberspace: The New Female-Bashing Universe

Of course, we cannot fully discuss this issue without looking at the Internet, the greatest technological achievement since man landed on the moon. With fully 70 percent of the Web devoted to the most graphic pornography, cyberspace has emerged as a female-bashing universe. Of the hundreds of spam e-mails I receive each week, not one says, "Come to our website and watch as we get black men to clean our floors and toilets." Not one entices viewers to "watch Jews chase quarters as we throw them in the street." Nor have I seen an e-mail advertising a website of live webcams showing Mexican immigrants trying to escape into America: "Come see a bunch of dirty spics as they try to infiltrate our country." Any such racist communication, however trashy in origin, would rightly be investigated by the government for racial incitement.

Yet every day I receive about fifty junk e-mails with headlines like the following: "Teen whores and sluts who want their mouths stuffed with_____"; "Tear her Womanhood Apart," "Dumb bitch blondes who are so stupid they only know how to_____"; or the especially inventive and disturbing, "This girl loves being ravished by her horse." The main complaint rallied about these unsolicited messages is that they are clogging up our hard drives. When did this become a culture where our computer memory space is more important than the way we depict the fairer sex? Child pornography on the Internet is highly illegal in every culture that calls itself civilized. So the message becomes "Exploit kids and you are going to jail. Degrade women and you make a buck." There are billions of e-mails a day maligning women as retarded whores who love being beaten while they are sexually abused, and to my knowledge, no government agency has investigated any of these sites. Worse, we don't hear of any high-profile women's organizations launching successful national initiatives to combat this abuse.

When No One Shows Up for the Protest

One of my principal concerns is that the rampant misogyny in our society is going unchecked by its victims. The complicity of women in their own degradation has made the situation not only possible, but also terrifying. Adversity has been known to make groups strong, to propel them to achieve great heights that they might never have striven for otherwise. But what makes me most fearful is that instead of facing the adversary and growing from that battle, the majority of women today do not even seem aware that they are being challenged. When the greatest assaults to their character and personhood are hurled directly at them, they barely notice.

This indifference was evident during a lecture I delivered on the mistreatment of women in America at the 92nd Street Y in New York City. A number of professional women in the audience took great offense at my insinuation that women are being portrayed as one step above hookers. But not because they felt my assessment was inaccurate. "What's wrong with being a hooker?" one irate listener instead asked. "It's an honest job, and if that's how a woman wants to earn a living, what's it got to do with you?

You just want to control women, like all religious people do." I asked this woman if she would object if every Hollywood film portrayed all black men as garbage collectors. When she agreed that it would be offensive, I asked her why. "Garbage collecting is an honest job," I pointed out, "and if a black man wants to spend his life hauling your trash, and Michael Eisner wants to show us that that's what most black men end up doing, what's it got to do with you?" Of course, it has everything to do with all of us. Such generalizations and stereotypes leave a lasting mark, and it is naive to think that they do not. The portrayal of black men as suitable *only* for garbage duties presupposes that, as a group, African Americans do not have the intelligence or perhaps the ambition to do otherwise, and the portrayal would thus be racist and dehumanizing. The same is true of women when their portrayal is always about their bodies and never their brains.

Why aren't women going crazy with objections to this onslaught against their character? Well, it appears that they are way too busy trying to live up to the negative caricatures. Object to it? Why, they are running to Victoria's Secret to purchase thongs worn over their jeans to *become* the stereotype. And this is why women are so blind to their own degradation. They think that by "doing what is expected of them"—wearing low-cut blouses and skirts with big slits (even in the office)—they are perhaps gaining control over men. Little do they realize that men evaluate this behavior in a totally different way. They see it as women accepting their rightful place as the walking fulfillment of male desire.

Worse yet, not only are grown women lowering themselves to embrace these negative ideals, but young girls are being malnourished by the unwholesome examples placed before them. The next generation is being taught that a woman's highest calling is to serve as a mindless nymphomaniac. They are learning that the best way to succeed in life—with success defined by the amount of male attention one garners—is to learn how to entertain men at the first possible opportunity. On October 26, 2003, the *New York Times* ran a story titled "Underdressed and Hot: Dolls Moms Don't Love" by Ruth La Ferla, reporting that girls ages eight to twelve are dumping their Barbie dolls in favor of a new line called "Bratz." Yes, the name is not coincidental. That is what these dolls look like: out-of-control teenagers wearing very little clothes. "Introduced in the summer of 2001, Bratz and their licensed products have already rung up a spectacular $1 billion in sales. . . . The Bratz' shrunken sweaters, shredded jeans and faintly glazed expressions are part of their allure." The *Times* then quotes a young girl from a Manhattan elementary school commenting about the new doll line, "Bratz looks sexy, but that's O.K., because that's what makes them look good." Get it? *Because* they look sexy, they look good. And that is the message being given to little girls: Look sexy and you will look good—even if you are only ten years old. The article also quotes Miriam Around, editor of *Child* magazine, who said, "These days many children of four and five are developing a fashion sense mirroring a society in which we're treating really young children as if they were much older." But can it be healthy for a little girl of four to be conscious of how she looks in front of boys? To utterly lose her sense of innocence, her sense of playfulness—the very art of being natural—at that tender age? To think one of her duties is to please boys with the way she dresses, in kindergarten?

This trend is not limited to Bratz. The big toy companies are now looking to catch up with slutty dolls of their own. Mattel has introduced Flava dolls, with stick-on tattoos and one thumb suggestively hooked in the waistband of her denim micro miniskirt. Perhaps, the most shocking thing in the *New York Times* story is a quotation from a real-life mother, Ellen Rosenthal, commenting on the popularity of Bratz and why she has no problem with it. "As a parent," Rosenthal says, "I would like to let [my daughter] Macie explore these things. Age eight is a perfect time for her to experiment with lipstick, fairy dust glitter and all of that. If the Bratz doll has a belly ring, I wouldn't care—they're just a phase." Are any of us surprised at this mother's blinded complicity? After all, she is part of a culture that degrades and demeans women, so she transfers that belief to her daughter, and allows it to spiral out of control. Amazingly, she is already getting her geared up for her most important role in life: to be delicious eye-candy for men.

2

∞

WAKING UP FROM THE
MISOGYNISTIC NIGHTMARE

I want this book to serve as a wake-up call to all of us. If the negative stereotypes of women do not stop, they will soon be so ingrained in the public psyche that they will become permanent. To a great extent, that has happened already. We seem to have become immune to the degradation of women and view its manifestations as nothing more than harmless entertainment. In fact, the most glaring transgressions make little impact on us. We are creating a world in which things that should be shocking are deemed to be innocuous and commonplace. We are developing a society in which the cheerleaders' outfits get smaller and beer commercials become more salacious. We are shaping a world in which more American beaches will become topless since even bikinis don't show enough flesh to gain some women the attention they crave. Even the Miss America pageant decided in 2004 to substitute swimsuits with thongs, becoming a near-pornographic program, in a desperate attempt to compete with more explicit shows. Not that it helped. CBS canceled the show anyway. But such is the desensitization of men, who have become so overexposed to women's bodies that they yawn unless the nudity is total and complete.

When I grew up in Miami Beach, it was illegal for women to bare their breasts. Now, it is taken for granted in South Beach.

The trend has less to do with avoiding tan lines and more to do with how many stares they get from men when they go naked. They do it to entertain men because they have begun subconsciously, and perhaps even consciously, to believe that they have an obligation to do so. Most women today understand that the only reliable means to attract male attention is to show flesh. Their intelligence and humor, by contrast, just don't seem to matter. For many men, such qualities may even be a hindrance to attraction.

When I speak at high schools and see the way many young women dress, I almost get the impression that someone has told the girls, "Now remember, you are in this school with the boys. You know what's expected of you. The boys have a right to be entertained. You do want to be popular, right? You don't want to be one of those girls who no one invites to parties. Now get out there and flaunt 'em if you got 'em." In response, the girls seem happy to oblige. They dress like tarts and learn to have that frivolous, flirty giggle that says to men, "Don't worry. My brain is certainly not my strongest feature. You have nothing to fear."

Putting on Your Own Shackles: An Answer to the Critics

I know that the sharpest criticism of this book will come from younger readers who think that I am dragging them back to the dark ages from which feminism tried to liberate them. Many professional female friends who first read this book have accused me of trying to put them back into the kitchen and laundry room, as if trying to restore male respect for women can only come in a domesticated role. This is an absurd protest. In raising my five daughters, I do my utmost to instill within them feminine dignity and character, but also every professional ambition. My message is that feminism has justly and righteously demanded respect for women as men's intellectual equals, with the right, even encouragement, to use their talents to prosper, just like men.

Why Is Taking Off Your Clothes for Money an Act of Liberation?

The second most vociferous critics will be resolutely secular women, who are going to argue that I am trying to use a theory of morality as a means of subjecting women to the control of men. I find it interesting that taking off your clothes for money has been sanctified as an act of liberation, so that when moralists or clerics insist that there are far more respectable ways of earning a living, they are accused of attempting to shackle women.

This is exactly the response I got from many of the women in the audience who came to hear me debate Lindsey Vuolo, *Playboy*'s Miss November 2001 (and advertised as their first Jewish playmate), over her choice to pose naked in that offensive magazine. I was raked over the coals by audience participants who told me that I had no right to preach to Lindsey about her choices. Women's liberation ensured that young women can make up their minds for themselves. One woman even said that Lindsey was a hero, brave and spirited about her body, and women should emulate her courage. Now I know that Clara Barton was valiant for dodging cannonballs on the battlefields of the Civil War to aid injured soldiers. Similarly, I recognize that Susan B. Anthony was bold and audacious when she defied the male lawmakers who denied women's rights, and she was steadfast in facing jail during her fight for women's suffrage. But what act of courage is involved in subordinating oneself to the leering eyes of lecherous men who need to see a woman's breasts while they masturbate? In extolling a woman who submitted to the basest instincts as being heroic, these women had the inverted idea of heroism proclaimed by the Marquis de Sade, "Has not nature proved, in giving us the strength to submit to our desires, that we have the right to do so?" Courage is not putting yourself through college by taking off your clothes, the justification Lindsey Vuolo used for her centerfold. Courage was what I saw at Morehouse College, the premier African American men's university in the United States, where I received one of the great honors of my life when I was invited to be a keynote speaker at a convention of students in the Martin Luther King Hall, with Coretta Scott King as part of the program. The kitchens of the college are staffed by young men from Morehouse and young women from neighboring Spellman College, who hold honest, dignified jobs in the kitchen to pay for their tuition, get an education, and forge a better life for themselves and their families. That is courage.

I have noticed that it is not overweight or older women who oppose my message. On the contrary, when an abstract of my thesis ran as an editorial in several newspapers around the world, I was inundated with praise from women in the thousands who thanked me for finally taking a stand against the misogynistic spew that they found themselves wading through daily. These were dignified, impressive women who were being disadvantaged by the misogyny to which I am referring. They were treated as ugly or obsolete. They were made to feel as if they had failed at their principal purpose in life: to serve as a thrilling specimen to entertain men. Since they did not fit accepted male criteria for attraction, they were treated as second rate.

If one is young and good-looking, one is more likely to get a job and more likely to attract men. Thus the misogynistic system works to the advantage of the nubile beauties among us. Human nature often dictates that as long as the system benefits a group, the members will have no major gripe with it. This is just as it was with the majority of whites in the old segregated South. The civil rights movement was not fought by many Southern whites because, after all, why would they choose to give up their position of privilege?

In this new misogyny, pretty, busty women are akin to Southern whites while the fat, short, or pimply women fill the position held by blacks. Indeed, there was a story recently about flight attendant Ellen Simonetti, who was fired from her job with Delta Airlines for posting saucy pictures of herself in her uniform on her weblog, which she called, "Diary of a Flight Attendant." In some of the photos, her skirt was pulled way up, revealing a whole lot of leg. In others, she was leaning over the seats, her blouse unbuttoned,

exposing part of her bra. Delta said that she had degraded her position by sexualizing it and had embarrassed the company. They sus-
pended her in September 2004 and fired her a month later.

Amazingly, she retaliated by accusing Delta of hiring ugly
flight attendants. Speaking to the *New York Times*, Ms. Simonetti, a
twenty-nine-year-old blonde, said from her home in Austin, Texas,
"In the past people expected flight attendants to be young and attractive. Maybe I represent the flight attendants of the past." She
said there was nothing wrong with her playing up her attractiveness in her uniform on her website. Apparently, Ms. Simonetti is of
the opinion that working as an air hostess should be the exclusive
domain of the young and the beautiful. On October 20, she posted
a question from a male reader that asked, "Why are all of my
flight attendants so unattractive when you are so very good looking?" Simonetti's arrogant response: "Because Anonymous Airlines [her euphemism for Delta] fires or indefinitely suspends all
of its good-looking flight attendants. They prefer them fat and
ugly." Simonetti also played down the scandal of her posted photos, by telling the *Times*, "Gosh, it's a little tiny sliver of my bra,"
she further told the *Times*. "It's not like a bright red push-up bra,"
she said. "It's not like I worked the flight like that."

What is particularly shocking about this arrogant woman's
comments (what will she offer the world once her looks wear off?),
is that she appears to be wishing for the airline industry to return
to the pathetic days of the seventies and eighties, when airlines
discriminated outright against women who may have been completely competent, but were not "beautiful."

To give you an idea of how effective women once were in combating discrimination against less beautiful women, the *New York
Times* writes in the same article, "The women's movement played
a large role in the elimination of the overt sexualization of flight
attendants like those portrayed in National Airlines' 1974 television ad featuring attractive stewardesses beckoning mostly male
business travelers to 'Fly Me' and Continental Airlines' similar invitation to ogle the flight attendants, with its promise, 'We Really
Move Our Tail For You.'

"Airlines discovered they were on the wrong side of that issue twenty years ago. They've gotten religion. And deeply ingrained in their corporate culture and human relations practices is an aversion to that kind of sexualization.

"'This change is welcomed by many in the profession,' said Tim Kirkwood, a flight attendant for twenty-seven years and author of *The Flight Attendant Job Finder and Career Guide* (Planning/Communications, 2003). 'Flight attendants over the years have fought hard to get rid of the image of the sexy stewardess,' he said after reviewing *Diary of a Flight Attendant*, 'and it does tend to regress back to that a bit'" (*New York Times*, November 16, 2004).

But in almost any other industry, the pendulum has swung the other way. Younger, thinner, particularly buxom women are the immediate beneficiaries of the system we have today, and they are able and ready to manipulate that system to their advantage. A friend of mine who works on Wall Street, where beautiful female assistants are common, hired a blonde-haired bombshell as a secretary and agreed to pay her 30 percent more than he had advertised for the position. He explained his actions to me by saying, "Well, if I have to look at someone throughout the day, it may as well be something that's nice to look at. And I'm prepared to pay extra for that." When I asked him why that didn't also apply to the men he hired—"Shouldn't they have to be tall and handsome"—he told me I was being ridiculous because he was not attracted to men. "But you're not attracted to furniture or bookcases either, but you want them to be aesthetically pleasing. On the contrary, the reason the women have to be pretty is that you do treat them like the furniture. You can't help but objectify them."

The hiring of beautiful women and the marginalization of ugly women have become so rampant that they essentially served as the underlying theme in an important lawsuit brought against one of the worst offenders, Abercrombie & Fitch. Walk into any store and you'll find that the women are usually young, beautiful, white, and college age. A class-action lawsuit was brought against Abercrombie for taking the ones that look ugly or insufficiently appealing—in this case it was black and Latino women—and giving them such important jobs as cleaning the toilets and dusting off the merchandise.

On November 16, 2004, the court granted preliminary approval to a settlement of the class-action lawsuit, *Gonzalez v. Abercrombie & Fitch.* The settlement required the retail clothing giant to pay $40 million to Latino, African American, Asian American, and women applicants and employees who charged the company with discrimination. The settlement also required the company to institute a range of policies and programs to promote diversity among its workforce and to prevent discrimination based on race or gender.

Still, it will be a cold day in hell before you see any overweight woman, or a woman with a double chin, selling clothes in any of their outlets.

While all this goes on, and attractive females receive blatant employment favoritism, women still mistakenly believe that their sex appeal is empowering, granting them control over men and the ability to manipulate the reception of their misguided wants.

By seeing this kind of behavior as nothing more than a harmless means to achieve their greater goals, these women rationalize and perpetuate their own degradation. Jennifer, an acquaintance of mine, is an attractive, leggy, blonde. She was thrilled to get an internship in a trading firm, where her ultimate dream was to make a lot of money as a stockbroker. The office, a small boutique, was filled with men throwing around constant sexual innuendos. But Jennifer was not offended; in fact she decided that catering to the role of the pretty girl the men could flirt with would get her far. When she saw her boss looking at a porn picture on his computer sent to him by a colleague, rather than just walking out, she made a point of commenting on the woman's body.

After being asked by her boss whether she thought she could succeed permanently in the testosterone-driven culture of New York traders, she went with two of her girlfriends one night to the firm, after everyone had left, and took a picture of herself in the company gym, in her bra and panties, working out. In the morning, she sent it to her boss and three of his associates with the words, "Just in case you didn't think I was daring." She got the job, only to discover that, while the firm's young owners were prepared to pay her more than $120,000 a year to be eye-candy and a great flirtatious tease, they were never going to take her seriously as a trader, and she mostly ended up running errands for the men. After six months, when they tired of her, they told her she could stay but at a 50 percent pay cut. She left in hostility and bitterness.

Men Can Look Up to Women without Patronizing Them

I am sure that some of my readers are inwardly accusing me of being a throwback to the Stone Age, with rigidly defined roles for men and women. They could not be more incorrect. When I speak of an era in which women were placed on a pedestal by men, and treated as their superiors in nobility and refinement, I know that students of women's history will say, "That pedestal only provided a very small area on which one could stand!" This is undoubtedly so, and while being placed aloft on a pedestal was probably a better position than being cast down in the muck, the notion seems to have an inherently patronizing premise if we do not understand what the pedestal really symbolizes.

I have had the good fortune to be acquainted with many intelligent, educated, successful women, especially over my eleven years as rabbi at Oxford University. When I have approached this topic with them, many women, in no uncertain terms, have let me know that they think I am clueless. Each and every time that this conversation unfolds, I have to defend myself, explaining that I *do* understand that being treated like a china doll is simply not enough. (I shall wax lyrical, later in the book, about the olden days when women inspired men to great heights, when they were honored for their dignity and natural grace, and when they were perceived as innate superiors by men who aspired—through acts of gallantry, daring, and courage—to become worthy of them.)

But even as I hunger for a bygone age of innocence, I am not naive in thinking that this was a golden age for womankind. In the

Middle Ages, peasant women were fair game for abuse. Only the noble ladies, who could be levied and deemed valuable in marriage alliances, were protected and placed on a saintly pedestal. Up until the modern age, women had few, if any, rights. Property and political rights were certainly denied them, and the United States would not even grant them a vote until the passage of the Nineteenth Amendment in August 1920. It was a man's world. On a macrocosmic level, men controlled everything. In ancient times, great men demonstrated their superiority on the battlefield. They were great conquerors and military commanders. This masculine-aggressive ideal persisted long into the medieval period and beyond, and in such societies, there certainly were few opportunities for women to express themselves or be leaders.

To some degree, this kind of thinking prevailed well into our own era and that is why the feminist movement was critical. Today, no one of any intelligence denies the infinite capabilities of womankind. Women have abilities and desires that the male-dominated society has historically failed to recognize or understand. Immersed in a world where brute strength and power were deified, women's subtler qualities of refinement, wisdom, and grace were always treated as subordinate. In other instances, beyond just failing to acknowledge the talents of their female counterparts, many men were downright threatened by the power and skills of women. They did not want to believe that women were their equals. The idea of a softer, gentler creature being possessed of an inner strength that was greater than that of a man made men feel emasculated. All this contributed to the repression that women have experienced throughout history. I cannot emphasize how vital I believe the women's liberation movement was in addressing and overcoming the obstacles that prevented women from actualizing their potential.

In the sixties and seventies, the nation confronted the issues of job discrimination and limited professional opportunities for women. I remember hearing a story from a professionally successful woman about her early days in the business world of the sixties. Applying to be part of a long-term trainee program that would eventually lead to a lucrative career, she had to struggle for each and every step she took into the profession. With a shudder, she recalled her final interview, the last hurdle she had to clear to win a pivotal entry position in her field. Seated in front of the recruitment panel, who insisted on referring to her solely by her married title, the woman was shocked when a committee member asked, "Tell us, Mrs. Gordon, why should we waste this position on you?" She actually had to promise her interviewers that she would not waste their time and investment in training her for the job they assumed she would abandon the moment she wanted to start a family. To protect against this kind of discrimination, valiant feminists have fought long and hard to establish a place for women in society that allows them to advance in every sector. Thanks to their efforts, women were no longer relegated to play the role of a man's sidekick, good only to stand by him and keep his house tidy.

While, admittedly, these battles were essential, the movement failed in one regard: It condemned the *lady* in favor of the *woman*. Somewhere along the way, instead of adhering firmly to the goal of attaining equal rights for women, the ERA (Equal Rights Amendment) agenda wound up pummeling the uniqueness of womankind. Femininity came to be associated with weakness and thus feminists urged women to negate their feminine traits, flattening down and essentially making them androgynous.

So here is an essential point. Although in times gone by, women were oppressed and made to be the inferiors of men, the *ideology* demanded that women be the fairer sex, more innately dignified, noble in all emotional and spiritual aspects, and the superiors of men. Their realm of inferiority was considered to be in intellect and physical strength. But along came the feminist movement, which addressed those wrongs. Feminists showed that women were men's intellectual equals, and, though not possessing perhaps the same physical strength, were equal to men as well in physical endurance and grit.

Where feminism went shockingly wrong was in deciding to dump the ideology of feminine emotional and spiritual superiority. Feminism mistakenly believed that the male paradigm of women being more noble and refined was merely a ruse to justify subjugation. It was a way to insist they not sully themselves with the professional, political, and monetary responsibilities of men, threatening the established hierarchy. But no matter how much this ideology was abused by men, it is still true. And once it was removed—once feminists insisted that part of being liberated was throwing off the shackles of dignity and encouraging women to be as crass and vulgar as men, if they so desired—the floodgates were opened for grotesque sexual exploitation of a kind that one could scarcely have imagined.

Have we not gone too far when Madonna and Britney Spears simulate masturbation at concerts that are being aired in prime time on national television? They are singers, not porn stars, right? In February 2005, during a concert in Auckland, New Zealand, Cher called Britney Spears and Jennifer Lopez "ho's." But how could women allow the female recording industry to sink so low? Or when a string of women appear on a show like *Who Wants to Marry a Multi-Millionaire* and parade themselves in front of some egotistical, shallow imbecile whose only claim to virtue is that he's got a couple of bucks? This dissolute behavior is showcased for young impressionable minds, and yet no protests are being staged. With this kind of stuff being rampant, we are no longer talking floodgates. We are talking a hurricane of women hatred.

Never in history have women been so negatively portrayed. But instead of combating this outbreak of misogyny, feminist leaders save their vitriolic uproar for things like the ban on women at the all-men's Augusta National golf course. When we look around at the rampant misogyny that assaults our eyes and ears daily, how can anyone underscore a men's golf tournament as the epitome of the evil facing today's women? In fact, these misguided feminist causes have led to a loss of following in the overall movement. Maureen Dowd, the noted *New York Times* columnist, lamented that Brian Williams, a white man, succeeded Tom Brokaw, another white man, to the anchor's chair of NBC News. It's funny that this is the kind of thing that bothers her, whereas the fact that tens of millions of e-mails are sent daily to people's accounts calling women "sluts," "bitches," and "whores" seems to have escaped her notice. Or the fact that woman-as-prostitute is becoming commonplace on American TV. Comedy Central's *South Park* aired an episode about Paris Hilton in 2004. The name of the episode was "Stupid Spoiled Whore." The highlight is where the Paris Hilton character puts a pineapple in her vagina to compete in a "Whore Off" with a gay sadomasochistic teacher from the local school. To top her stunt, he then puts the entire body of Paris Hilton into his anus. This edifying spectacle is followed by his speech about the horror of becoming a stupid spoiled whore. How could a national network get away with portraying women in such a negative light? Easily. They could say that Paris Hilton has already portrayed herself this way. They're just following her lead.

Throwing Out the Lady with the Bathwater

But the real tragedy of all this is how, as a result of the incessant assault on feminine dignity, women have become so ordinary. The reverence and respect that men once had for women—the whole concept of a fairer and nobler sex—has been erased, with women maintaining adamantly at the forefront that they are just like the guys. But whether women want to accept it, they are not just like men. Much more than men, when women behave in a sleazy fashion, they compromise something essential within. Sex without love for a woman offends her most innate sensibilities, even if she is not fully conscious of it. Lovemaking for a woman, unlike for a man, is an internal rather than external undertaking. It is literally opening oneself up for invasion, and it is far more difficult for a woman, therefore, to compartmentalize her emotions from her body in a manner that men have found so easy over the centuries. A woman's very anatomy proclaims that she is not built for casual carnality.

I maintain that men and women are *not* equal, and I base my view on various ancient, practical, and spiritual ideas. I believe that in the most important areas of life, women are men's superiors, and men have a lot more to learn from women than vice versa.

In fact, insisting on this farcical notion of equivalence devalues the distinctions of women and, moreover, has made it uncomfortable for any woman to embrace traditional roles.

We will return to the notion of feminine superiority later, as it is a crucial component of this book. But for now, it is worth noting that the assault on the ideal of the lady has made it difficult for women to embrace traditional roles without being frowned on. Mothering is the most important example. Women who give up their careers, or put them on hold, to nurture their children are seen as second tier to those women who get up every morning and work in an office. It seems incredible that any woman would feel she has to apologize for prioritizing parenting. While the battle for open access and opportunity in the professional world was waged without hesitation, why wasn't part of the program to gain respect for the work women had been doing all along? Why did feminism throw out the lady with the bathwater?

Many feminists shifted from protesting discrimination and rigidly proscribed gender roles to discriminating against the feminine woman and her choice of a traditional role in family or marriage. It has gotten so bad that in the 2004 presidential race, Theresa Heinz Kerry even suggested that because Laura Bush had always been a mother, she never had "a real job." And while she later apologized, this was only because she was mistaken—Laura Bush had been a librarian and teacher. The fact remained that a woman who nearly became our first lady did not consider mothering to be an honorable profession.

3

∞

IN A WORLD WITHOUT LADIES, THERE CANNOT BE GENTLEMEN

Four Archetypes of Women— Glorious Past, Ignoble Present

In past ages, four noble attributes characterized a woman. She was deemed to be:

1. A creature of superior dignity and grace, interested in love over money, and in a rich inner life rather than a shallow outer life

2. A spiritual intimacy seeker, unwilling to surrender to a man who was not her soul mate

3. A strongly productive but nonaggressive team player

4. A nurturer and comforter, capable of uplifting man to heights of insight, nobility, and pleasure that he could otherwise scarcely comprehend

These characteristics were coveted, venerated, and cherished. Woman was looked at as a hallowed being with a profound influence and impact on the men around her. By contrast, women today are maligned, defamed, deprecated, and degraded in contemporary culture to a degree that is unprecedented in all human history. Instead of the noble characteristics of the past, the popular culture has shaped four essential portrayals of women. Watch television any night, especially reality TV, and you are bound to see one of these four modern female archetypes:

1. *The Greedy Gold Digger:* The woman who loves money more than love and romance, and will date or marry practically any guy who's got pockets full of cash

2. *The Publicity-Seeking Prostitute:* The woman who will do anything for publicity, including strip and sleep with strangers

3. *The Brainless Bimbo:* A dunce and an airhead who entertains with her jackass comments

4. *The Backstabbing Bitch:* The woman who will cut the heart out of another woman for social advancement or in a catfight over a guy

In fashioning these distinct personas for womankind, our society has left little room for alternative noble renderings, and the result has been the utter demoralization of the female spirit and the burial of her nurturing power. It is because of this very degradation of the female energy that our world faces the crises that it does.

This ferocious assault on the dignity of women has undermined male respect for women and made it almost impossible to create gentlemen. In previous generations, a man's love for a woman was believed to lend him limitless nobility, as Andreas Capellanus expresses beautifully in his thirteenth-century classic, *The Art of Courtly Love:*

> Now it is the effect of love that a true lover cannot be degraded with any avarice. Love causes a rough and uncouth man to be distinguished for his handsomeness; it can endow a man even of the humblest birth with nobility of character; it blesses the proud with humility; and the man in love becomes accustomed to performing many services gracefully for everyone. O what a wonderful thing is love, which makes a man shine with so many virtues and teaches everyone, no matter who he is, so many

good traits of character! There is another thing about love that we should not praise in a few words: it adorns a man, so to speak, with the virtue of chastity, because he who shines with the light of one love can hardly think of embracing another woman, even a beautiful one. For when he thinks deeply of his beloved, the sight of any other woman is relinquished to nothing.

But today, the caricature of a man being refined into a gentleman through exposure to a woman would be laughable. Instead of the passionate lover or the refined gentleman, what we have instead are four categories of men that demonstrate just how low the gender has sunk. Allow me to present to you the four general classifications into which too many of our "boys-next-door" now seem to fit:

1. *The Crotch-Scratcher (aka the Belly-Belcher):* The man utterly devoid of any human refinement; a gross slob bereft as much of dignity as he is of manners

2. *The Harem Gatherer:* The lecherous man who has made it his life's goal to bed as many women as possible

3. *The Selfish Spouse:* The all-too-common uninterested and self-absorbed husband

4. *The Porn Addict:* The guy who is able to relate only to fantasy women

We come back to each of these stereotypes later in the book, and point out the TV shows, films, and electronic media that sustain them. But I am mentioning the four foul stereotypes of women and how they have bred four rancid archetypes of men to make a vital point here: In a world where there are no ladies, there can scarcely be gentlemen.

There are strong consequences for a world in which men have little respect for women and women have little respect for themselves. With the neutralization of women as a nurturing and softening force, our world is becoming more aggressive, more ruthlessly ambitious, less compassionate, more vulgar, and more insecure. It is a world of harsh judgment, bereft of gentle creatures to soothe the pain. It is a world of manipulation, calculation, and judgment, rather than acceptance, confidence, and openness. It is a world of sharp elbows instead of soft hearts, spiked shoes instead of outstretched hands. The kinder, gentler nation promised to us by George Bush Sr. in his famous 1988 "thousand points of light" speech (written by a woman named Peggy Noonan) is a distant dream. In the Middle East, the brutal belligerence of the once great Islamic world is a supreme example of the consequences for a society that denies women public roles and influence. Arab mothers regularly extol their suicide-bomber children as martyrs and one wonders how, in a culture where even the nurturers have become bloodthirsty, we will be able to bring civilization back from the brink.

In the West, the disparagement and the defamation of women have already fostered a generation of loutish and unrefined men who have no incentive to become gentlemen. With women so significantly devalued, and with men subtly taught to despise women as worthless playthings created for nothing but their personal entertainment and pleasure, men are making little effort to ennoble their character to be worthy of a woman. After all, who tries to make himself worthy of his own servant? Who would seek to refine their character for a creature that they perceive to be innately crass? Imagine for a moment that you're a guy who is dating Christina Aguilera and you accidentally burp at dinner. She scolds you and tells you that you're a slob. Do you take her words to heart, or do you think to yourself, "Look who's calling the kettle black?" So the rule today is that a man can act like a complete jerk and still get a girlfriend. You can two-time the woman you are dating—as boys as young as high school age routinely do—and even have a reputation as a complete womanizer, and still find a woman who wants to be in a relationship with you, especially if you're perceived as exciting or have a couple of bucks in the bank. What woman, forty years ago, would have tolerated a man dating her for four or five years without popping the question? When would it have been acceptable for a man to string a woman along without committing himself to her? And what woman was dumb enough, or insecure enough, to accept such a rotten deal?

In 2004, the biggest-selling relationships book in the United States was coauthored by a man and a woman, both of whom were screenwriters for *Sex and the City*. The book is called *He's Just Not That into You,* and its premise is that a man who treats a woman poorly does not have a real character flaw, but rather "he's just not that into her." The book tells women to stop blaming men for being jerks, and just accept that they have a right not to like any specific woman that much: If he doesn't like you, move on and enjoy life. Amazing, isn't it? A book that says if men treat women like garbage, it is because, essentially, they are just not hot enough. So we have come full circle. Rather than asking men to take responsibility for their selfish behavior toward women and finally become gentlemen, we are telling women that they empower themselves by being honest enough to admit that, when men dump them with barely an explanation, it is because, in the men's eyes, they are no great catch. Presumably, if they were supermodels, they would be treated a whole lot better. But even greater than my outrage at such an immoral argument is the unbelievable fact that there was no protest from women at this abominable idea. On the contrary, women bought the book in the millions and then set about going back to the gym and watching their weight, hoping, somehow, that the next guy would finally be into them.

Women come to me all the time telling me about their live-in boyfriends who will just not commit to marriage. These women are in a lot of pain and are confused about what to do. They are damned if they break up—because they love their men—and damned if they stay with them, because their hopes of getting married and starting a family are being dashed. I was having my teeth cleaned one day when the dental hygienist suddenly said, "I hear you're a relationship expert. Please help me. My boyfriend and I have been living together for three years. He never talks about marriage and gets all bothered if I even bring it up. My parents say

I should leave. Please tell me what to do?" I had sharp metal instruments in my mouth and could not utter a word, but her despair was such that she hungered even for the mumblings of help.

More than ever, men are disappointing women—even though standards seem to get lower with each generation. They barely know how to be faithful, have little clue how to be husbands, and, as a result, have little idea how to be fathers. After all, children are a lifelong commitment, just like marriage. And if you fail at the latter, you usually fail at the former. Men routinely burp and break wind in the presence of their wives, and then laugh hysterically as if being a brute is funny. Is it any surprise that women are more fed up with men than ever before? Is it a surprise that, women routinely delay marriage themselves until they are in their thirties because they "could not find Mr. Right," and then wind up initiating 74 percent of all divorces?

That's right. Three-quarters of all divorces in America are initiated by wives. And unlike husbands who, when they leave their wives, are nearly always going to the arms of another woman, less than 10 percent of wives who leave their husbands are entering into another relationship. Indeed, the vast majority never remarry. But they would rather be alone than be with a husband who is seldom affectionate, rarely helps with the housework, and stares at other women's cleavage to boot. Since the chances of divorced women remarrying are statistically remote, these women are prepared to be alone, perhaps for the rest of their lives, rather than continue to live with men who seem incapable of valuing them.

The devolution of the male character today is beginning at younger and younger ages. A woman called me recently asking me what to do about her thirteen-year-old son, who attends a Jewish day school, and whom she recently caught Instant Messaging a girl in his class, "Hey lesbo, wanna f—k?" Is this how we are raising the future men of our society? When will we realize that the denigration of women not only harms a specific woman or group of women but also spirals out to irrevocably scar society at large?

Fighting Negative Images

Men are not going to start respecting women until the disgustingly negative portrayal of women as consisting primarily of breasts and a vagina is replaced with something more wholesome, respectful, and human.

When Mel Gibson released his film *The Passion of the Christ*, which depicted Jews as demonic Christ-killers who pressured the Romans to nail Jesus to a cross, the American Jewish community raised hell to have him modify the false portrayal of Jesus' Jewish brethren as god killers. American Jewry understood this negative depiction of Jews as, "blood-thirsty, sadistic and money-hungry, forcing the decision to torture and execute Jesus, enemies of God and the locus of evil," to quote from a press release issued by the Anti-Defamation League (ADL) was inherently harmful to Jews. They understood that this depiction was bound to have a negative effect on how Jews are viewed in today's society, even if it did not lead to outbreaks of anti-Semitism.

The same is true of how African Americans have been depicted in films for decades. The common portrayal of blacks in movies was that they were stupid and simple, like Mammy and Prissy, the characters in *Gone With the Wind*. The black community was outraged at the proposed depictions of slaves and the attending ramifications that such perceptions would have on their place in American society. Cautionary letters about the impact of the characters that David O. Selznick was preparing to put on the screen flooded the producer's studio in 1938 including one from Walter White, the secretary of the National Association for the Advancement of Colored People. The film's depiction of African Americans galvanized the black press, and when the movie was finally released, black activists took action, organizing their communities to walk picket lines in front of box offices. Once these vocal rallies took hold, images would be adjusted and soon "Mammyism" would disappear from the silver screen in favor of more dignified black performances and portrayals such as Dooley Wilson in *Casablanca* and Leigh Whipper in *The Ox-Bow Incident*. Ultimately, it was the protest, the insistence on a more venerable image of black Americans, that evoked positive change.

Likewise, the foul word *nigger* has been obliterated from nearly all speech, except for committed racists. Black Americans took a stand against this disgusting and dehumanizing term. Today, it is inconceivable that an American politician would use the word, even in private, and be able to continue another day in office. And yet, the word *bitch*, an equally offensive and loathsome term, is used by even the most sophisticated and enlightened men on a daily basis, which gives you just a small idea of how much work there is to be done. Yes, I am aware that "nigger" is an all-encompassing racial slur that denigrates all blacks as one, whereas bitch has the connotation of a mean-spirited woman and is thrown at women on a more individual basis. But that distinction is losing validity as more and more men use bitch as a generic term for all women.

Women need to rally together to produce a serious alteration of their public image. If television, film, magazines, and the Internet continue to portray the female gender as publicity-seeking prostitutes and mindless nymphomaniacs, this impression will become permanent. With that image at the fore, college men will continue to think that all they have to do is buy a girl a slice of pizza and take her to a movie and she will automatically bring them back to her place for a romp in the sack.

I don't mean to portray myself as the champion of women's honor. I know that as a man this is not exclusively my fight. But I *am* the father of five daughters. I am also the son of a single mother who raised five children completely on her own with great sacrifice and courage. And I have already written several books, and hundreds of articles, about male-female relationships. I believe that my wife is my superior in her humanity, goodness, and wisdom, and that I have much more to learn from her than she from me. I have been taught by my Jewish faith that women are the superior sex and have much to teach men about spirituality, refinement, and human dignity. I am writing on this subject because I am scandalized and terrified by the society in which my girls are growing up. But it is women, rather than me, who should be leading this charge.

True, Abraham Lincoln freed the slaves. But many were still afflicted by a slave mentality until great black leaders came along, challenged the status quo, and taught African Americans that they had no one to rely on but themselves. That is why the African American redeemer had to be a black man, and came in the form of Martin Luther King Jr. The allies could save the remaining Jews from Auschwitz, but only Jewish armies could fight for and create the modern state of Israel. And the same is true of women. The fight to reclaim their dignity from a world that has so desecrated it is a woman's battle, not a man's. The battle will not be won unless it is seriously led and fought by the women themselves. In the final analysis, everybody must redeem themselves and only women can redeem other women. A cry of outrage must go out from women around the world to reclaim their dignity.

It is no longer acceptable for women's organizations to watch in silence as Abercrombie & Fitch employees all but admit to the *New York Times* that they only hire beautiful women as sales attendants. Apparently, in their shallow corporate estimation, only about 10 percent of the female population conforms to media-driven ideals of being thin, leggy, busty, and scantily clad. Although Abercrombie & Fitch settled the race suit that was brought against them, why is it still acceptable to hire only "gorgeous" women, especially when *the corporation* subjectively determines who is gorgeous?

Likewise, women's groups must make their voices heard against the cable news networks that, it seems, care far less for a woman's credentials than for her high cheekbones. Try to find a female anchor who is new to cable news these days who isn't young, blonde, and beautiful like Deborah Norville and Paula Zahn. Even Greta Van Susteren, a noted legal expert, felt that she had to have plastic surgery when she moved to anchor her own show on Fox.

Plastic surgery that helps women achieve that cookie-cutter, big-breasted, wide-eyed, tight-skinned look is becoming not just a rite of passage for older women, but is increasingly becoming a hallmark of youth for the millions of young women who are made to feel that they are just not beautiful enough. The movie *Malcolm X* powerfully demonstrates how, prior to the civil rights movement, many African American men and women spent large sums to have their hair straightened because they were ashamed of their distinctive African American looks. Likewise, when my wife and I visited Senegal in sub-Saharan Africa, one of the poorest countries on earth, we were amazed to see enormous skin-bleaching advertisements on billboards. But how different is this sad denial of ethnic pride from the explosive trend among American women to undergo surgery to conform to accepted modern standards of beauty? This trend is becoming so pervasive that, according to the American Society for Aesthetic Plastic Surgery, Americans under the age of 18 accounted for 223,594 cosmetic and plastic surgery procedures in 2003. *Teenagers* are getting liposuction, breast implants, and reshaped facial features to be thin, busty, and beautiful.

Where will the next generation of women's leaders come from? When will they appear on the scene? Well, maybe you will be one of them. Maybe today will be the day. As the ancient Jewish sage Hillel said: "If I am not for myself, then who is for me? And if not now, when?" The ancient rabbis also said, "You are not required to finish the entire job. But neither are you absolved from beginning the process." Look around at the billboards the next time you take a walk, and look at what is on TV when you come home. Decide if the time for new leadership and change isn't right now. Decide if we can even wait one more day. And decide if you can afford to sit this one out.

TWO

THE NOBILITY
ACCORDED WOMEN
IN AGES PAST

4

VENERATION FOR WOMEN
IN TIMES GONE BY

I grew up in a single-parent home, and I watched my mother work two jobs a day to put a roof over the heads of her children and send us to a good school. She gave her life to us, and she instilled within me veneration for women in general, and for women like her in particular. No sacrifice was beyond my mother. I remember one night when she was driving us in the midst of a terrible storm, and the jalopy she drove broke down. She left us inside to protect us from the torrential downpour as she stood on the street, soaked to the bone, trying to flag down someone with jumper cables. When no one stopped, she pulled the hood open, tearing open her hand in the process. With blood dripping from her fingers, she tried to get the car started so she could get her children home. Such were the heroics of what seemed otherwise to be an ordinary woman.

My admiration for my mother caused me to grow up in awe of womankind. I saw women as divine creatures who exhibited a unique nobility of spirit. I observed their consummate devotion to all that is precious in life, and I noted that they were garbed with a dignity that made them appear almost angelic. In my class at an orthodox Jewish day school, the girls were just different. At lunch, the boys would have burping contests. My friend Larry could string one out for nearly thirty seconds without taking a breath (after which he would pass out). Sure, the girls would sometimes giggle at his grossness, but it was unthinkable that they would copy it. We boys would entertain ourselves with the usual locker-room humor. But there was no chance that one of the girls would emulate us by asking her friend to "pull my finger."

When I went to study at an advanced rabbinical college in Jerusalem at the age of sixteen, our training took place in an all-male environment. In orthodox Jewish education, the sexes are strictly segregated and we were not allowed any female friends or even acquaintances. Distant and elusive, women became even more divine in my eyes. My yeshiva in Jerusalem was at the bottom of a hill and perched atop that hill was Beis Yaakov, the largest young women's seminary in the city. Every day at about 4:00 P.M., approximately 1,000 teenage girls, dressed modestly from head to toe in their light and dark blue uniform, would amble past the windows of the auditorium in which we studied Talmud. There were about two hundred of us boys and we worked together in animated pairs. At four o'clock, however, the room would become much quieter as we all paused to secretly catch glimpses out the windows. The head of the yeshiva, a scholar who was not quite five feet tall, would scramble to close all the curtains. But despite his efforts to minimize the distractions, the wind in that hot city would blow the drapes apart and we could see the girls walking by, although each of us pretended not to notice.

I still remember what it was like. We looked at these girls as if they were seraphs of heaven whose gentility moved us even from a distance. I remember, too, that our gazing was devoid of lust. We weren't looking at them like horny teenagers. Instead, we looked at them with a sense of jubilant wonder. We knew that these heavenly creatures had emotional softness and comfort to offer that could take away our loneliness and pain. They could make us feel cherished and worthy. As they strolled by, they seemed so mysterious. Their modesty thrilled us. Their femininity pulled us. They seemed always beyond our grasp, which only increased the sense of awe. Their inaccessibility increased our desire for the day that we would be able to date and marry, most likely in our early twenties.

Our yeshiva gave us Friday afternoons off and we would often go to the commercial district of Ben Yehuda Street, where we would give out Jewish religious paraphernalia to less religious Israelis and lay *tefillin* (ritual leather with parchment which Jewish men affix during morning prayer) with the soldiers. Afterward, I would buy myself uniquely Israeli treats for the Sabbath, like marinated spicy lemons and fire-pickles. Once, in a small store at the Kings of Israel shopping street, there were three girls wearing the distinctive Beis Yaakov uniform of light blue tops and dark blue skirts. When I saw them, the store owner was berating them for touching the merchandise and putting it back. I was in shock. How could a man raise his voice to young women? Did he realize to whom he was speaking? These were not men at whom he could yell. These were young ladies: beautiful, gentle young ladies who deserved reverence rather than chastisement. How could he be so blind to the aura they carried?

It was this gentility that we in the yeshiva all longed to add to our lives. We were conscious that these women had what we lacked. Whereas we would just throw our clothes on in the morning and run down to the study hall where we had to appear by 6:30 A.M., we knew that the girls dressed in a refined and ladylike manner that reflected their gracious characters. They were softer, both literally and figuratively, and they shone with the light of the divine countenance, reflecting God's transcendence, as we had been taught. Whereas we prided ourselves on how our studies made us smart, I knew that they were being taught how to be wise. And whereas we worked so hard on being holy and spiritual, I knew that to them it came naturally.

The elation that my seminary classmates and I anticipated when we thought of the time it would be our turn to marry was based on a sense that, on our own, none of us was complete, and that our lives would never truly be fulfilling without the specific female energy invited into our daily existence through marriage.

You may feel that I am describing a world that is either utterly foreign or false. Worse, you might say that glorifying women and placing them on a pedestal is just as dangerous as degrading them, a point I addressed earlier. But what I have described is classic Jewish teaching and constitutes the manner in which women were viewed for millennia in our tradition. It was my rabbinical training up to that point that had taught me to revere the feminine and to admire women. In fact, the adoration of women was pervasive in all ancient mystical thought.

The Veneration of Women in Ancient Tradition

Early cultures conceived women as being superior rather than equal to men. The ancients perceived women to be the fairer sex, more naturally noble, innately spiritual, inwardly secure, and romantically committed. Catholicism allotted distinction and reverence to the power of the female spirit with its emphasis on the sanctity of the Virgin Mary, according a unique place in that religion for the veneration of the sacred feminine. It went even further, moreover, by describing Jesus as a nurturing male, a feminine man, whose principal ethical teachings pertained to forgiveness, meekness, love, and humility. But Catholicism did not suffice itself with the feminine side of Jesus, because even Jesus, while described as loving and gentle, also had a judgmental side. In response to this, the cult of Mary arose. Jesus's mother Mary is depicted as being the embodiment of unconditional love, devoid of any judgment. She is venerated as the consummate protector, shielding all her children within her comforting bosom. The present Pope is a strong advocate for the cult of Mary. He credits Mary personally with having saved his life after Mehmet Ali Agca tried to assassinate him in 1981. It is particularly noteworthy that the Pope credited his salvation not to Jesus, a man who is the Christian savior, but to Mary, a woman.

Catholicism's emphasis on the blessedness of the Virgin Mary recognized the importance of worshiping the feminine energy and supported the idea of a woman as a sacred object to be treasured. The cult of Mary conditioned men to respect feminine sanctity and to guard feminine piety and purity.

Likewise, the ancient Hindus said that Yab (feminine) was greater than Yum (masculine), and the Tantric masters taught that the feminine Shakti was the source of divine energy for Lord Shiva. The Chinese placed Yin, the feminine, above Yang, the masculine. And in the Jewish faith, the divine radiance was captured in the feminine *shekhina*. Based on this assessment, the ancient rabbis maintained that Jewish women have fewer ritual observances than men because their congenital piety necessitated fewer external reminders of God's presence. The feminine influence in Judaism was always seen to be profound. When Abraham, the founder of monotheism, disagrees with his wife, God commands him to follow her instruction. In all these traditions, woman is understood as an elevated, lofty creature, an earthly vessel who uniquely captures the divine radiance. Woman is revered for her ability to refine, soften, and complete the masculine force that is coarse and brutish on its own.

Courtly Love and the Unattainable Woman

This idea of the supremacy of woman over man reached its zenith in medieval times in the realm of Provence, and the invention of courtly love in the court of Eleanor of Aquitaine, the mother of Richard the Lionheart. According to the ideals of courtly love, a woman was seen as an unattainable prize, an exquisite treasure high above man's reach. *Fin' amour*, or "fine love," as it was referred to when the culture of courtly love developed in southern France and Italy, was an expression of the knightly worship that a lover had for the refining ideal embodied in the person of his beloved. They were lovers only in the sense that he longed to be worthy of her affection, not that there was to be physical consummation of their emotions. In this way, while women may not have been able to move and shake the world because power during these times was based primarily on physical and military strength, they were certainly expected to be the inspiration behind the movers and shakers. They made men better, they tempered the bestial nature of man, added softness and cultivation and directed his efforts toward grander horizons. Their exalted influence was meant to guide the swords, scepters, or pens of those men who went out to mark the world.

The troubadour poets, those wandering minstrels who began to sing about courtly love in the late eleventh century, idealized womanhood and the power of loving. As Bernart de Ventadorn wrote in the mid-twelfth century, "By nothing is man made so worthy as by love and the courting of woman. For thence arise did light and song and all that pertains to excellence. No man is of value without love." It is clear from verses like these that it was the act of loving a woman that provided the ennobling and refining features within an otherwise loutish man. This was the fullest expression of what was potentially fine and elevated in human nature. Although social historians claim that the culture of courtly love had little effect on actual women in the early period of its development, aristocrats in the Middle Ages began to act out their own lives along the patterns of *fin' amour* as they learned of it in romance poetry and love lyrics. In this realm, women were given preeminence in courtship and marriage and were made into the arbiters of love and passion. But this love and passion surpassed the mere physical world, for in their adoration of a woman, the writers of courtly love were expressing a greater, spiritual love linked to God and the heavens. In a man's love for a worthy woman, he was transported beyond the earthly realm.

What Dante implied, when he wrote his thirteenth-century masterpiece *The Divine Comedy* for the unattainable Beatrice, was that a woman is superior in character. And in knowing her and being exposed to her natural goodness, Dante was inspired to produce greatness and work on his own intrinsic being to be worthy of her attention. In a period where men and women were overtly unequal in the day-to-day lives that they led, or could lead, because so much of survival and advancement depended on militaristic strength, it was somehow easier to see the differences between the sexes. Men were stronger and more powerful in terms of directing history, but women were loftier, purer, better—and this seemed evident to all.

Feminine Sanctity Inspires Masculine Dignity

The effect of women being placed on a pedestal in Judaism and other ancient cultures was that men had to work to be thought worthy of a woman. Capturing the attention of a damsel was a life-long pursuit, and a man would spend a lifetime refining his character to win a woman. Even after marriage, a wife maintained her status of lofty honor. Outside of worshipping God, honoring women was life's highest ideal. A man devoted his existence to honoring and protecting the woman he was lucky enough to have as his wife. Like a man who is taken aback by the site of a majestic mountain peak, he complimented her because he was in awe of her.

The ancient rabbis declared in the Talmud that the worth of a man is determined by how he treats his wife. An honorable man, they said, was a man who dressed his wife in far better raiments than the ones he wore himself. Having his initials on his collar meant nothing compared with the wedding ring that told the world a glorious creature such as woman was prepared to accept him as a husband. Marriage, therefore, was the ultimate sign of status because every time a man married, it was akin to being accepted into nobility. The ancient rabbis said that greeting a woman was like greeting the divine presence (not exactly the first emotion that comes to mind when seeing a picture of Paris Hilton). When Moses first encounters God in the desert, he is commanded to take off his shoes lest he trample on holy ground. Chivalry, too, was once predicated on the idea that men had to mind their manners in the presence of creatures who reflected the divine presence. The firm belief in times of old was that it took feminine sanctity to create masculine dignity.

This ideal carried on and, as late as 1936, the world applauded King Edward VIII for forfeiting a kingdom of 600 million subjects and a quarter of the world's surface for the love of a single woman. Today, wealthy businessmen routinely dump a devoted wife for the young, loose, social climber with a boob job. Significantly, these men suffer no social censure for doing so. Donald Trump, who has discarded two wives already and is now on his third young bride, remains one of the most admired businessmen in America.

Before I go on developing this argument, let me briefly, once again, preempt my critics. I know that some will be fuming in anger at the golden age for women that I have described. They will say that it never happened, that women were men's chattel for thousands of years, treated as nothing more than an insignificant appendage. They had few rights and, even in developed democracies like the United States, they couldn't vote. This was indeed so in many, perhaps most, cultures. I have no illusions at just how badly women were belittled in many societies and how badly they were treated in many countries throughout the centuries.

But here is a crucial point. In the past, the mistreatment of women was the corruption of an ideal. Women being treated as inferiors *betrayed a fundamental philosophical and religious premise that maintained that women were more lofty than men*. The very same cultures that afforded women few rights still all maintained that women needed to be cherished and protected because they were the more refined and noble counterparts to men. So the ideal was there even if its implementation was utterly corrupted. But today, it is the very ideology that has changed. Women have lost their mystery and elegance in men's eyes. They have become utterly ordinary.

Well-educated men use the word *bitch* almost as a generic reference to women. The reason that men today treat women poorly in relationships has little to do with *the corruption of an ideal* and everything to do with what they really believe about women, which is that they are stupid, sleazy, materialistic, and bitchy. You date 'em, you get bored, you move on. In the marital counseling I do, I am often amazed not at how many husbands cheat on their wives, but at how many actually believe that not cheating is for idiots. They challenge the very premise of being faithful to a wife, as if a woman is simply not deserving of devotion. Men today are interested in women mostly as *womankind*, rather than as individuals. They need a great many women to keep them interested.

The pornography industry understands this mind-set and gets men addicted to it on the Internet by giving them an infinite number of pop-up images. But men are quickly losing the ability to remain stimulated by one woman for the duration of their lives. In men's minds, there simply isn't enough content there, either on the inside or on the outside. The thought today of a man serenading a woman with poetry for many nights outside her home, or spending years courting a woman without consummation, would be laughable. Great novels like *Cyrano de Bergerac* could never be penned today because everyone would dismiss as absurd the premise that men could spend years winning a woman over without sex.

Western women are letting all of this happen, closing their eyes to the dangerous trend before them all in the name of no longer being willing to be seen as property. They decry the old stereotypes of the stand-by-your-man kind of woman and say that what we are seeing today is progress. Women too can go to strip clubs with their boyfriends and watch porn videos with them. Many women today mistakenly believe that being portrayed as loose and uninhibited is a form of feminine independence that they should embrace with pride. But this image—far from empowering—represents the ultimate triumph of men. In essence, it represents female surrender. After thousands of years of domesticating men, women seem to be saying, we are now going to throw in the towel and allow men to shape our behavior to be in line with the vulgar male libido.

This perceived correlation between the unrestrained woman and progress in gender relations has become so ingrained in our culture that no woman wants to be called a lady anymore. That term has been misconstrued to connote a submissive or somehow demeaning code of behavior. But without ladies there can be no gentlemen and without gentleman there can be no true feminine companionship. Only feminine sanctity can recreate masculine dignity, and without that balance there is devastation in every aspect of life.

5

∾

DISRESPECTING WOMEN IS THE PRINCIPAL CAUSE OF THE WORLD'S DEVOLUTION

Amid the good things happening in American culture, like the rise of the morality-based voters, much of what is going on is outrageous and disappointing. Pop culture grows more crass and decadent by the day. Nobody even blinks any more when a Miami radio station changes its call letters to WFCUK. As I pen these lines, the most successful American TV show is *The Apprentice* starring Donald Trump, a man loaded with money but bankrupt of class. The highlight of the show is when Trump humiliates potential employees by barking at them "You're fired." One can only grieve over a culture that promotes a coarse womanizer, who regularly dumps wives in favor of young models, as its very symbol of professional success.

Watching people be humiliated is big business on American television. Shows like *American Idol* feature judges such as Simon Cowell—known as Mr. Nasty—who shoot the middle finger at contestants they don't like. Public degradation has become as American as apple pie with programs like *Fear Factor* garnering huge ratings by having participants eat cockroaches and swim with feces.

The divorce rate is insanely high; our kids are largely ignorant, shallow, and undisciplined; the Arab world is erupting in monstrous terrorism; and the leaders of our domestic political arena are consumed with attacking one another rather than solving problems. The United States has divided into warring camps of right and left that often fight over trivialities at the expense of national unity. It is possible that we could find individual causes for all these tribulations. We could say that divorce is high because men and women live much longer these days and therefore experience more marital breakup (an interesting argument when you consider that it is based on the idea that people used to drop dead before they had the opportunity to divorce). We could say that kids are growing up faster than ever and are experiencing a sense of dislocation that exhibits itself in errant behavior. As far as the aggression in the Islamic world, we could explain that the Arab world is suffering a decline based on its rejection of modernity and the humiliation it feels at being bested by the West. And we could add that politicians are becoming more polarized because of the increasing emphasis on partisanship. No doubt all these factors play a role in society's ills, and some would say that the problems we are facing have always existed.

But I have a far simpler explanation, a single cause that accounts for the devolution of society's very civility. I submit that something brings together all these problems and roots them into a single malignant growth. That something is the growing hatred and disparagement of women: the assault on femininity, womanliness, the nurturer, and all things maternal in the world.

The Feminine Energy

Feminine energy has guided the world since creation. When God created the world, he began with the simplest formations and built up to the most complex. Thus light and dark emerged first followed by water, land, and air and finally living things, beginning with plant life and only then moving on to complex life-forms of the animal kingdom and humans. Notice the growth in complexity in what the ancient Jewish philosophers referred to as four stages of creation: the mineral, vegetable, animal, and intellectual. Eve was the last entity that God created before he surveyed his world and concluded that it contained everything that it needed. Woman was the very top of creation's ladder. Once woman was created, God could rest, for he had now brought the force that could orchestrate all the other disparate elements. With the creation of woman, God acknowledged that the world now had a healing component and was therefore complete; the world had what it needed to survive and thrive.

The biblical sages comment that it is no coincidence that Eve was the final creation, for she was the most intricate, the most complex (we all know how complex women are!), and the most complete being. In addition, the creation of Eve made the world perfect, and was therefore the last of God's creations, because it brought harmony and balance to the otherwise aggressive and unbalanced male energy of Adam. Eve represented the healing force that could ensure a harmonious future for everything that preceded her creation. Women are the glue of the world. Men compete against each other for honor and recognition, what the German philosopher G.W.F. Hegel called the thymotic urge. But women have a natural instinct for cohesion, and keep it all together. Notice that a man's anatomy resembles a line, indicative of a linear nature that is competitive and sometimes violent. The male line manifests itself in the swords of the battlefield and the baseball bats of professional competition. A woman's anatomy resembles a circle and is indicative of all-encompassing unity and the healing togetherness of the feminine energy. Woman is the glue of the world.

In creating Adam, God addressed the universe's requirement for raw masculine energy to sift through the chaos and construct an orderly world. God used the strength of a creature like Adam to drain the swamps, fell the trees, irrigate the land, and build cities and civilizations. But a world of only Adams would be highly imperfect, even dangerous. All that necessary testosterone, without anyone to temper it, would have led eventually to an aggressive and brutal world in which war would be the norm and fighting an everyday occurrence. Indeed, look at what happened as soon as Adam and Eve had two sons, instead of a son and a daughter: Cain and Abel immediately begin to bicker about who is more worthy in God's eyes until finally Cain kills Abel. And this is before history even begins.

God created the female sex as the counterbalance to the male, to soften and civilize man, because what is the point of building cities if a bunch of uncouth brutes inhabit them? Men may chop down trees to shelter themselves from the cold. But who is going to cultivate within them an appreciation for nature and sensitivity to the environment? This is what made Eve the jewel of creation and the last to be created. With Eve, harmony and peace came into the world, a nurturing character that could take away, rather than inflict, further pain. Through Eve, a healing energy flowed into the universe. That is also why, immediately after the creation of Eve, the Sabbath sets in. Peace can finally come to the world. There is a softening influence that brings harmony. Even the Sabbath is referred to in womanly terms, as a bride.

The Talmud tells a famous story of how every week ancient great rabbis, like Akiva, would go to the outskirts of the city, late on Friday afternoon, and stand to watch the sun go down. The disappearance of the sun over the horizon was a signal that the Sabbath, with all its holiness, was coming in. As the rabbis invited the Sabbath into their lives they would say, *Boi Kalla, Boi Kalla*, meaning "come, my bride, come, my bride." They naturally used the metaphor of a woman in describing the Sabbath because only a woman could capture the Sabbath's natural transcendence, healing, and sanctity.

The ancient rabbis point out in the Talmud that although the world was created in six days, there are many biblical references to it having been created in *seven days*. They explain that, true enough, the physical components of the world were created in six days. "But the world was still missing peace. But when the Sabbath came, peace came. Hence, the world was created in seven days." As anyone who has lived through wartime has learned, you can have all the blessings in the world, but if there is no peace in the land then all those blessings become negligible. Prosperity without peace is like having a vault filled with the most precious gems, but no light source by which to see them. In essence, they might as well be limestone.

So although God placed Adam in the Garden of Eden amid purest beauty and delight, Adam needed a nobler, more comforting presence alongside him to appreciate and absorb the beauty. By bringing nurturance and peace into the world, women bring light into the world. Eve is the Eden of which God speaks. Until her creation, Adam inhabited a beautiful garden. But it was not Eden. It became paradise when a woman whom he loved came into that cold world to soften his pain and excite his senses. Only when he shared the world with a woman he loved did Adam create for himself heaven on earth.

Male creativity is only realized through feminine expansion. A man only has children through a woman. The male seminal drop is actualized only in the feminine incubator. By nature, the female force is secure and unflappable, while the male force is capricious and vulnerable. Together, the power of these two forces can bear fruit, but on their own, each is lacking.

America: A Giant Truck Stop

In our society, the feminine energy that is so essential for ensuring productivity without brutality has been all but squashed. As a consequence, ladylike influences have diminished in every aspect and area of life—influences that might otherwise make this a kinder, gentler universe and make the United States a more compassionate and understanding society. Simply stated, there is very little to temper and ennoble male aggression and crassness.

My family loves to go camping. We love the outdoors, and we travel around the country in our RV. To buy diesel fuel in places that can fit a large vehicle, we often stop in trucker posts. Walking into a trucker post is like walking into a new and different universe. It is totally a man's world. And it shows. The truckers don't mean any real harm, but it is a world where most women would feel immediately uncomfortable, with ubiquitous decals and mud flaps of naked women to stick onto the trucks. There is an aggressive feel walking into these places, and you can almost sense the lack of any kind of nurturing presence. Looking at the American cultural landscape today is like looking at a giant truck stop.

Does this sound like an exaggeration? Well, think about it for a moment. Aren't men and women failing to bond in the first place and drifting apart after marriage because the masculine goal of professional success has taken precedence over the more feminine inclination to love? Is it not a glaring coincidence that the Arab world, a society which largely denies any public role or influence to women, is becoming much more aggressive? Aren't our children messed up because neither parent is focused on raising and nurturing them, and aren't politicians behaving like a bunch of spoiled jocks motivated as they are primarily by ego?

Professional fields that have a preponderance of men and dearth of women are often the most vulgar. Two cases in point are professional athletes and rock stars. Professional athletics has become famously misogynistic. At a professional football or basketball game, women are scantily clad accoutrements who jump up and down when a man scores a touchdown or a basket. Furthermore, professional athletes attract groupies by the hundreds with whom they often have casual sex. Both Wilt Chamberlain and Magic Johnson claimed to have slept with literally thousands of women. And just look at how these athletes, especially the NBA players are behaving: In the November 2004 riot between the Detroit Pistons and the Indiana Pacers, the players climbed into the stands and assaulted the drunken fans—a particularly disgusting example of male excess. And the rock stars? Why, female groupies literally throw themselves at these drugged-up wretches, which is why it should come as no surprise that most of them are on their fourth or fifth marriage. Men who are not conditioned to respect women, and whose characters are not tempered by women, are more often than not loutish, barbaric, and uncouth.

Femininity, more than merely being a womanly quality, is a panacea for solving nearly all the world's ills. Again, perhaps you think this a simplistic exaggeration. But if Arab countries gave women an authentic voice, I believe they would speak out against their children dying as human bombs, just as in the United States it was women, not men, who organized the Million Mom March against handgun deaths. If women indulged their innate feminine virtue and refused to sleep with men on dates, men would be forced to treat women with greater respect, and to marry them before bedding them. They would have to become gentlemen before being allowed to possess a woman. If wives did not just turn their bodies over to their husbands in the false belief that marriage is about sex on tap, then husbands would be forced to help more around the house to win over their wives and the divorce rate would plummet. In the presidential debates between George W. Bush and John Kerry, the pundits made the point that both candidates were on their guard to treat each other respectfully and cordially for fear of otherwise alienating "the female vote." Women make men behave better. But if there are no women, or if they are silenced or subtly encouraged to emulate men, their tempering influence is compromised.

This is nothing new. In fact, it is a very old concept and I am far from the first to articulate it. The ancient Jewish prophets long ago predicated that that the hard-nosed, masculine aggressiveness that led to war and strife would one day be replaced in a messianic era of peace and brotherhood. Men would take their phallic swords and beat them into more maternal ploughshares. According to the Kabbalah, maintaining the correct balance between the masculine and feminine presences in the premessianic era enables the dissolution of masculine aggression so that its positive characteristics can be enjoyed without being swallowed up by its own destructive potential. What is promised in the postmessianic period, however, is more than just an alleviation of potentially damaging masculinity, but rather an utter transformation. Humanity will not only learn to live together in peace, but to thrive off each other's differences.

While the Messiah is supposed to be male, he will be a very feminine man, a nurturer, a teacher. Many of the most revered men in the Hebrew Bible—leaders like Moses and Abraham—were nurturing teachers who fought when they were compelled to do so but were, by nature, soft and compassionate. This is why from ancient times all the way to modern Israel, there isn't a single triumphant military arch. Conditioned by the Bible to bring out the nurturing side of their characters, the ancient and modern Israelites never celebrated military victories. Indeed, even the Hebrew Bible's greatest warrior, King David, is better remembered for having sung the Psalms with harp and lyre than for fighting his enemies with bow and arrow. The Jewish festival of Chanukah celebrates the ancient Hebrew triumph over the Assyrian Greeks, the successors to Alexander, who defiled the Temple and sought to suppress Judaism. But the Jews, conditioned to be a studious and nurturing people, did not celebrate with a military parade, but with the warmth of the lighting of candles, a practice that continues until this very day.

Similarly, the New Testament, asserting the messiahship of Jesus, portrays him in very feminine terms; a nursemaid attending the sick, a maternal figure curing people's pain. He is depicted as a prince of peace in contrast to the powerful Roman emperors—raw masculine figures—who dominated his day. Ultimately, contrary to his depiction in the latest installments of the popular *Left Behind* book series by Tim LaHaye and Jerry B. Jenkins, the Jesus of the New Testament is not a warrior nor does he revel in some classical, militaristic, heroic status. He is portrayed as going silently to the cross rather than attacking his aggressors. As a Jew, I may not believe that Jesus is the Messiah. But I can still appreciate the purposeful depiction of Jesus as a nurturer instead of as a combatant.

The prophet Isaiah said that the Messiah would, "not judge after the sight of his eyes, neither reprove after the hearing of his ears. . . . And righteousness shall be the girdle of his loins, and faithfulness the girdle of his reins" (Isaiah 11:5). Rather than mete out harsh judgment, the Messiah would be a nurturer. Men judge almost everything based on visual evidence. That is primarily how they select a woman. Moreover, they rush to judgment. Women, on the other hand, are naturally deeper and their nature is kinder. Like God, they are more long-suffering. Thus, the perfect world foretold at the end of days appears to be a deeply feminine and nurturing world whose hallmark will be the end of aggression:

> The wolf also shall dwell with the lamb, and the leopard shall lie down with the kid; and the calf and the young lion and the fatling together; and a little child shall lead them. And the cow and the bear shall feed; their young ones shall lie down together: and the lion shall eat straw like the ox. And the sucking child shall play on the hole of the asp, and the weaned child shall put his hand on the cockatrice' den. They shall not hurt nor destroy in all my holy mountain: for the earth shall be full of the knowledge of the LORD, as the waters cover the sea. (Isaiah 11:6–9)

You do not need to be religious to accept this image of a more refined, gentler world. Secular lore has its own version of this purification. In fairy tales, a princess's kiss turns frogs into princes, signifying the age-old belief that a woman brings out the best qualities in a man. In more realistic scenarios, boys became gentlemen to win over a lady. But we have become too cynical for all this, and too masculine to believe in fairy tales and courting rituals. The saying used to go "behind every great man there is an even greater woman." Today's women have rejected this adage because of the word *behind*. To them, it sounds as if women are being asked to play second fiddle to a man. They refuse to do this, and rightly so. But in truth, they have missed much of the point of the adage. It doesn't merely suggest that a woman facilitates a man's success. It also asserts that whereas a woman can be a woman without a man, a man cannot be a man without a woman. Currently, our society lacks a nurturing feminine influence, and as a result, men are behaving more aggressively and brutishly and seem to be devoid of manners. Without the feminine foil, men can be hard as steel.

6

∾

THE LINE AND THE CIRCLE:
THE MASCULINE AND
FEMININE ENERGIES

Women were created to embody the feminine energy that checks the negative and destructive qualities within the otherwise productive male energy. However, when women are maligned and disparaged in a society, they cannot be the effective, softening counterforce that balances men, and the consequences are severe.

Before we break down the dual energy forces to their affiliation with gender, let's first talk about the concepts of feminine and masculine in general. The insights I offer are straight from the ancient mystical wisdom of the Kabbalah.

The Bible refers to God in both masculine and feminine terms, thus illustrating the ultimate marriage of opposing energies. Moreover, by embodying both male and female characteristics that correspond to what I call the God of the Line and the God of the Circle, the Godhead itself becomes a metaphor for relationships. A successful relationship will combine the line and the circle in the same way that these two forms are linked within God.

Kabbalah explains that there are two energies to God, one masculine and finite, the other feminine and infinite. When the Bible refers to God with either a masculine or a feminine term, the particular usage of one term over the other conveys different attributes of God. On the one hand, we hear of God's awesome might in such references as the *King of Kings*. The Kabbalists explain that this sort of identification describes the masculine, aggressive, history-shaping aspect of God. On the other hand, the sustaining and mothering identification of God is revealed when the Bible refers to the Creator by such designations as *The Merciful* and, most famously, the *shekhina*. This latter instinct is conceived by the Kabbalists to be the feminine, nurturing energy within the Godhead. This is the part of God that envelops all of creation in a giant cosmic womb, giving life to, and sustaining, the infinite expanse of the universe.

These two energies roughly correspond to a line and a circle, the cosmic geometry of divinity. The masculine God is the God of the Line, resembling, as it devolves down in our world, the phallus. The God of the Line is the God of history, which itself occurs in a straight, chronological fashion. Known in the Kabbalah as *memaleh kol almin* (the light of God that fills the universe), it is linear insofar as it is connotes the aspect of God that comes down from the heavens, like a ray of light onto the earth, illuminating the cosmic darkness and inspiring the activities of humankind. This is the manly God of strength and revelation who, like the majesty of a king's scepter, descends from the heavens into our world. He intervenes directly and at times unexpectedly in human affairs, rewarding the righteous and punishing the wicked. Like a stern father, this characterization of the Godhead reacts directly to human choice, rewarding and scolding humans in accordance with their actions. Like a king, the God of the Line metes out justice, rewarding the deserving and punishing the iniquitous. This is the God who uses the rod of justice and the scepter of kingly rule to teach man to turn from his foibles and embrace sanctified living. This God of history is a stern God of justice.

Yet this is only one side to God's energy. In addition to the God of judgment and history, there is also the feminine God of creation. This divine radiance, unlike its linear masculine counterpart, is represented by a circle that resembles the female anatomy. This aspect of God, known in Kabbalah as *sovev kol almin* (the light that encompasses the universe), is circular and cyclical, surrounding and sustaining creation. Like a circle, it is infinite, knowing no beginning or end. And this aspect of God is the spiritual source of women, which is why their anatomy reflects the circle. Just as a woman's sexuality is hidden in comparison with a man's, which is overtly visible, this dimension of God is cloaked and veiled behind the curtain of *Mother* Nature. This God of the Circle encompasses all of creation at once and is infinite, mysterious, unknown, symbolized by a spherical shape, with no origin or point of completion. This is the aspect of God that nourishes the universe in its bosom, hovers above creation like a protecting angel, nurturing humankind throughout the continual struggles of life—not intervening, but rather, silently accompanying man through his endless travails. This ever-patient force is permissive even in the face of human corruption and darkness, for it is always awaiting man's repentance and is confident that he will eventually embrace the path of righteousness and light. This is not the God of justice but rather the God of empathy and love. It is the God who is prepared to forgive man and embrace him even in failures, sin, and moral wretchedness. This infinitely compassionate side of God is the one that has given birth to universes and all that is contained within them. It is the aspect of God that endows all creatures equally with life, regardless of merit. It allows for and awaits man's repentance and rebirth, for this aspect of God, like a mother who forever broods over her young, is prepared to give man another chance.

Hence, the Hebrew Bible has two names for God, which are used interchangeably throughout the five books. First there is *Y-H-V-H*, otherwise known as the Tetragrammaton—the name connoting God's feminine and compassionate presence, which is God's holiest and most mysterious name. But the masculine name for God, connoting judgment, is *Elokim*, and is used specifically in the context of events like the ten plagues that an irate God visits on wicked Egypt.

Masculine and Feminine Pervade the Universe

Throughout the universe, we see the masculine and feminine energies in operation. Donor and developer, provider and recipient, heaven and earth, Chinese yang and yin, Tibetan Yab and Yum, Hindu Shiva and Shakti, Buddhism samsara and Nirvana, justice and love, prose and poetry, form and substance, body and soul, intellect and emotion, and of course, man and woman. Heraclites said that God is day and night, summer and winter, war and peace, and satiety and hunger—all masculine and feminine opposites. Everything in our world, such as computers, is run by lines and circles—units of digits opposite ones and zeros. Perfection is found when the masculine and feminine cease opposing each other and instead come together. Line and the circle join together, thereby creating the number 10, a line and a circle, signifying perfection and completion.

The medieval Christian scholar Nicholas of Cusa called the unity of the masculine and the feminine *coincidentia oppositorum* ("union of opposites"). Since the opposites coincide without ceasing to be themselves, this also becomes an acceptable definition of God, who mystically encompasses masculine and feminine traits but remains indivisibly One. The Hindu *jivanmukta*, the liberated individual, is he or she who is liberated from the duality of masculine and feminine, harmonizing the best traits of both. Tantric masters strive for the union of Shiva (a Hindu god) and Shakti (Shiva's consort) in one's own body and consciousness and engage in appropriate practices to this end. In Kabbalah, the union of masculine and feminine is known as Yichud Zah and Nukvah, or *yichud zun*. The ancient Greeks believed in the unity of masculine and feminine as well as a sign of completion. As Heraclites said, "Between all things there is a hidden connection, so that those that are apparently 'tending apart' are actually 'being brought together.'"

In Buddhism, the masculine and feminine are represented by *yab-yum* (Tibetan for "father-mother"). In Buddhist art of India, Nepal, and Tibet, the representation of the male deity in sexual embrace with its consort is the mystical union of the active force with wisdom (*prajna*, conceived as feminine)—a fusion necessary to overcome the false duality of the world of appearances in striving toward spiritual enlightenment. And in the West, we believe in the unity of masculine and feminine through society's most important institution, marriage, which in turn brings forth the continuity of civilization through the production of life.

Linear Men and Circular Women

Men and women stem from the two distinct energies that we find in God. In obvious, physical ways, men represent the line. A handsome man is thought to be one with an angular facial structure and a hard, solid physique—all this in addition to the obvious sexual equivalence of the male phallus. Men who are too circular, with rotund beer bellies, are not as attractive as the man with a flat stomach six-pack. The stereotypical alpha male is aggressive and assertive, looking straight ahead and always keeping his eye on the end goal. Men are the human embodiments of the God of history, who invades the human world, performs overt miracles, shapes society, and exacts justice from humanity. Like the proud and jealous God of justice who wields a gavel or performs impressive feats that mark the earth as if with a magic wand, men have always fought antagonistically to distinguish themselves, taking pride both in their own achievements and the vanquishing of their competitors. Men are into mastering nature instead of communing and becoming one with it. In fact, idle men are rarely attractive to women. Relationship books will tell you that women are attracted to "the man with the plan." Men become appealing to women through their accumulated accomplishments and their impressive resumes. Henry Kissinger was absolutely correct when he said that power, not good looks, is the ultimate aphrodisiac. Men embody this ethos with their competitive spirit in all areas of life.

Unlike the linear, goal-oriented man, women are celebrated for their curviness, their rounded breasts and hips, their full, voluptuous lips and wide eyes. Of course, their principal anatomical distinction from men is their genitalia, which form a circle instead of a line. The God of the Circle is hidden and seemingly passive. Likewise, women are, in the words of psychologist Warren Farrell, genetic celebrities who can draw men to them simply by looking radiant and attractive. They draw men in their passivity; their principal strength, in terms of their appeal to men, lies specifically in the passive qualities of natural beauty and feminine mystique. Like a gorgeous mountain range produced by Mother Nature, women are appealing in what they are rather than in what they do.

Goal Orientation versus Means Orientation

Whereas men have a linear approach to life, women have a cyclical approach. Men are goal oriented, but women are means oriented. Take the average man's preoccupation with sports, most of which consist of lines dominating circles: baseball bats hitting balls, hockey sticks slapping a puck, footballs being kicked through the uprights. Men love linear subjects like politics (who is higher on the ladder than who), money (represented by the linear market graphs), and finally women, whom they reduce to lines and measurements (Stacy becomes a 36-24-36). But women love talking primarily about relationships, circles of intimacy. They talk about their boyfriends, their husbands, their children, and their friends. They also love talking about shopping, another circle, this one not of intimacy but of acquisition, the one spiritual, and the other materialistic. (Indeed, when women fill the circle of their existence with love, they are not as dependent on filling it with material things.)

Since men stem from the God of history, they have traditionally built civilizations. Since women stem from the God of creation, only they can bring forth life. Between the two of them, therefore, men and women represent the essential components of the universe wherein every kind of interaction, to be healthy and maximize its potential, requires the synthesis of both the energy of the line and the energy of the circle. The heaven's rain comes down like a line into the embracing circle of the earth, thereby producing the greenery of nature. The sun sends its rays like a perfect line into the planets that circle it and that depend on its light for sustenance.

To elaborate this point, let us look again at one of the primary, identifying characteristics of men: competitiveness. The spiritual origin of men is the God of the Line, the God of history and justice. This is the finite aspect of God described in the Bible as being jealous of other gods. God exacts punishment from those who worship idols. Similarly, men view the world in a finite way that breeds their own competitiveness. When one of their colleagues succeeds, they see this as having taken away from the earth's limited abundance. Unlike the circle aspect of God, which connotes the infinite, the line is the source of the finite and limited world that God creates, thereby inducing a deprivation mentality in men, who emanate from God's linear light. From this perspective, men feel they must compete for their share of any pie. And if their colleague has taken a piece, he is treated not as a colleague, but as a competitor, an enemy even. They therefore cultivate an aggressive stance toward the world around them, seeking to grab all that they can. It is this attitude that has allowed men, throughout the generations, to cut down forests to make room for progress, or to declare their own ethnicity superior to another. Men seek to emblazon the earth with their name, and any obstacle that stands in the way of that immediate goal is seen simply in oppositional terms, as a foe to overcome and subdue.

Although I might seem to be painting this characterization of the masculine in purely negative terms, I do not mean to imply that there are not advantages to this kind of behavior. This single-mindedness has helped to establish civilization, has been responsible for advancements in science and technology and, in general, has created a modern world that, compared with the difficulties and dangers of the ancient world, must make each of us feel blessed to live in the twenty-first century. Male aggression was needed to clear swamps and forests, as well as to fight bad guys like Hitler and Saddam Hussein. But male aggression can also be a frightful thing when it goes unchecked. Advances in civilization have almost always been accompanied by war. All of us would probably prefer that future advancements not come about at such high costs. Don't we most admire the people who have been tremendously successful in their professional life, but have reached the pinnacle of success without stepping callously on everyone below them? How did he or she accomplish that? The answer lies in balancing the feminine and the masculine energy.

The Circle Envelops the Line

Unlike the Greek thinkers who postulated that dualistic and antagonistic energies steered the universe, the mystics understood that harmonizing is the objective of the energy of the line and the energy of the circle. The two are always longing to unite. These are not conflicting energies, but rather, two aspects of the same entity, in the same way that God embodies both of these aspects. There is an underlying unity when men and women come together, when the line and the circle unite, and as sparks and life are created. The Kabbalah calls this the unity of *memaleh kol almin* and *sovev kol almin*—the light that fills the world and the light that surrounds the world—a blazing cacophony of radiance. The key to success is to understand that the two seemingly opposing energies harmonize without ever ceasing to be themselves. Rather, in their union, each distinct energy is meant to enrich the other. But even as they harmonize, even when they meld together, it will be noticed—and this is crucial—that the line becomes enveloped by the circle. The feminine is predominant.

When a man and a woman make love, the man may often be on top. But it is the woman who always encircles the man. Amazingly, at the exact moment of union between masculine and feminine, there is no equality. No line and circle stand as equals side by side, as symbolized by the number 10. The masculine is subordinate to the feminine. The very nature of the circle is to encompass the line. I cannot overemphasize this point, because it exposes the lie of the whole notion of the equality of the sexes. In sex, the woman encircles the man. In the quintessential act of congress between masculine and feminine, it is the masculine that is subordinate to the feminine and it is the feminine that envelops and dominates the masculine.

The misleading notion of the equality of the sexes is predicated on the patently untrue idea that the line and the circle match up together. But in reality, when the masculine and feminine unite, when men and women come together to become one in sexual congress, they are not side by side. Rather, the line is inserted into, and thus completely enveloped by, the circle. The feminine is predominant. They are not equal, the masculine is subordinate.

How does this work in reality? Well, let's go back to this idea that man's competitive nature has led to civilization. Again, while this development, in theory, has been positive, the means of progress have often been brutal. This is what happens when the energy of the line functions without the soothing input of the circle. Combined with the energy of the circle, progress is infused with conscience and patience. In terms of men and women, this means that a woman is a man's redeemer. Women rescue men from the pain of competitiveness and the tribulations of an existence where they are measured solely by their productivity. Being in a relationship with a woman exposes a man to a higher reality, to a being who is naturally in touch with things that are superior to the everyday grind of acquiring status and power. Men are firmly ensconced on earth, and exposure to women inspires men to reach for something higher.

Sure, women are first attracted to men who are successful. But once they choose a man, they soothe him. They learn to love him for who he is rather than what he does. They transform his feeling that he's just a "human doing" into the firm conviction that he is a "human being." A woman for a man is like a hot bath, immediately soothing him of all his aches, encompassing him with a warm embrace.

In practical terms, the feminine elevates and redeems the masculine. Men without women are insufferable. Don't believe me? Just go into the average bachelor's apartment—or even better, a male student dorm room—and see for yourself. The place smells.

:re is green mold growing on the half-lemon in the fridge. There are urine stains on the toilet seat. Masculinity without femininity is ugly, chaotic, and brutal.

Tyrannical Regimes Have Little Feminine Influence

In tyrannical regimes led by men like Hitler or Stalin, there was never a single high-profile woman. These were cruel men over whom women, with their gentler nature, had no influence. Hitler purposely did not marry his mistress Eva Braun to show that no woman controlled him. Indeed, he hid her away. As his architect and war minister Albert Speer revealed in his famous memoir, *Inside the Third Reich*, on the rare occasions that Hitler brought Eva Braun out in public, he would make a point of giving her an envelope filled with money, in full view of his guests, to publicly demonstrate that she was nothing more than a whore to him. The Fuhrer would not be subjugated to any woman. Unlike other men, he did not need feminine companionship.

The same is true of the Soviet Union and its sadistic dictator, Joseph Stalin. You would be hard pressed to name a single prominent woman from the Stalinist era. Indeed, Stalin had essentially no feminine influences in his life, lest they curb his demonic lust for power and his unbridled brutality. His first wife, Ekaterina, died three years after they married. His second wife, Nadya, unable to handle the extreme torment to which her husband subjected her, committed suicide. After her death, historians have noted, Stalin became more violent, more bitter, and more consumed with vengeance. As Bunting Institute Fellow Patricia Blake notes, "[Stalin] killed almost every member of his immediate and extended family, leaving only his second wife's parents, her brother, and his own children."

By contrast, the world's greatest statesmen, who fought aggression and later established peace, were usually happily married and greatly cherished their wives. Theodore Roosevelt, Winston

Churchill, and Ronald Reagan, all of whom were extremely happily married, come immediately to mind. Even Franklin Roosevelt, who famously cheated on Eleanor and broke her heart, still looked to his wife as one of his principal advisers, giving her authority no first lady had ever enjoyed before.

A woman brings salvation into the life of the male. She teaches him that he can be hungry and competitive, but remain nurturing and kind. She softens his rigidity. She links love and emotion. She takes the man's strong electrical current and grounds it, ensuring that he will use his energy to produce light rather than shocks. In short, women domesticate men. A princess must kiss a frog to make a prince.

The Sexual and the Sensual

The synthesis of the masculine and the feminine is immensely beneficial to men. A woman can take her man's love of the sexual and teach him to appreciate the sensual. She takes his love of sexual conquest and teaches him the pleasures of fidelity and monogamy. She takes his hunter-gatherer instincts and domesticates him into a refined gentleman. She takes his love for conquering and bedding women and exposes him to how much more thrilling monogamy can be, as he devotes his time to fully exploring one's woman's sexual nature, instead of having shallow interactions with many. She takes his love of acquisition, power, and money, and gives him the far more lofty love of devotion and children who are created in his own image. She takes a creature who enjoys the sexual, and raises him to the delights of the sensual. In short, women civilize the brute in man.

Before you conclude that only men benefit from this synthesis of the masculine and feminine, let me elucidate how the fusion enriches women as well. A woman, the embodiment of the circular energy, also gains by being joined with the linear spirit of a man. Without a man in her life, a woman could easily have a satisfying routine, an orderly home, a great career. She would have order in the midst of chaos. But it would be an existence that lacked passion. Sure, she could be passionate about her hobbies, her career, and all the things that interest her. *But she would not be passionate about herself.* It is specifically when a man makes a woman feel intensely desirable, when a man lusts after a woman, that she feels her blood boil and her skin tingle about her very being. Without a man desiring her, a woman would have passionate pursuits, but in and of herself she would be living a life without sparks, in a home with no electricity. Men bring zeal into women's lives. They serve as the detonator to release a woman's hidden passion. That is why so many women make the mistake of loving bad boys. They may not be worthy, but their penchant for discarding rules makes them (falsely) exciting. A woman can use a vibrator to give herself an orgasm. But it takes a man to send her careening through the rafters of the ceiling, to the moon and back.

A woman seeks a line, a man to whom she can bequeath her love. Because she is capable of giving love, she must give it to feel complete. She wants not only her soothing qualities of the circle, but the passion and excitement of having someone who, through his focus and attention, makes her feel intensely alive. Like a magician's magic wand, the linear nature of man is immensely exhilarating. Men bring magic tricks to a woman's life. In nearly every relationship survey conducted, women said that the quality they most admired is "a man who can make me laugh." Women, possessed of a strong maternal instinct, are naturally responsible. But a man teaches her how to let go. With a man, she gets out of the predictability of life. He brings her pleasure. If there was only Mother Nature, there would be no God of history: no miracles, no drama, no excitement, no special moments—just the slow grind of the natural order. A woman wants a man who can bring marvels into her life.

Even in the sexual realm, the line plays an important role. Sure, women want love, the circle of intimacy. But they also want passion. They want men to lust after them. They want raw sexual brutishness, a man who makes love with raw energy out of his unquenchable thirst for the woman. True, a woman rescues a man from his activity, teaching him to be more comfortable with himself. But, conversely, a man rescues a woman from her *passivity*, which is not to say that women are passive, but that they attract men even in their passivity. They attract men just by being. But men excite women and teach them to quake and thunder. There is nothing like romance to set a feminine heart on fire.

Nevertheless, while masculine energy improves the quality of a woman's life, it can still be a dignified, gratifying existence without such additives. It will not be as exciting, and it will not lead to new life. But there is no danger of causing harm, and it will not take life. By contrast, the secret to male nobility is feminine dignity. Without women, men *can* be dangerous. Masculine energy that is not tempered by feminine poise is bereft of majesty. It may be productive; it may accomplish great things and indelibly score the earth; but it will most likely do so in a callous and brutal manner. At the end of the day, a man may have an impressive résumé but a deadened spirit. And perhaps some dead bodies as well.

The Natural Osmosis from Masculine to Feminine

If we go back to the notion that the male energy and female energy are representative of that which God possesses, then we need only look at the chronology of the God we see in the Bible to understand the linear male spirit, and that it was always meant to give way and be guided by a circular spirit. These two energies have a natural sequence. In the beginning, the God of history was most manifest. The Bible relates how God performed great miracles, revealing his might and strength and suitably impressing humankind. But as time passes, God retreats more and more into the background. He wants the earth's inhabitants to find him even when he is not overtly present. He wants humankind conditioned to finding him hidden behind every blade of grass and every falling leaf. This is an unlimited quality that is constantly renewed.

The same applies to world history. It, too, gravitates from the masculine to the feminine. Thousands of years ago, great men were the warriors wielding swords, strongly masculine men who subdued their enemies in battle. Their names remain legend: Alexander, Hannibal, Caesar, and Attila. Yet amazingly, if any of these men were alive today, they would be dismissed as gangsters, dictators, and thugs. The modern-day Alexanders are Slobodan Milosevic and Saddam Hussein. The most respected men in the world today are feminine men, what I call "circle men": individuals who beat their swords into ploughshares, who took their lines and made them circles, who transformed their aggressive male energies and became peacemakers. Their names are Gandhi, Martin Luther King Jr., and Nelson Mandela. Thus, in our time, the triumph of the feminine over the masculine is complete. It is no longer conquerors, but winners of the Nobel Peace Prize, who are most respected in the world.

Three thousand years ago, the ancient Jewish prophets foretold that the redemption would come to the world when women took the lead over men. Likewise five hundred years ago, Rabbi Isaac Luria, the greatest Kabbalist of all time, predicted that the Messiah would come in an age when husbands began listening to their wives. He predicted that the world would be redeemed by women, and women would teach men how to bring forth their more nurturing, harmonious energy. Women would help men create a messianic era based on peace and prosperity by teaching men to see all beings as brothers instead of as competitors, teaching them how to love rather than conquer. This was the intended role of the feminine facilitator.

Death of the Feminine Facilitator

The world, as God intended it to function in his image, was to embrace the line and the circle, the masculine and the feminine energies and synthesize them to promote the best interests of both. This was the formula that was meant to lead to optimal productivity and healthy relationships. This was the secret of the world's inevitable perfection. And with the birth of feminism, there was the possibility that this might occur. Women began demanding their rights. They demanded to be taken seriously, to have a role in shaping the culture and the body politic. They asserted the truth of their intellectual equality to men, and demanded access to the traditional male professions of medicine, law, and politics.

How did it all go south? How did it transpire that, instead of women influencing men to be more nurturing, men ended up influencing women to be more aggressive and vulgar? Likewise, how did it come about that, instead of women helping men understand that their children were more important than their jobs, men ended up influencing women to believe precisely the opposite? Here we are, forty years after feminism, and the primary depiction of women in mainstream Western culture—on TV, in music, and on the Internet—is not woman as an intellectual being, but as a creature solely of the body. Not woman as a professor, but woman as a prostitute. It seems that few individuals in our culture today want to be feminine any longer. Even the women themselves, the embodiment of this circular, feminine energy, have chosen to go the way of the line.

The *New York Times* reported, on December 6, 2004, that Princess Sayako of Japan had finally decided to marry, at age thirty-five. The women of Japan were thrilled, not that she was getting married, but that she was breaking convention and marrying late. The article quotes Yuko Matsumoto, an author who writes about social and gender issues, as saying, "She's wonderful because she has waited until she became thirty-five years old and then found the best person at the best time for her. I assume that she had been pressured to marry when she was twenty-five or thirty years old." What an astonishing development. For thousands of years, men made the terrible and selfish mistake of believing that real fulfillment and personal greatness were to be found in power and money. They neglected their wives and farmed out the raising of their children to others to pursue their dreams of money and conquest. Now, the women have become just as dumb. They too now believe that becoming a vice president of an accounting firm is superior to finding love and nurturing life. They too believe that the purpose of life is to live to work instead of working to live. Why couldn't Princess Sayako pursue her passion as an ornithologist with a husband at her side? Isn't it more exciting to climb a mountain when one has a partner with whom to share a view? Have the selfish pursuits of a person's own interests really trumped the selfless dedication to family, community, and kids? And now that our nurturers have become money-grubbers as well, who will teach us values? No wonder American's kids are confused, ignorant, drugged up, and sex-crazed. There is no one to teach them what is truly important.

The shallow criteria that men employ in choosing a spouse is likewise being copied by women, with women becoming as calculating and cunning as men. Today, 93 percent of women say that they will not marry a guy who earns less money then they do. This seems like the same kind of shallow appraisal of the opposite sex for which men have been rightly indicted. In the past, the hope was that men would be influenced to shed some of the distinctly masculine characteristics that made them assess everything with a physical rather than a spiritual eye. Exposure to femininity helped men soften their hard edges, so that the two energies, masculine and feminine, could live in harmony, bolstering and enriching one another. But instead of finding harmony and learning balance, today's men and women have both become linear. They exist in parallel lines that never meet, with no interlocking of line and circle. Men and women still marry, and still have sex, but they rarely achieve deep and lasting emotional intimacy, thereby perpetuating the widespread loneliness that has become the hallmark of a vacuous society.

We cannot really be surprised by all this when we look around at the offerings that popular culture puts forth. Women are no longer depicted as treasures worthy of immense effort, nor as lofty, inspiring creatures of mystery. Instead, they are portrayed as insignificant objects to be acquired. Since men (the line) tend to constantly evaluate women like an architect with his ruler, more and more men are not falling in love. They refuse to "fall," to let go of rational evaluation and comparison, and allow emotion to take over. Few women today feel adequate or good about themselves, because even the men who love them view them through the objective lens of unending judgment. What motivation, then, is there for a woman to embrace her feminine energy?

FORTY YEARS OF FEMINISM ERASED IN A SINGLE DECADE

PART
THREE

FORTY YEARS OF
FEMINISM ERASED IN
A SINGLE DECADE

7

AN UNEQUAL EQUALITY

When the second wave of the feminist movement began approximately forty years ago, it was motivated by important factors such as the need to ensure equal work for equal pay, which promoted the overall notion that a woman is a man's equal in the workforce. While objectives such as this were crucial and paved the way for women to achieve equal rights with men, the movement lost its way because it failed to acknowledge the intrinsic difference between men and women. In the rush to make sure that women were not repressed, that they were treated as well as men, it tried to claim that men and women, apart from their plumbing, were identical. This idea is not only misguided, but demeaning to women.

Men and women are not equal. Let me say that again so that we are all clear: In terms of their intrinsic essence, *men and women are not equal*. The equality of the sexes is a modern-day myth, born of a misguided, though well-meaning, objective. The thinking was that promoting men and women as equals would ensure that women would be treated as such. Little did those who promoted the idea of the equality of the sexes realize that if women are treated *only* as men's equals, then they would be forced to emulate and become like men in order to succeed in a man's world. Rather, the respect of men for women was always predicated on the idea that women were not equal but superior.

79

This may sound like a strange idea, but it is empirically verifiable. Women are not equal to men. In the most important aspects, they are more advanced. Yes, generally speaking, men are physically stronger than women and can outrun them in a race. But in every *human* area that really counts, women come out on top. Men are responsible for 97 percent of violent crime in the United States. They are many times more likely to abandon their children than women. Women represent more than 65 percent of all people who go to synagogue and church. Women commit easier in relationships than men and cheat less often in marriage. Men spend $15 billion a year on pornography. Women spend virtually nothing. And while men are frequently more accomplished than women in subjects like mathematics, engineering, and science, women are wiser than men, understand life better, mature faster, are much more gifted in languages and the humanities, and are far less likely to mess up their lives with things like drugs and alcohol. Women get significantly less depressed than men, and are seven times less likely to commit suicide. And this is just a tiny sampling of feminine superiority in the range of the emotional and the spiritual, the areas that most define our core humanity. The superiority of women is also manifest in many other ways: Studies show that girls cheat less on tests, exhibit fewer behavioral problems in school than boys, wait longer to have sex, are more likely to help around the house, and are more likely to volunteer for charitable work

None of this should come as any surprise. It is self-evident just by hanging around both genders (although I admit that in this age of feminine masculinization, the distinction between the sexes has become far more blurred). I have always been aware of the primacy of the woman. I was raised by a mother who sacrificed everything to raise me and my siblings. And I am not alone. Millions of American boys and girls are today being raised by single mothers who have utterly ignored their own needs for happiness as they put their children first. Women are simply better at being selfless than men. To be sure, men are also good at sacrifice, although usually of the variety that comes with glory and classic heroics, like jumping on a grenade. But women will sacrifice even when there is no glory, when the cameras are not rolling.

I know that a lot of people will argue and say it is counterproductive to elevate women onto a pedestal. They will insist that it is better to focus on the sameness of the sexes than to glorify one over the other. I often receive letters like the following one:

> Dear Shmuley,
> I always enjoy reading your articles. Where I take issue with you is your treatment of men. You are always bestowing virtues on the female character. I just read your article on misogyny and there you go at it again. It is like you are some kind of an apologist for the bad characteristics of men. I believe you have an important message to spread but that message will never be spread if you turn off your audience, as you have done for me.
>
> Allow me an example. Say I am about to address a group of people dealing with man/woman relationship issues and I start with this comment. "The men in the group are brutes, motivated by impure desires and they really need to listen to their pure counterparts that have the real message to give." Don't you think the men in the audience would just leave? As a strategy, Shmuley, your panning of the men is a poor one.
>
> Think about it.

I did think about it, and I concluded that this writer misunderstood me. I believe that men are just as godly and goodly as women, but a man needs a woman to help bring out his righteousness. Woman is the catalyst that unearths masculine virtue. Women refine men and make them better people. That is why mothers and wives have such a profound effect on their husbands and sons. That is also why the existence of gentlemen is predicated on the prior existence of ladies. Look even at the word: *gentle*man. A man who is more feminine, more gentle.

While the feminist movement wanted to elevate women from the lower rungs of discrimination, to which society had relegated them, the movement should have been seeking to reclaim the lofty, dignified perception of women that existed in the past, instead of seating women on the same level as men.

A passage from Baldesar Castiglione in his renaissance classic *The Book of the Courtier*, gives you some idea of how in former times women were seen as the powerful motivation behind masculine virtue:

Who does not know that without women we [men] can feel no contentment or satisfaction throughout this life of ours, which but for them would be rude and devoid of all sweetness and more savage than that of a wild beast? Who does not know that women alone banish from our hearts all vile and base thoughts, vexations, miseries, and those turbid melancholies that so often are their fellows? And if you will consider well the truth, we shall also see that in our understanding of great matters women do not hamper our wits but rather quicken them, and in war make men fearless and brave beyond measure. And certainly it is impossible for vileness ever again to rule in a man's heart where once the flame of love has entered; for whoever loves desires always to make himself as lovable as he can, and always fears lest some disgrace befall him that may make him be esteemed lightly with her by whom he desires to be esteemed highly. Nor does he stop at risking his life a thousand times a day to show himself worthy of her love: hence whoever could form an army of lovers and have them fight in the presence of the ladies they love, would conquer all the world, unless there were opposed to it another army similarly in love. And be well assured that Troy's ten year resistance against all Greece proceeded from naught else but a few lovers, who on sallying forth to battle, armed themselves in the presence of their women; and often these women helped them and spoke some word to them at leaving, which inflamed them and made them more than men. Then in battle they knew that they were watched by their women from the walls and towers; wherefore it seemed to them that every act of hardihood they performed, every proof they gave, won them their women's praise, which was the greatest reward they could have in the world.

Do you not know that the origin of all the graceful exercises that give pleasure in the world is to be ascribed to none other than to women? Who learns to dance and caper gallantly for aught else than to please women? Who studies the sweetness of music for other cause than this? Who tries to compose verses, in the vernacular at least, unless to express those feelings that are inspired by women? Think how many very noble poems we should be deprived of, both in the Greek tongue and in the Latin, if women had been lightly esteemed by the poets. (Waller Newell, *What Is a Man?* [New York: ReganBooks, 2001], 9)

Many will say that this is ridiculous. They will say there was no golden age for women. Women were treated as men's property, could not get an education, and did not have rights. To be sure, if women had it so great in days gone by, there would have been no need for feminism. I, of course, acknowledge that women were indeed prevented from maximizing their intellectual and professional potential. Women were consigned to a secondary role in society, were not even allowed to vote, and feminism emerged as a backlash to such revolting discrimination. So why do I say that, in the past, women were so much more respected than today?

Because they were. There was a widespread understanding that women were superior to men, even if its implementation was thoroughly corrupted. Men believed that women were the fairer sex, much more emotionally developed, more naturally spiritual, and in possession of an innate nobility of character that a man could never match. It was for this reason that men always felt it was their obligation to protect women, just as a man puts a fence around a precious garden. Men took off their hats to ladies, were careful not to utter profanities in their company, and got up from the table when a lady arrived. To be sure, they also abused the concept of a lady by saying that such a gentle creature had to be protected from the rough-and-tumble of the professional world, and thus for the most part, women were denied careers. But it wasn't the philosophy of feminine superiority that was misguided, it was the implementation. Rather than men controlling women because they were the fairer sex, or wrongly treating them as being too emotional for serious intellectual pursuits, men should have been following the lead of women for that very purpose. Feminism could have been, should have been, the liberation of feminine potential as women assumed leadership positions in a world yearning to be better. Instead, it became about women adopting a masculine model of achievement and emulating it.

Feminism should have striven to teach men and society at large that a woman could be a great lawyer or a successful politician, but still take great pride in being a wife or a mother. Women demanded that in addition to being respected, they had to be taken seriously as intelligent and highly capable people. And women insisted that they could do all the things that men did (true). All these accomplishments of the movement were undeniably positive. However, instead of infusing the raw and competitive professional world with a nurturing energy, women for the most part made the terrible mistake of assimilating into the previously male-dominated environment, becoming hypercompetitive, living for money, delaying marriage, fearing commitment, ignoring their family, becoming greedy and materialistic, becoming social climbers, and using ruthlessness to achieve their ends.

Men's philosophy about women has changed. Men think that women are even greedier than they are, and that they will marry a man for his money. They think women are so stupid that they are only good for spreading their legs, and so bitchy that even their own husbands can't trust them completely. Think I'm exaggerating? We are beginning to see the actualization of these ideas more and more frequently. We see it in the number of men who now *insist* that their brides-to-be sign prenuptial agreements. In 2001, the *New York Times* reported an increase of 1,500 percent in prenups over the preceding ten years because men are suspicious that the women they are marrying only want their money. We are seeing the male belief that women are just as mean and untrustworthy as men. That is why more and more movies like Tina Fey's *Mean Girls* are being made. That is why so many books like *Queen Bees and Wanna Bees*, *Odd Girl Out*, and *Fast Girls*, which allege overall that girls in school are much cattier and more mean-spirited than boys, are being published. As a culture, we seem to like seeing women degraded. We love painting a picture to undermine the idea of the female nurturer. We love ripping women from their pedestals and shoving them to the ground. We love showing that they are no more refined than men.

Donald Trump: American Hero?

Men are coming to believe that women really are shallow gold diggers and empty vessels. After the runaway success of the NBC show *The Apprentice*, I published an article saying how lamentable it was that Donald Trump was being touted as an American hero, when he repeatedly dishonored women by marrying them and dumping them the moment they put on a couple of pounds or a couple of years. I argued that it was impossible for a man who wasn't a gentleman to be a hero. "At best, Trump is half a success, having succeeded in the far easier and far less important half of life, namely business and making money," I wrote. "But in the personal realm—the far harder half and the one that really counts—Trump is unfortunately a dismal failure." At a Manhattan kosher restaurant a month after the column appeared, I bumped into Marla Maples, Trump's second wife, who thanked me for writing the article.

But notwithstanding how many women welcomed the column, I was amazed at how many of my male friends flipped out and accused me of always blaming men. They said that I was blind to the real dynamic at play: that women are the ones who chase guys like Trump for their money. A typical response was this one from Mark:

> Shmuley,
> You are really losing the plot. Trump is amazing. And your focus on women's rights is ludicrous. When a woman, such as his first wife, meets a guy like this, they see dollars. Then there's sex and romance. Then there's living with that witch. Then the bitch who was an air hostess capitalizes on her boobs and her sex appeal, and she woos this guy and has his kid. Then you come and say how wrong he is. Please. Most women have dollar signs in their eyes, and success and power as their messed up priorities in choosing husbands. It's like the famous French leader said, "All women are fickle." Women want a guy's money, yet you blame Trump. Now, you'd have a point if this was a

poor man who married a woman before he was rich, and then discarded them when he'd made it. But no, not Trump. Most women, let's not kid ourselves, look for the wrong thing. Just look at all the beautiful women who marry bald, fat men just because they have money. Women are awful in this regard and you must lecture them. The majority of women are dependent on their men to produce money for homes, vacations, lifestyle, kids, education, etc. Hence they are forced to look for a rich man. This is the real problem.

To be sure, there is some truth in what Mark writes. There are a heck of a lot of shallow women out there who would love to marry a man with money. But men like Trump often attract gold diggers *because* they flaunt their money. By his actions, he is saying to women who meet him, "All I have to offer is cash rather than character." How can men complain that women only want their money when it is all that men shove in their face? This is another example of our culture's downward spiral. In an effort to create equality between the sexes, women are deprived of their natural primacy and are thereby dragged down to the baser levels of men. Men, without the ennobling influence of women, devolve to embrace a cruder lifestyle. If women are struggling to equalize themselves, then there is little wonder they are no longer regarded as lofty, refined creatures. In this environment, women as gold diggers make sense!

8

∞

THE FALL OF EVE

Women have been disempowered, disparaged, and degraded in a slow, gradual descent. If we look at the process that today's men and women engage in as they go out with one another, we have a prime example of this devolutionary change. Up until the social upheaval following World War I, men courted, rather than dated, women. In many ways, women were in the driver's seat. A man would come to a woman and present his card as a means of asking for permission to enter her company. And a man had to become a gentleman before he could even *think* of being received. The woman would then be in a position to determine whether she would receive him. Men had to overcome all kinds of barriers before they could even approach a woman, not the least of which was her mother. By contrast, today, women writhe and wriggle on a nightclub's dance floor to attract male attention. The onus is now on the women to be magnetic enough to draw a man. When I lectured at Yale on the subject of misogyny, one woman identified this as the principal degradation that she experienced as a female university student. "I don't like how men have their choice of women. When it comes to love and relationships they can sit there picking us out, like a man sifting through a jar of jellybeans for the colors and tastes that he likes, leaving behind all the ones that don't appeal to his taste buds at the moment."

Women will take issue with this point and say that part of the liberation that has occurred in our society is that the social convention has changed and now allows a woman to ask a man out instead of waiting for him to take action. This point of who asks whom is not the issue, however; it is the whole dynamic of dating that has degenerated. No matter who starts the relationship, it is the women who have to paint their faces for the men. It is the women who are expected to go to the gym to tone their muscles for the men. It is the women who are expected to diet and conform to fit into the pinup girl image men demand. Men are also asked to take care of themselves, but if you take five minutes to randomly watch couples on the street, you will observe that if a couple has disparate looks, it is almost always the man who is out of shape, bald, or dumpy, but nevertheless draped by a hard-bodied woman.

Putting the issue of physical appearance aside, that women take care of themselves and can be cultured and gentle has never been in question. Therefore, we are not worried about women expending sufficient effort to make themselves presentable and desirable. Men, on the other hand, have always needed help. So many of my male friends, and I would include myself in the group, improved our style and decorum after wedding, because we had a woman to tutor and refine us. Yet to attract that woman, we had to begin the process ourselves and show a desire for change and improvement. Heck, we had to prove that there was raw material with potential! In the general population today, the entire dynamic has been reversed. Women are actually devolving to appeal to men, rather than inspiring men to reach their elevated plane. When men courted women, it was the man who did the work. He had to refine his character, to work on becoming a gentleman. He had to learn manners, dress immaculately, behave chivalrously, and only then was he deemed worthy of courting a woman. Without having developed most of these qualities, his chances of getting a lady were virtually nil.

Today, while the woman goes through her two-hour routine getting ready for a date, all the man does is shave, scratch his crotch, jump in the car, belch, and pick her up. This is certainly not the way a man would treat someone he prized.

When "courting" ended and "dating" began, somewhere just after the social upheaval of World War I, the locus of power in male-female relationships shifted from the women to the men. In courting, it was the women who selected which men they would receive. In dating, it was the men who began to choose which women they would take out. And the power of the men in relationships has since grown substantially.

My Personal Sense of Awe for My First Date

When I was twenty-one, having just returned from a two-year tour of duty as a student-rabbi helping to found the first rabbinical college in Sydney, Australia, I was incredibly lonely despite an abundance of male friends. A rabbi with whom I was close suggested that I take out the daughter of a couple I knew in Australia, who happened to be studying in New York. I remember the first time I picked her up in the car. She was the first woman I ever dated, and I could not believe I had a young lady sitting next to me. My brother had lent me his sports car for the occasion, and I was driving incredibly fast without paying much attention to the road. I was just staring at her. I was not fixated on her beauty, but rather, on the light that shone from her face. Without paying heed to the fact that I was clearly entranced by her, she chided me over and over again: "Look at the road and drive." I felt like Moses, who had suddenly encountered the divine presence in the burning bush. I was in the presence of something transcendent. Having a woman on a date mesmerized me. I felt unworthy. And without discounting the special qualities that were unique to this woman, the awe I felt was not for her in particular, but for womankind. I felt she was a hallowed creature, and it humbled me. We married a few months later, and God has since blessed us with seven children.

I do not tell you this to promote the fact that marriage came to me without the pain and confusion of constant dating. I do tell you so that you recognize the reason it came easier than it does to most was that extra sense of awe I had when I went on my first date with a woman. I wasn't sitting there searching for flaws the way many men do. Indeed, because I had never been out with a woman before, I had nothing by which to compare my future wife. But unlike most men today who have dated so many women that they have become like diamond dealers, experts at spotting imperfections and flaws, I was like a new bride given her first diamond, for whom the stone only glitters.

"Women Are No Big Deal"

Not only is the sense of awe that I felt on my first date nonexistent today, but most men would positively laugh at my description and think that I have a few loose screws. *Sense of awe on a date? You crazy? Women are not that big a deal.* Those are the words I hear all the time. Women aren't a big deal. Sex isn't that big a deal. Oh, they'll admit, *some* women are a pretty big deal. The really gorgeous ones. The supermodels. The *hot* ones. But all the other women, cut the crap. Grow up. Wake up out of your romance-induced fantasy.

I remember when I noticed the earliest murmurs of this new world dominated by a brutish and dismissive masculine spirit. It was 1992, and by then I was into my fourth year as the rabbi at Oxford University. The city of Oxford has miserable winters but beautiful summers. And every year, the thirty-nine colleges that make up the university compete against each other in a rowing regatta that is known as "Eights Week." There I was, walking among the beer-guzzling students at the Oriel College boathouse, Oxford's premier rowing college (which has produced many Olympians), listening to them cheer their boat crew, when I heard the following tune:

A-bor-tion, A-bor-tion . . .
Lay that lady on her back. Pull that baby from her crack.
A-bor-tion, A-bor-tion . . .

Several other songs along these lines followed. The so-called panty-raiders were also out stealing women's underwear and hoisting them up the boathouse flagpole. The panty-raiders were a proud crew, wearing both hats and T-shirts to identify themselves. Interestingly, when they would pull a woman's knickers up the flagpole, she would usually stand by laughing hysterically. I guess both parties thought this was pretty funny.

I didn't know what was more shocking: that male students at the world's most prestigious university were chanting such misogynistic rhymes and pulling off such disgusting stunts, or that hundreds of female students sat there laughing as they did it. At the other boathouses, men pulled off women's brassieres and flew them up the flagpole to the amusement of all. The women who were their victims did not seem the least bit distraught. In fact, they laughed the heartiest.

This kind of acceptance of the degradation of women could not be merely chalked up to a lack of maturity on the part of drunken college kids. Today, the internalization of misogyny seems to start from a young age and carry on to adult life. A female advertising executive, with whom I am friendly, and who attended Harvard Business School, told me that when her male and female classmates from HBS would go out for drinks together, the men would routinely play a game of dividing the women into three groups: the women they would like to marry, the women they would "love to f—k, and the women they would love to shoot."

"What did you do when you heard them talking like that about women?" I asked her. "Nothing," she replied, shrugging her shoulders. "It was gross, but I didn't want to make a big deal of it."

Here was an intelligent, accomplished woman who did not feel entitled to object to an obvious assault on her gender. At least she was honest enough to admit that the discourse was offensive, instead of insisting, as many women do today, that it was all just harmless fun. I have too many personal stories that illustrate the problem of women yielding to a relentless barrage of misogyny with nary a complaint. In fact, many women actually facilitate the unacceptable behavior.

A case in point was a discussion I had with a newly engaged male friend of mine in Australia. I took him out for lunch to celebrate his happy occasion. "Do you have cold feet? Any hesitations?" I asked him.

"Nah, we actually have a really good relationship," he told me. "We never even fight. The only thing that Samantha sometimes gets upset about is my porn collection of DVDs. She'd rather I get rid of it."

"She'd rather you get rid of it? You mean she hasn't *demanded* it?" I asked.

Without the slightest real embarrassment, he simply responded by shrugging and saying, "She knows that it relaxes me when I watch, but she won't watch with me. I might get rid of it. I have to think about it."

In another age, it would have been unthinkable for an engaged man to speak so nonchalantly about his collection of pornography with his fiancée. Most men would have been embarrassed to have an entire collection of garbage catering to their basest instincts. Today, however, the self-esteem of women is such that they feel that they have to put up with this humiliating treatment. They actually have internalized the belief that they have no right to demand any erotic exclusivity from their spouses. While I was appalled when I noticed this trend, I found that I had to ask myself whether it was really all that surprising. Given that men are exposed to such explicit and relentless sexual exploitation of women, is it really shocking to find that men expect their wives and girlfriends to accept the permissive role in which they are cast?

But pornographic DVDs seem positively innocuous compared with the Internet. Each day, millions of American men receive e-mails with subject headings like the following:

"See insane bitches stalk men, they f—k 'em, suck 'em, and leave 'em for dead!"

"Screw her right" (an advertisement for performance-enhancing herbs)

"Horny farm girls. Watch 'em Get It All Over the Face"

"I forced her to"

"Watch These Sloppy Young Girls Get It All Over"

"Young Girls Taking It You-Know-Where for the First Time"

"Girls Getting Nasty with Animals"

"See Where This Guy Shoves His Arm"

"See What I'm Making This Girl Drink Gallons Of"

"See What I Do with These Drunk Girls"

"See How Deep I Shove My Pr—k into This Tiny Girl"

"Horny Teen Sluts Getting It Anal for the First Time"

"The most demented bitches ever found"

That this sort of material is circulating by e-mail every single day in the United States, without any serious outcry, beggars belief. We have become so inured to the offensiveness of such e-mails that we merely glance at them and then nonchalantly delete them (or at least I *hope* we delete them). This resignation is scandalous and shows how desensitized we are to the violence against, and the deprecation of, women.

It has become commonplace for men to refer to a woman who refuses their advances—say at a bar or on an airplane—as a bitch. It is as if they have a sense of entitlement; if they are interested in a woman, it is her duty to reciprocate. When she doesn't, she is a vile bitch. Similar to an African American man who used to be called "nigger" because he did not know his place, the woman is called bitch so that she learns hers.

9

~

WOMEN BEHAVING LIKE MEN

Instead of admitting that men and women are different by nature, that those differences are complementary and vital to our successful continuation, we have chosen to smear women, to drag them down to the low levels of men and, in so doing, to deny the female nature that inspires and elevates its male counterpart. We have worked so hard to turn women into men, and fearfully, we are getting closer and closer to making this a full-scale reality.

Nevertheless, even today, there are proofs all around that hint at what we are so anxious to deny. Women are naturally nobler, their softness, far from being a signal of weakness, is part of their lofty character, and we deny this reality to our own peril. If we create a society that does not nurture women, we will watch them slowly become like men. They will become as ruthless and as independent as men traditionally have been. It is a bit like raising kids. Children are tender and innocent. But if their parents neglect them, abandon them, or worst of all abuse them, the children slowly coarsen. They grow up before their time; they lose their innocence. They become vulgar and undisciplined. In short, they learn to rely on themselves. When the vulnerable elements of society are not protected, they have to give up their vulnerability. They become harsh and unpleasant. Go to a woman's prison and you will discover that an overwhelming number of the inmates have had a horrible, negligent, or absent father. Look at the very characteristics of the different sexes.

Man, by nature, is more violent than woman. Whereas once upon a time, it took a horse and a pike to be dominant, today the tools of destruction do not require physical primacy. Yet, even though women now have the capability to be as brutal as men, we find that men still reign over the darker corners of our civilization. Now that crude force is no longer the only means of asserting dominance in a violent situation, there should be no excuse for men being overrepresented in these statistics. The only explanation, therefore, must be that, by their very nature, men are more violent than women. Men, after all, are the ones with testosterone.

If we move out of the obvious realm of crimes and violence, there are other areas where the morality of women versus men seems to point to a disparity in their innate makeup. I mentioned earlier that men are many times more likely than women to abandon their children. We might try to explain this by saying women have a maternal instinct, but this accepted cliché is in itself proof of my point. We would all agree that the maternal role is an illustrious one. Mothering is the most selfless of undertakings in that its sole function is to toil endlessly for the welfare of another human being. It looks toward the future generation and labors to ensure its survival. I do not mean to imply that women have cornered the market in working toward these goals. But generally speaking, they are better at it by nature. A woman who abandons her children is an anathema in our society even today. On the other hand, while we have become better about calling men to task for such behavior, we are not necessarily shocked by it. Deadbeat dads are all too common in our culture. Therein is a small testament that even in our more equalized society, we do, at some level, recognize that women are far more reliable and committed than men.

This example falls under the rubric of morality, a realm over which women have traditionally maintained dominance. We are certainly working hard to change that. Prior to this generation, men were far more likely to have affairs than women, but today those numbers are changing. *Cosmopolitan* magazine maintains that wives are more likely today to cheat than their husbands. My friend Susan Shapiro Barash, who wrote a book on women's infidelity, maintains the same. Instead of viewing this trend as a tragic consequence of our popular culture, reflecting just how dissatisfied women are in their marriages, some claim it is a sign that women are becoming sexually freer and catching up with men in a healthy way. But there is nothing healthy about women becoming as unfaithful as men. The film *Down with Love*, starring Renée Zellweger and Ewan McGregor, was a narrative based on encouraging women to be as emotionally deadened and sexually promiscuous as men. This storyline was meant to be comical but I found it downright terrifying. It was too true to life to be funny, because the subversion of the innate female nature, away from love and onto empty sex, is actually happening.

Indeed, even ardent feminists like Sheer Hite have shown that, unlike men who cheat on their wives even if they love them, women only cheat if they are ignored or miserable in their marriages. If they are happy and satisfied, they almost never cheat.

Where is the sanity in celebrating that women have become as sexually capricious as men? Imagine you had two children: one who was very successful in school, smart and studious, and another who was lazy and an underachiever. Would you attempt to equalize them by coaxing the motivated child to slack off so that her sister would not feel badly? Of course not, you would want both children to succeed and excel. Why then do we consider it progress when women feel free to be as morally loose and crude as men? Why is the goal not about holding men to a higher morality? Why are we denigrating women in the popular culture instead of chiding men for being lasciviously drawn to such derogatory images of womanhood? Ultimately, why are we denying the natural order of our universe? This is what our present, racist misogyny does by hating women and negating the superior and inspirational energy they embody.

10

∞

THE PORTRAYAL OF
WOMEN AS THE
WALKING MALE ORGASM

Emmanuel Kant said that the definition of behaving morally is treating all human beings as if they are an end in and of themselves rather than a means to an end. The essential immorality of slavery was that white men and women looked at blacks as the means by which their labor could be accomplished—not as individual human beings with their own aspirations and dreams.

The relationship between men and women today is similar to this picture. Whereas the Bible refers to Eve as Adam's "helpmate, who is opposite him," today men have been trained to see nothing but the walking fulfillment of their erotic needs. Feminists complain that Sigmund Freud denied woman an intrinsic identity by portraying her as a castrated male. Yet they seem to be oblivious to the far worse modern depiction of women as a walking male orgasm. For many men, the answer to the question of why women exist is that they were created by God to be man's toy. Like sports on television, their primary existence is to serve as an instrument for male amusement and fantasy.

Let me submit some examples for your consideration. Women today are used primarily to sell products, from beer, to cars, to dandruff shampoo. What they are really selling is not so much the specific product, but sex itself, and this is done in the most debasing and crass manner. Arguably, the most popular television commercial of the 2002–2003 TV season was the beer commercial known as "Catfight," produced by Miller Lite. The ad showed two women wrestling with each other in a swimming pool and then in mud over the question of whether the beer was good because it "tast[ed] great" or was "less filling." The popularity of the commercial stemmed from its being the ultimate male fantasy, with breasts bouncing, underwear showing, and women rolling around on top of one another. But what made the commercial really memorable was that, at the end, the whole scenario turned out to be the reverie of two men talking in a bar, in front of their girlfriends, about the kind of television commercial that would truly capture their attention. In other words, just when you thought this commercial couldn't get any more misogynistic and offensive, guess what? It turns out that the real premise is that these two guys are talking about their erotic fantasy in front of their dates! Few objected to this commercial. On the contrary, it has become routine for boyfriends and husbands to display their lechery for other women in front of their girlfriends and wives. The women are expected not only to be "adult" enough not to object, but to laugh and enjoy the joke as well.

Women as a Human Plate

In another grotesque display of women being sexually exploited to sell a product, *The Week* magazine reported in November 2003 that Asian women were protesting a Seattle restaurant that "serves sushi off the body of a nearly naked woman." Patrons at Bonzai restaurant get to pick pieces of raw fish off a sexy model. She lies there very still wearing only a thong and plastic wrap. "It's dehumanizing to be treated as a plate," said protester Cherry Cayabyab. But not all women agreed that it was demeaning for a woman to be shrink-wrapped, topless, and have men pick sushi off her boobs. Nope, some women thought that it was no big deal. Promoter

Cheresa Nemitz said that this was not only harmless fun, but art as well. Performance art to be exact. "I think there are bigger fish to fry," she said. Astonishing. Who would imagine that women would consent to lie naked and have men select food off their bodies? And who could have imagined that *any* woman would see this as anything less than appalling, let alone come to the defense of this humiliating stunt?

Could you imagine the reaction if the story was that a jewelry company had decided to create a "ghetto" theme? Patrons could walk into the store to find an African American man, covered with tattoos and dressed as a rapper. The man would just stand there with hundreds of gold chains draped all about his body and the customers would come over and take the chains or bracelets off, try them on, and put them back, all the while using him as a human jewelry showcase. Would we consider this degrading? Or if asked, would black leaders say, "Hey, we've got bigger fish to fry." And if they did say that, would they survive as leaders of the black community?

As I keep insisting, a primary problem is that the women themselves are not objecting. In fact, the new genre of reality television combines all the issues that I have been talking about. For some inexplicable reason, average American women agree to submit to the foulest forms of degradation to participate in these shows and be in the spotlight for a moment. Not only do they consent to various humiliations on screen, they compete vigorously for the right to do so.

Most reality television revolves around sexual exploitation and the denigration of women. ABC's runaway hit *The Bachelor* was popular for showcasing the backstabbing, excessive emotion, and desperation of twenty-five beautiful single women jockeying to attract some reasonably good-looking guy. While the women on *The Bachelor* came off as weak and pathetic as they wept inconsolably over a failed two-week relationship, the beauties on Fox's *Joe Millionaire* were far worse. There we found the most glaring stereotype of the female gold digger—a money-grubbing, lewd parasite—and the crux of the show's entertainment was the suspense over whether the chosen hussy would dump the professed object of her affection the moment he revealed the true balance in his bank account. These women cut one another down and manipulated their way through the game, barely bothering to pretend that it was the man they were after. What they truly craved was the delicious, decadent lifestyle he seemed to offer, and if they had to feign love to get it, so be it. Doesn't it just warm your heart? Their mothers must have been so proud!

The list of similar shows goes on and on with creations like *Paradise Hotel* or *For Love or Money*. *Paradise Hotel* was particularly disgusting, with women being offered continuity on the show only if they shacked up overnight with complete strangers. Yup, having sex with the complete strangers is paradise. But for whom? A man or a woman? In all these shows, the women are asked to debase themselves over and over again, offer themselves up for physical perusal and clamor for attention by being as morally loose and intellectually simple as possible. NBC got into the reality relationship show frenzy with a new twist on the genre called *Average Joe*. In this offering, a host of out-of-shape, nerdy, socially inept men are presented to a beautiful woman to see if she can get past her desire for good looks and find the real man beneath the gawky packaging. Even here, it is the woman who comes off as shallow and disreputable. In fact, in the first season, our heroine dumps the goofy but lovable guy who has been around for six weeks in favor of the hunky specimen of a man brought in during the final two weeks. This proves, yet again, that women are superficial and petty. Let us not even dwell on the obvious point that, while presenting a bunch of average Joes sounded like a hit, parading around a slew of average Janes would never be considered. (True, they did do a show where the first, rejected average Joe guy returned to pick through the women. But even though all the women were not supermodels, there were plenty of beautiful ones and almost no truly ugly ones as had been the case in the average Joe male lot.) There is no point in showing that a guy is going to go for the hot woman in a bikini and not look twice at the slightly overweight woman with a heart and mind of gold. Where is the sport in that? And who would watch it?

We never ask the guys to dig deeper, to be more than a bundle of walking hormones. Certainly the women who submit themselves for these shows are not requiring them to be better men. Rather, these "ladies" seem more than happy to fit into the stereotype of a disposable doll to be used and discarded at whim. What has happened in the past few years is that this derogatory imaging of women that was popular in movies and television—where fictional characters represented generalizations about womankind—has now become an accepted norm for real women. No longer scripted figments of a writer's imagination, ordinary women are now living "up" to the stereotype in all its glory.

11

GENTLEMEN PREFER BIMBOS

The depiction of women as money-hungry sex objects is only one of the stereotypes to replace the ladylike image that used to prevail generations ago. There is also the broad characterization of women as vapid, shallow clods. I do not mean to imply that these personas are a sudden invention of this generation. This kind of labeling has always occurred, but it used to be relegated to the boys' bathroom or the superficial chatter of disdainful men. Today, it is the subject of popular television shows that, in themselves, give such personas legitimacy.

Fox television's reality creation *The Simple Life* has become a wild success by showcasing the disturbing characterization that most dominates the self-image of women today, their mindlessness and imbecility—after all, where is the entertainment value in seeing a smart woman? The series follows socialite Paris Hilton—arguably one of the most wince-worthy women in all of America—as she agrees to spend a month "living with [and condescending to] a farm family in Arkansas." She is joined by Nicole Ritchie, Lionel Ritchie's daughter. One of the principal purposes of the show is to demonstrate just how stupid and out of touch Paris and Nicole are. In one episode, Paris wonders if Wal-Mart is where you go to buy "wall stuff." Then Nicole muses about having some laughs by dragging the farm family's innocent-looking nineteen-year-old son into a sexual "threesome." Here, again, is the imaging of women as mindless nymphomaniacs, brainless bimbos, without an intelligent thought in their heads. Certainly, these women brought the stereotype on themselves, and maybe these particular girls are really like that. But why does this seem to be the constant depiction of women on television?

Why are we fascinated by cookie-cutter molds of blonde women like Jessica Simpson, whose show, *Newlyweds*, was a smash MTV success—mainly for her idiotic musings (most famously, whether Chicken of the Sea tuna was made of chicken). Is there not a single woman in the United States who has a brain? Then there is Jessica Simpson's positively stomach-turning references to her stool as "children" who go swimming in the pool, meaning the toilet. Man, let me throw up. This is what feminine dignity has come to? Talking about excrement and sitting on the can, on TV? The proliferation and popularity of television stars such as Paris, Nicole, and Jessica would seem to imply that we prefer to be entertained by women who are the incarnation of the blonde bimbo.

A November 18, 2003 *New York Times* piece titled "The Season of the Airheads," Dwight Garner reported this about Paris and Nicole: "Lately, the gossip-page chatter about these two has been heavier and more cringe-inducing than usual. Nicole was charged with heroin possession earlier this year and, therefore [wasn't] taking part in her show's publicity junkets. Paris's public relations army has had to explain why she allegedly appears in an amateur porn tape, à la the infamous Pamela Anderson and Tommy Lee video, that's reportedly making the rounds. . . . Paris and Nicole are city-slicker degenerates in need of rehabilitation . . . the show casts them as rich bitches and they embrace these roles with scary enthusiasm. 'This is so ghetto,' Paris gripes when she's forced to drive a weather-beaten pickup truck. Later she asks, with a space-cadet ditziness that feels calculated, 'What are wells for?'"

How Many Moronic Men Get TV Shows?

But if she is such a half-wit, which her actions seem to confirm, why does she dominate the airwaves and gossip columns? There are plenty of men who are imbeciles as well, but how many get their own TV show? Alternatively, the entertainment appetites that we have cultivated in the United States reveal that there is something particularly compelling about a truly stupid woman. There is something compelling about celebrities who feed into the stereotype of women, especially attractive ones, as empty numskulls who are only good for sex. Use them for their bodies while they are still ripe, and then discard them for something even younger and stupider. How deeply embarrassing for women everywhere.

Anyone who watches this show should end up loathing Paris and Nicole as tedious bimbos and snobs to boot. The show almost invites you to despise them. But here is an interesting spin. What if the show, instead of employing female stereotypes, played to Jewish stereotypes and invited you to hate them? What if the show was about Jewish CEOs from Manhattan who have to live among the good people of the American heartland. What if the public tuned in to see the Jewish business tycoons complaining incessantly about the uncouth country bumpkins with whom they are being forced to live? The message of the show would clearly be that Jews love money, love the good life, and have contempt for honest, hard-working people. A show like that would, thankfully, never be allowed on the air. It would incite hatred against Jews and would, rightly, be identified as anti-Semitic. Yet to make a show like that about woman is perfectly acceptable.

Perhaps you feel that I'm taking two isolated examples—Paris and Nicole—and casting them as representative of all women. I *wish* Paris and Nicole were two isolated examples. I wish they weren't evocative of the larger trend. But the facts remain: These two women represent the very same stereotype of rich, materialistic, horny nymphomaniacs that we find depicted by Samantha and her pals on *Sex and the City*. And it is this image that is becoming increasingly common.

To be sure, the moron-man is also a TV stereotype, and there are plenty of examples—especially on sitcoms—of generating laughs by depicting a single male character as an utter bozo.

Whole genres of film, including *The Naked Gun*, are based on this type of character. But here is why depicting women that way is a different matter: First, women have now completely eclipsed men in the portrayal of stupidity. Second, and more important, the neutralization of women as a civilizing force in society has had horribly destructive consequences for our world. When men are portrayed as stupid, nobody really suffers. It is still a man's world. Men are not as vulnerable as women and there is no real fear that a negative portrayal of men will have a nefarious impact on the state of the culture. Less so is there the fear that the portrayal of men as clods will lead to discrimination against men. Discrimination by whom? Men are not the vulnerable ones. But the constant portrayal of women as imbeciles causes men to lose respect for women and neutralizes women's influence over men. It means that men will not be asking a woman for her advice. The result is a less gentle, less refined, less nurturing world.

12

THE MUSICAL "AXIS OF EVIL"

A primary contributor to the degradation of women is that we have become an overwhelmingly visual society. Nowhere is this more evident than in the impact of visualization on the music industry and, in turn, the powerful reverberations the music industry has had on the imaging of women in general. Jewish law contains a concept of *kol isha* ("the voice of the woman"). As part of modest behavior, women refrain from taking center stage in vocal performances. Traditionally, female singers in Orthodox Judaism perform for all-women crowds, otherwise preserving the allure of their singing voices for their husbands and families.

I am in no way suggesting that we do away with female recording artists. I am simply pointing out that the voice has always been a powerfully feminine instrument. However, society is no longer sensitive enough to appreciate the allure of the female voice. In virtually every leading female recording act today, it is the singer's body that receives the most attention. The music industry has become much more of a visual medium than an auditory medium and, as a result, the quality of the music suffers. A more perilous consequence is the lesson learned from the new incarnation of the pop diva—a creation nowhere more evident than in "The Musical Axis of Evil": Madonna, Britney, and Christina.

My friend Joey Reynolds is the host of New York's leading overnight radio show, and I often appear as a guest on his program.

One night he had on a talented singer named Melissa Errico, a Broadway star who had just released her first CD, and who, incidentally, is married to the tennis player Patrick McEnroe. She played tracks from her album on the radio show and it was clear that she was gifted with a rich voice of unusual sensitivity and range. Still, I told her on the air that she has no chance of selling the album to a large market. She took offense at the comment and asked me why I would say that. "Well," I told her, "because although you're a very beautiful woman, you're also a woman of dignity. You're not prepared to undress in order to pimp your album, so you're doomed. Oh sure, you may be one of the exceptions to the rule—a woman like Norah Jones who miraculously enjoys commercial success without showing her boobs—but the odds are strongly against you."

When we went to a commercial break, she told me that I had really made her think and had given expression to the deep-seated frustration that so many female recording artists feel when they see the Britney Spears of this world succeed while singers like Melissa are largely ignored. The commercial ended and we came back on the air. Joey chimed in, "Shmuley, why make Melissa feel bad about her album?" Before I could answer, Melissa interrupted. She said that I hadn't made her feel bad. She had come on the show to promote her album, and here she had met me who told her that the reality of her industry is such that only those women who are prepared to expose their bodies will rise to the top ranks of the profession and get the most attention. She acknowledged that she probably would not receive as much consideration or notoriety. She said that she hated to admit it, but I was right. This is the state of the recording industry today.

For two decades, Madonna and others have been allowed to destroy the role of female artists in the recording industry by erasing the line that separates music from pornography. Before Madonna, it was possible for women more famous for their voices than their cleavage to emerge as music superstars. But in the post-Madonna universe, even highly original performers such as Janet Jackson now feel the pressure to expose their bodies on national television to sell albums. This in turn has spawned the lascivious careers of

Madonna copycats, such as the vulgar and crass degenerates, Britney Spears and Christina Aguilera.

How tragic that forty years after feminism rightly demanded that women be accorded the dignity of an equally intelligent and dignified member of society, these performers have been allowed to undo so much of that progress—and they have been met with barely a whimper of protest.

Five Senses?

Every human being is possessed of five senses by which we perceive our world. Each of the five gives us a different form of pleasure. Each sends a different signal to the brain that then computes the signals to form recognizable impressions. The sense of sight is the most immediate, and the most superficial, hence the aphorism "Don't judge a book by its cover." From sight, we move on to the more sublime and deeper senses—the sense of touch, the senses of taste, sound, and smell. In the field of female recording artists and music, we presuppose that men can get beyond taking pleasure from a woman's looks and actually appreciate her voice, a different pleasure from a totally different faculty. But what happens when men are conditioned to be so shallow, so base, that they cannot get beyond the superficial sense of sight? Then what? What happens when a whole slew of new artists comes along who, rather than trying to elevate men to that higher plane of being entertained and deriving pleasure from a woman's musical talent, just caters to their animalistic instinct to derive pleasure from their visual bodies?

What would have happened if Madonna, Britney Spears, and Christina Aguilera—who, when measuring the harm they inflict on teenage girls, have earned my nickname of the "Musical Axis of Evil"—had come along four decades ago? Does anyone really believe that someone like Ella Fitzgerald, who has a divine voice but is overweight, would have been a successful recording artist? Or even someone like Barbra Streisand for that matter, given that she has a big nose and hasn't had breast implants?

About ten years ago I met with Streisand. At the time, I was the rabbi at Oxford University and she was thinking of producing a movie about the friendship that I shared with Cory Booker, an African American Rhodes Scholar who served as one of the presidents of our Jewish organization in Oxford. Cis Corman, head of Barwood films, who is also one of Barbra's closest friends, took us to Barbra's Upper West Side apartment overlooking Central Park.

The meeting started at 3:00 P.M. and did not end until I had to rush to Kennedy airport to catch a flight back to the United Kingdom at about 8 o'clock. Barbra, who was filming a movie at the time, met us in her bathrobe. She had no makeup on and her hair was not done up. I have to admit that at first her appearance was a bit of a disappointment to me. After all, I had grown up with her movies and music and expected to see the great film star in all her glory. What we met instead was someone who seemed to be an ordinary, middle-aged woman. But as the afternoon went on and she spoke to us about her life's experiences and had us laughing and thinking, she came alive in all her glory. Here was a woman whose personality amplified her already pretty looks and made her unimaginably beautiful. She was mesmerizing and I understood why she had such longevity in the public eye. But would her stupendous success have been possible had she started out today in our overly visual media, in a world of talentless exhibitionists who take off their bras to sell music albums?

How sad that Madonna is the most famous female recording artist in the world today, a woman who, while possessing some real talent, wound up making her name primarily with outrageous antics such as simulating masturbation in front of teenagers on MTV. Madonna has been studying Kabbalah now for a good many years. The same woman who helped debase the dignity of women everywhere with her mainstreaming of sadomasochism, who helped launch a decade of decadence and misogyny with her music videos, and who, in her 1992 book *Sex* bared every region of her body for money and publicity, is now a devoted student of the most sacred mystical texts in Judaism.

Has it made her into a better person? Has she ceased her contemptible portrayal of women as merely a temptress for perverted men? Was an ennoblement of character in evidence in the 2003 MTV Music Awards, where the publicity famished star "swapped spit" with Britney Spears, while millions of teenage girls looked on? (She defended her coarse performance as "the kind of kiss you would give your sister," thereby insulting our intelligence as well as our morals.) And what of her most recent film, *Swept Away*, which itself was swept away by critics who described its embarrassing amalgam of "vulgarity, nudity, adult situations, sex, bad taste, bad acting, bad judgment." Here was Madonna at forty-four, years into her Kabbalistic journey, proving, in the words of an online reviewer, "that she is still willing to strip for the cameras with a couple of peeks at her breasts and her bottom."

Kabbalah argues for the spiritual supremacy of women over men, for feminine transcendence over masculine imminence, and feminine radiance over masculine expediency. Yet Madonna has spent her career dishonoring women, portraying them as chunks of meat bereft of personalities or even souls. The stupidity of the Kabbalah Center, for whom Madonna serves as unofficial spokesperson, desperate enough to highlight Madonna as its principal star, would be akin to the Catholic Church touting John Gotti as an exemplary representative of the Church.

More significant for talented artists like Melissa Errico, Madonna has set back the cause of female recording artists by a generation through showing, more than forty years after the second wave of the feminist revolution, that a woman today cannot sell a record unless she bares her breasts and butt. If you have any doubt about Madonna's legacy, just look at the sleazy imitations she has spawned, foremost among them being her make-out partners, Britney and Christina. One's heart might even go out to them as being nothing more than three desperate women reduced to disgraceful publicity stunts because, in their insecure minds, they have so little actual talent. But somehow, I do not remember the Beatles having to gyrate on the floor or flash a thong to sell out a stadium.

Britney—The Woman Who
Made Music into Soft Porn

To be honest, I do not follow Britney Spears very closely, but I did have the occasion to meet her once in Michael Jackson's hotel suite in New York City. My teenage daughters, although raised in a religious home and enrolled in a very religious, single-sex school, were still excited that I had met the pop princess. "What was she like?" they asked me when I got home. I told them the truth. "She was absolutely ordinary. Her looks were ordinary and her personality was ordinary." I did not want to belabor the point and put her down in front of my daughters, whom I try to raise to be gracious to all, but Britney is really destroying young girls by portraying herself as an adolescent sex provocateur. She learned that role from those who came before her, as she credits Madonna for influencing her to be the bad girl that she is. "I remember being in my living room and watching her on TV," Britney gushed. "I'd dance around in my short tops and sing and dream about being her" (*Newsweek*, October 2003).

Had I told my daughters the truth, I would have said that Britney is embarrassingly ignorant. Like fellow blondes Paris Hilton, Nicole Ritchie, and Jessica Simpson, Britney is little more than a buxom babe who displays a dearth of brains. *Newsweek*, in the same issue, ran an interview with her in which they asked her whether she had been influenced by Hinduism. She responded, "What's that? Is it like Kabbalah?" Here is a twenty-one-year-old woman who has not heard of a religion that is followed by one out of every five people in the world—not to mention that it is one of the world's oldest faiths. So what, you ask, if Britney is not one of the brightest candles on the Chanukah menorah? You're right, and I shouldn't fault her for being uninformed. My point is that her fame, despite her ignorance and lack of exceptional talent, is yet another example of the tremendous degradation of women. Certainly we must see it as debasing when Britney, whom even *Newsweek* compares with Madonna in that "she cannot sing," has risen to the top of the female pop charts by simulating masturbation on Showtime. This turns from being merely perplexing to being downright disturbing when we see how young girls dress in imitation of her. Moreover, her fame sends a message to all women who want to break into the music industry: Forget the songwriting or voice lessons and, instead, take some erotic dance lessons!

People who defend this sort of behavior fail to acknowledge that there is no end to the devolution once it starts. Now that Britney has done her striptease on MTV, she must push the envelope even further to sustain the shock effect. That is why she is becoming filthier all the time. Here is the *New York Times* reporting on the release of her 2003 album, *In the Zone:*

> "Mommy, this is nasty." The voice was that of a nine-year-old girl watching Britney Spears tape an "ABC in Concert" special at Gotham Hall in Manhattan. Performing a new song, "Breathe on Me," Ms. Spears wriggled out of a sheer crew-neck shirt. With bra exposed, she proceeded to writhe on top of bedroom furniture as several of her dancers followed suit. "It's just stripping," the girl complained.
>
> ....On her forthcoming CD ... she continues her very public sexual evolution.... Here, she is the siren of the party scene, hooking up with random men, declaring that she doesn't want to be a tease and offering "whatcha need all night long...." In promoting her new CD, she upped the ante, posing bottomless and topless for magazine covers.

How wonderful that a twenty-one-year-old music star is posing bottomless and promising men that she can accommodate their needs "all night long." What this has to do with music is utterly beyond me. If the subject were prostitution, it would make sense. Now it becomes clearer why so many women feel that they have to come across as prostitutes to succeed in the recording industry.

As for Britney's personal morality, *Newsweek* reported in November 2003 that she was "hook[ing] up with a married backup dancer." Fabulous. She could clinch her public sexual persona by playing the role of the predator who wins the other woman's man. But as of October 2004, Britney, now a divorced woman (or was it annulled?) after her deep and committed fifty-five-hour Las Vegas marriage to a childhood sweetheart that she undertook while reportedly drunk, has now married a man who already has a couple of kids with another woman whom he couldn't be bothered to marry. Apparently, for Britney, your first marriage is something you do while intoxicated. The second one is where you get serious. Here is a woman who really understands and respects traditional values and morality. Why wouldn't any mother in America yearn for her daughter to follow in the footsteps of Ms. Spears?

Now, I am not as extreme as Kendel Ehrlich, the wife of Maryland's governor, who told an audience at a conference against domestic violence that if she had a gun she would shoot Britney (although I do wonder how many moms are prepared to lend Kendel their pistols). Many a mom in the audience applauded. As for Britney, she has no clue why people find her so offensive. After all, a female recording artist doing full frontal nudity is now par for the course. "Why? Why are they mad at me?" Spears wailed to *Newsweek*, claiming not to know about the incident. "Why are they not going at Christina [Aguilera]? Have they seen what she has on? I know I'm acting like a four-year-old right now. Well, look at her! . . . Beyonce dresses provocatively. Why don't they say something about her? What is too sexy to them? My family, we walked around the house naked, we really did. By the time I was thirteen, my dad was like, 'Uh, Britney, it's time to start covering yourself up.' I'm very free like that."

So indeed it all does start with the parents. One wonders why her father woke up only when she was thirteen and told her to stop walking around the house nude. (I kid you not. This is a real story and brings new meaning to the term *dysfunctional family*.) It is primarily a father who can influence his daughter to be a lady. Britney's dad had no problem with her looking like a tart and made no effort to teach his daughter feminine dignity and modesty.

Another interesting nugget from the *Newsweek* interview was the following: "At the *SNL* rehearsal, she finishes a frenetic dance number and plops down on the stage, her legs wide open to a crew of at least thirty people, mostly men. She appears oblivious to the effect she's having." Nice, very nice. You finish your dance number and you flash your privates at the male crew. How very classy. Now just imagine if a man had done this? He finishes a dance skit and flashes his crotch at the female crew. Wouldn't he have been sued for sexual harassment? But Britney can get away with this revolting behavior because, I assume, the men enjoyed it. Which of them was going to complain? Men have become so accustomed to women exposing themselves to get male attention that they have come to think of it as their right. Britney was just doing what she has been programmed to do. Amazingly, Britney is convinced that her vulgarity is actually spiritual, which is not surprising. The narcissism of people like Britney Spears ensures they not only justify their behavior, but also associate it with divine will, since people treat them like gods. Forget criticism for their disgusting antics. On the contrary, people pay thousands of dollars to watch it live!

Britney actually believes that her behavior is sanctioned by God. "What effect do you think your steamy performances are having on kids?" the *New York Times* reporter asked Britney. She replied, "It's a visual thing. That's why I'm here right now, because I dreamed of these moments. Kids need that. If they don't dream, they have what? That's what makes you feel spiritual, connected with God." Apparently, Britney's god is a peeping Tom, perhaps one of those ancient Greek numbers who come down to earth, seduce women, and impregnate them. Personally, I shudder at the very notion that little girls are lying in bed dreaming of becoming mind-numbing peep-show performers. Or even worse, that they equate it with going to church.

As for the *Esquire* magazine cover photos of Britney virtually nude, she had this to say: "I did feel kind of weird after those photos. I was in a moment. I had, like, eight Red Bulls and said, 'OK, let's do it.' I learned my lesson and you won't see me like that for a while. I'm kinda over it myself. Not that it's dirty or tacky, but it is really revealing and I wouldn't want my kid, at twenty-one, to be dressing like that."

Yes, exposing your teenage-looking body to the world is neither dirty nor tacky. It is art. Mind you, while that kind of revealing art would be inappropriate for her children, Britney and her entourage think that it is perfectly okay for yours. It seems that she will not be irresponsible with the people who really matter, but the "peasants," well, let them eat cake! As the "pop princess" she would never allow her own royal offspring to degrade themselves or be exposed to such vulgarity. Stripping is not for mummy's blue-blooded darlings; only our own ordinary daughters are supposed to watch these crude displays.

The notion that someone like Britney could lead such a depraved life and still hope to raise moral kids is dubious. Kids are influenced by their parents' actions. There is just no way around it. Under the best circumstance and with the most caring parenting, kids grow up looking for hypocrisy, looking for places to challenge their parents' moral center. Certainly, if you do not do as you preach when you are a parent, you do not have a shot. But let's not think about Mommy Britney, the idea is just too frightening.

Britney's idol Madonna has suddenly jumped up on her soapbox to criticize how destructive television has become. First, she helped to vulgarize and sexualize American pop culture by being the world's most successful pop slut. When she became a mom, however, she quickly escaped to Britain, complaining that American culture had too many negative influences on children, which is a bit like Saddam Hussein complaining that Iraq has become too violent. Madonna even had the nerve to go on ABC's *Good Morning America* to complain about there being way too much sex on American television and how harmful this is to children. When Madonna published a children's book based on the Kabbalah, she gave several interviews in which she disparaged the terrible and explicit violence on television. This immediately called to mind the time that Muammar Qaddafi decried all the tyranny and lack of freedom in the world. It appears that while studying Kabbalah, Madonna has not only learned the word *chutzpa*, but she has found new ways to demonstrate its meaning.

Madonna complained that she was very concerned for the welfare of her two young children, whom she feared would be marred by too much sex and nudity on television. That is pretty rich coming from one of the most vulgar women in the history of Western culture, who didn't seem to care a whit when the kids she was influencing were someone else's.

And lest you think that these porn-star rock divas aren't having an effect on our youth, here is how the *New York Times* summed up the trickle-down effects on high school girls:

> After a half-century during which generations of young women were advised to never call a boy on the telephone, it is now teenage girls who not only do the calling, but who often initiate romantic and even sexual activity. Whether they are influenced by the trickle-down effects of feminism, which has taught girls to be assertive in all areas of life, or have internalized the images of sexually powerful women in popular culture, American girls are more daring than ever.... The teenage girl as sexual aggressor is a recurring character in music videos, almost macho in her pursuit of sex and advertising her pleasure in it. (*New York Times*, November 3, 2002)

No wonder Madonna doesn't want to raise her daughter Lourdes in the United States, in the culture that she was so instrumental in creating.

13

∽

BECOMING FAMOUS
BY BECOMING NAKED

If we take a step back from the outrageous examples of woman-hood that we find in the elite celebrity set and think about the effort that went into winning women an equal opportunity to excel in any given career, we must realize that among feminism's early goals was the need to create an appreciation for women as something more than just a pretty face atop a great body. Women of the feminist movement legitimately asserted that a woman is everything a man is and more. Women are as smart as men, as ambitious, and as visionary. A woman is something more than an object for a man to ogle. Women demanded to be taken seriously. That is why it is so bizarre that, more than forty years after the second wave of feminism took shape, and despite great strides in professional achievements and education, women are still, first and foremost, treated as hunks of meat who get ahead by baring it all for men.

The *Girls Gone Wild* Videos and Other Standard Fare

The *Girls Gone Wild* videos are a prime example of this trend. Even if you have never seen the actual videos themselves, any insomniac will be familiar with the concept of the series (if you can say there is a concept behind something like this) from the blaring

121

late-night television commercials. These ads promise wild revelry as stone-drunk coeds flash their breasts for the camera. The young women who appear in these productions are virtually all college girls. Peculiar, isn't it? They spend tens of thousands of dollars a year to develop their minds—but still seek to be appreciated for their busts?

Dateline NBC aired a report about how some of the companies that produce such forms of "entertainment" were going so far as to get college students drunk, film what followed, and put the lurid action up on a website. In fact, according to a March 2004 article by the Associated Press, when the producers of the *GGW* videos wound up unknowingly filming underage girls baring their breasts, the courts deemed that it was not child pornography because there had been no actual physical contact. No one seemed to be horrified that girls under the age of eighteen were already anxious to flaunt their bodies for strangers. The bottom line is that with young girls so eager to project a depraved image of womanhood, it ceases to be a surprise that even when they go to college to get an education, they cannot escape being seen as a piece of ass. Moreover, they become complicit in this appraisal of themselves. The movie/documentary *The Real Cancun* was a shocking exposé of college coeds on spring break: The young women are all too eager to strip for the libidinous boys who accompany them, and then they jump into bed with them at the drop of a condom.

If you want a taste of how bad it's getting and at how young an age the degradation of women is beginning, consider that Hyperion has just put out a new book by Natalie Krinsky (who just graduated from Yale) titled *Chloe Does Yale*. The book is a remix of Krinsky's sex columns, which she wrote as a Yale undergraduate, detailing the amount of "hooking up" that young women at Yale were doing. The book has wonderful and inspiring scenes, such as the renting of a keg-erator-equipped RV to take to the debauched Harvard-Yale football game.

Amazing, isn't it? This is at Yale University, one of the top universities in the country; women work extremely hard to get accepted there. Yet women at Yale are portrayed these days as sleazy sluts and easy harlots. And don't think that the Yale women mind this portrayal. On March 3, 2005, *USA Today* described the reception of the book at the university as largely positive.

On the publisher's part, Hyperion was very proud of their portrayal of all the slutty women at Yale. "The book has huge potential because it is a very charming, funny, sexy look at what really goes on at college," says the publishing house's editor in chief, Will Schwalbe. He's anticipating it will be a big beach read in the successful vein of *The Devil Wears Prada.*

Krinsky's sex column at Yale received 350,000 hits a week at its peak. How silly we were to believe that women who went to college (especially the top Ivy League institutions) expected to be appreciated for their brains.

In light of this kind of revelation, can it be said that feminism succeeded? We have come a long way from the Victorian prudishness that advised women to endure sex by "lying back and thinking of England," but is this where we wanted to end up after the battle of women's liberation? Is this the freedom, equality, and respect that women toiled for so selflessly? Again, the problem is that the myth of feminine equality has come to mean simply that women can be *as bad as* men. If anything, Hugh Hefner's vision of women, as captured in his slogan for *Playboy*—"Entertainment for Men"—is what has actually materialized. How is this a feminist statement?

Graduating into the Celebrity Nude Photo Spread

Hef's world vision of the fairer sex is perhaps most evident in the shocking number of female celebrities who have decided to pose naked. Everyone knows that many women become famous by posing nude, but the trend now is for women who are already famous to give their career a quick hit of sex appeal by stripping. The only thing we can conclude is that these women feel that the only way to *remain* famous is to cater to the insatiable male appetite for flesh. Some of the celebs who have ventured down this path are fading starlets, prepared to do just about anything to hang on to the public's attention, but what of the rest? It seems to come down to something as simplistic as that men demand their pound of flesh, and in a male-dominated society, women are often willing to comply with these demands. And that is one of the great tragedies of the feminist movement. It simply pounded out a new, more aggressive and sexualized persona for women within the sullied world that men had already created.

In that arena, the rules are well known. Any woman in need of attention knows that when all else fails, just go for the shock factor and take off your clothes! Look at the commotion caused by Janet Jackson's "accidental" baring of her breast at the 2004 Super Bowl. While Ms. Jackson claimed that her flashing was the result of a "wardrobe malfunction," the buzz for weeks after was how this would affect her career. The conclusion, for the most part, was that *any* publicity, even bad or shocking, was positive, and moreover, when you have a body as nice as Janet's, flaunting it is never a bad thing. Oh, and she also had a new album to flog, of course. So what if six-year-old boys were sitting next to their dads passing along the tradition of Super Bowl Sunday?

Let's just have a quick look at recent bare-all actresses. There was Shannen Doherty, who did a ten-page nude pictorial in *Playboy*. Maybe she saw her profile dropping significantly so she rushed to take it all off, but what about the others? Britney Spears, Madonna, Christina Aguilera, Christina Applegate, Charlize Theron, Gwen Stefani, Demi Moore—what were their excuses for doing nude or semi-nude magazine pictorials? There is also perennial exhibitionist Carmen Electra, who has produced a how-to-striptease video, and young pop stars, Lil' Kim and Mya, but even Academy Award–winning Halle Berry did an *FHM* (For Him Magazine) spread which, while she was clothed (barely), was incredibly provocative. The latest graduate of the you-may-think-I-have-a-brain-and-talent-but-let's-instead-focus-on-my-bust school of celebrity includes 2004 Academy Award nominee Scarlett Johansson, who acted so superbly in *Lost in Translation* and *The Girl with the Pearl Earring* that she became famous enough to qualify for a cleavage-baring photo-op.

Career Development

Now, I understand why less naturally talented women like Britney writhe and wriggle on stage. They have been trained to believe that is all they have to offer. In the same way that Barbra Streisand offered another aspect of her talent to the public every year—singing, acting, comedy, a new song, a new genre—Britney offers a new part of her body. That is what career development means to young Britney. One year she will show you the bra, the next year the cleavage, and finally her nipples. Sad, isn't it? But it is not only those with mediocre talent who feel compelled to take it all off. Halle Berry is an actress with indisputable talent and a genuine range in her acting—and even she felt the compulsion to strip. The same is true of Demi Moore, who twice posed nude for the cover of *Vanity Fair*, once for *Oui*.

In Naomi Wolf's article "The Porn Myth," which appeared in the October 20, 2003, issue of *New York* magazine, she writes, "The porn loop is de rigueur, no longer outside the pale; starlets in tabloids boast of learning to strip from professionals; the 'cool girls' go with guys to the strip clubs, and even ask for lap dances; college girls are expected to tease guys at keg parties with lesbian kisses à la Britney and Madonna."

Somewhere along the road to asserting themselves as men's equals, women went overboard and flaunted their independence by pandering to the most banal characteristics in men, shunning the genteel personas their presence used to bring forth. It is perfectly comprehensible to want to break away from the strict, prescribed, and limited role of "Angel in the House" that prevailed in the nineteenth century. The answer, however, was not to become the "liberated" call girl on the street. Now, women must band together again to redress the problem.

The Victoria's Secret Fashion Show

Following Hollywood's lead, our entire popular culture has robbed women of every semblance of respect and mystique, and instead dresses them to look like streetwalkers even in their early teens. How can we be surprised by this when we're bombarded with images of female denigration over the airwaves and on every billboard? I am a step away from having my kids wear eye masks when we drive through New York City! A case in point, I was standing on a Manhattan street corner one day, speaking to a friend, when our conversation was suddenly interrupted by a giant pair of breasts unlike any I had ever seen. Gargantuan and incongruously sitting atop a New York taxicab, they looked like giant bowling balls invading the Big Apple from another planet. To be sure, exposed breasts are a penny a pair on billboards all around the United States, and we have grown so desensitized to them that they, at most, evoke a momentary and instantly forgettable thrill like a field goal in a professional football game. But what made these particular breasts so memorable was that they were unattached to any face. Like a prosthetic leg lying on the floor or a wig thrown on a dresser, the breasts were hovering there, disembodied and alone, as if someone had left them there by accident. They were restrained by a little piece of flimsy gold and black lace, evoking images of a bursting dam struggling against a great body of water. And on top were the words, "Don't miss the Victoria's Secret Fashion Show on CBS."

Fast-forward a few days later to the Sunday *New York Times* where readers needed no coffee to wake up as they were confronted by a full-page, color ad of three supermodels in sheer, almost see-through underwear, standing in a provocative pose of legs open and butt cracks showing. This time, the caption read "The Sexiest Night on Television: The Victoria's Secret Fashion Show."

What struck me in both of these ads was how Victoria's Secret—not *Hustler*, not *Playboy*, but a clothing company—was no longer promoting undergarments or lingerie. Rather, like pornography, they were highlighting body parts. I once admired Victoria's Secret as a store that could enhance the attraction between husband and wife by giving "ordinary" women the tools to feel desirable and look sexy. But not a semblance of that early idealism remains. They never feature everyday women, but only the world's most famous supermodels. The intention of the ads is not to make women feel good about themselves, but to make men salivate after the supermodels who wear their clothing. Rather than enhancing a woman's self-image by giving her lingerie that can make her feel feminine, Victoria's Secret creates an added pressure to live up to the supermodel standards that fuel male desire.

Like cheap pornography on the Internet, the clear message from the Victoria's Secret Fashion Show is that women are the libidinous guy's toy, created by God to amuse men by parading around in their underwear. Adorning the outside of Victoria's Secret's retail stores are their window displays replete with explicit pictures of women in see-through bras, their breasts spilling out, and thongs that barely cover their private parts. That pictures like these are being displayed on Main Street, USA, instead of being confined to adult stores, is astonishing evidence that the degradation of women has gone mainstream and that Victoria's Secret has gone from high class to low gutter.

When a spokeswoman for Victoria's Secret came on my radio show to promote romantic gifts for Valentine's Day, I told her that the company's alleged purpose of promoting romance was belied by their advertising campaigns, which promote women as brainless bimbos and horny harlots. But what is even worse is the *New York Times*, "the newspaper of record," prostituting itself by publishing these pornographic pictures for money. Not to mention, CBS deciding to become the Playboy Channel by airing the fashion show; but I don't expect much from Viacom, its parent company, which first gave us the soft porn of MTV to destroy our youth, and then helped to invent trashy reality TV on CBS.

A close male friend of mine told me excitedly that for $2,000, he had bought tickets on eBay to the taping of the fashion show, and that a whole bunch of his guy friends were going as well. Their wives weren't going with them, which is curious because the last time I checked, Victoria's Secret was a retail store for women.

Strippers in the French Bloomingdale's

When I worry about my daughters being exposed to the notion that a woman is the sum of her body parts, I guess I should be thankful that I am not trying to raise moral, dignified, confident women in France. On November 6, 2003, the *New York Times* ran a story with the headline, "Underwear seduction courses in a department store?"

The story was about Galeries Lafayette, "the closest thing France has to Bloomingdale's," and described how the store had invited hundreds of guests to sip champagne, stroll down a "street of temptation" named "Le Red Hot Boulevard," and examine eighty different brands of "strings" (the French word for "thongs") and other lingerie. There's something a bit disconcerting about the idea of getting shoppers to head down the path toward inebriation while they gawk at near naked mannequins in G-strings. Not only were the strings arrayed down the street of temptation but the store also started offering half-hour lessons by professional striptease artists so that "women can familiarize themselves with the art of revealing their new lingerie." In case you missed the point, let me repeat that. The French Bloomingdale's is teaching women how to strip. That's right. In France, even your family department store has become something of a strip joint. And who said husbands hated shopping with their wives?

It appears that the grand opening of this division of the store "coincides with a rash of sexually explicit advertising campaigns for lingerie that have enraged feminist groups and a few outspoken lawmakers who charge that they exploit women and potentially encourage violence against them." Whoa! It actually angered feminist groups. And they seem to have such long fuses.

"The pornography and the idea of woman as prostitute has become universal, ordinary," said Florence Montreynaud, the head of

La Meute, a feminist group. "What kind of a world are we living in when striptease artists give lessons at Galeries Lafayette? Is this the world of the chic and elegant Parisian? Is this a store I can feel comfortable shopping in with my grandmother?"

You tell 'em, Florence. Her little phrase was so powerful that, after reading it, I felt it had captured the essence of my book. Feminism was hoping that "woman as lawyer," or "woman as doctor" would become the norm. Instead, it is "woman as prostitute." Interestingly, Paul Delaoutre, Galeries Lafayette's president, who was delighted by the controversy and all the publicity it generated, said, "We want to be on the cutting edge. Your American stores are often so banal." Okay, *monsieur* Paul, if department stores you can go to with granny and the kids, department stores that merely sell clothing, are too boring and mundane, why stop at spicing things up with striptease lessons? Why not offer sex with the salesgirls? Think about it. Every guy who comes in and spends, say, $500, gets fifteen minutes with the salesgirl of his choice in the changing room. Now that's publicity, baby!

Lest I be accused of overreacting, just look at the facts. The store is bringing professional striptease artists in for the clientele. Why not bring in professional prostitutes? It would be a way to keep the guys from complaining while their ladies shop! Beats the hell out of the stores that have installed chairs and televisions to pacify the weary men who are dragged away from a Sunday football game.

Of course, even Mr. Delaoutre admitted that he was featuring the stripping instructors as a publicity stunt. "To bring in the press, that's the objective," he said. Great. So here we have it again, right back to women being exploited to sell something. By the standards of Delaoutre, and every other ad executive who ever draped a half-clothed woman on a convertible to up his sales, there is no problem in using sex to push product. It's a win-win-win-win situation. The strippers get paid; the store makes money; the husbands get to gawk at the strippers; the wives get to feel that their new underwear is going to save their marriage. And everybody goes home happy. Or do they? Yippy kiyay.

As for anyone who might want to claim that the primary cause that motivates most women to wear thongs is purely an issue of comfort, here is what the *Times* had to say about it in their article on strings and thongs: "Women's underwear has evolved into a full-fledged fashion statement, items to be shown off, not hidden under something else. The trend is particularly pronounced in France, where lingerie enjoys a lofty place in a woman's wardrobe. Last year, French females from the age of fifteen and older spent 18 percent of their clothing budget, or $2.9 billion, on lingerie, more than in any other European country. . . ."

What we are saying is that, from age fifteen, girls are already wearing lingerie—and that sure isn't about getting comfy. Do we really need to ask ourselves why it is that all these girls are having sex at such a young age and why a disproportionately large number of teenage girls have much older boyfriends? Well, maybe it has something to do with the early sexualizing of teens so that even their underwear has become mature. In every sense, we are portraying our fifteen-year-olds as twenty-five-year-olds, how are we then to ask them to act their age?

Enhancing Beauty versus Concealing Ugliness

Now, please do not get me wrong. I am no prude, and I am certainly no opponent of lingerie. In my book *Kosher Sex*, I argued forcefully for husbands and wives to spice up their sex lives by any means that would add to the novelty and excitement—with the exception of pornography or a ménage à trois, both of which compromise the intimacy in a marriage. Nevertheless, the idea of a young woman in high school wearing lingerie is disturbing and degenerate. We are talking about teenagers—girls who are enjoying the last years of their childhood—and what have we done? We have robbed them of their right to be carefree children. Instead, we have invited male exploitation in with open arms.

But let's, for a moment, put aside the issue of girls dressing inappropriately because even if we turn to more mature and married women, the obsession with lingerie has become excessive. There is something sad about what lingerie has come to represent for women. Women are not choosing intimate apparel to enhance their beauty, but rather, to mask their ugliness. They have been convinced, by a culture that inculcates a permanent sense of physical inadequacy, that they are never beautiful enough and that they have to wear the skimpiest things rather than be, even with their own husbands, in the raw. Don't believe me? Listen to the French women themselves, as quoted by the *Times:* "Lingerie is so important to a French woman's sexual self-esteem, it seems, that only 3 percent of French women believe they are seductive in the nude." Wow, only 3 percent think that they are attractive to men when they are naked. Is that surprising? Since men see thousands of naked women in their e-mail inboxes every single day, why would they be impressed with "just another naked women?" Especially one who exposes herself without the perfecting aid of the air brush. The sad part is that the women are convinced of their inadequacy, and this is why they go in droves to the strip classes offered at the neighborhood lingerie store.

The story does not stop here. The article goes on to say, "French public schools, already fighting a battle against Muslim girls who want to wear head scarves in violation of France's strict secular tradition, have opened a second front against girls who want to show their bellies and their strings. The problem is so serious that Xavier Darcos, the deputy minister of education responsible for elementary and high schools, has called for a study on the wisdom of returning uniforms to public schools. 'School is not a nightclub,' he told French television." Ah, I love the symmetry here. The French, the French. Is there anyone like them in the world? Muslim girls want to be modest and wear a head scarf, which should be their right and I applaud them. In France, it is their choice, unlike women who live under the Taliban regime and are beaten with a whip if they take off their head coverings. These French Islamic girls are exercising their free will in a democracy. But the French are fighting them along with the girls who want to wear the straps to their thongs on the outside for all the world to see. They're similar, right? A head covering and a thong?

So what does the future hold for French women? Well, read on. "A recent poster campaign for Sloggi strings, for instance, showed two long-haired women from behind, dressed in strings and red boxing gloves, their posteriors buffed and shined, playfully menacing a man in tight boxers. 'Be sexy. Be sloggi,' the caption reads. Not to be outdone, the most recent Bolero lingerie ad campaign showed a young woman removing what appear to be pants or a skirt, revealing her string. Turning toward the camera, she announces: 'I'm a virgin. Are you?'"

14

THE WIDE WORLD OF SPORTS

From the days of the ancient Greek Olympics, men have dominated athletic pursuits while women, until recently, have been relegated to the viewing stands. With great pain, and with important programs like Title IX, women have fought to open sports to women and to gain the respect they deserve as proficient and talented athletes. This is, undoubtedly, a real accomplishment.

But if the goal all along had been to assert the power of women and disseminate the idea that women have an elevating influence to impart to the world, even the heavily male world of sports would have been affected. In an overwhelmingly testosterone-laden field, however, where do we see women? Take football for example. No one is expecting women to slap on some shoulder pads and get out there on the field with the likes of Ray Lewis. So where do ladies come into play in this mainstay of American culture? Why, they get to be seen on the sidelines cheering on the athletes. They are cast as dimwitted go-go dancers, reduced, basically, to a pair of bouncing breasts in shorts so short they look like their underwear.

At least in college, one could argue that cheerleading is not about titillation, but is a genuine sport. First, college cheerleading also includes men, which shows that the spotlight is not only on women. Second, the women do not dress very suggestively. The focus is on their acrobatic skills rather than their cleavage. Any college that dressed its cheerleaders the way the National Football League dresses theirs would be sued for harassment and sexist discrimination. But NFL cheerleading highlights a woman's body over her skills, assuming she has any. Bouncing body parts are the highlight of the act, whose primary purpose is titillation. CBS has a network rejoin they often use as they come back to a game after a commercial break. Amazingly, it does not show a football player. Instead, it shows cutaway shots of cheerleaders, with a few pictures of these overly made-up dolls jumping up and down, and then one shot—I kid you not—of a woman's behind. A five-second close-up of a woman's ass: That is a commercial for football. The connection? I honestly couldn't tell you.

Then there is the annual *Sports Illustrated* Swimsuit Edition. Go figure what women in skimpy bathing suits sitting on a beach in Thailand with their legs spread-eagle have to do with sports. After all, you wouldn't expect to see a quarterback throwing a football on the cover of *Better Homes and Gardens*. And yet, the swimsuit edition is *Sports Illustrated*'s bestselling issue of the year. I watched Aaron Brown, the otherwise respected host of CNN's NewsNight, doing a serious interview with the 2005 cover model of the swimsuit edition, on February 17, 2005. It was honestly embarrassing to see him compliment this woman, who was virtually naked in the photographs. Brown commented on their tastefulness. He looked like a lecherous schoolboy, degrading both himself and his profession.

The bottom line is that this objectification of women caters to the basest instincts. On that topic, I found the replays of Brandi Chastain celebrating her team's victory in the 1999 FIFA Women's World Cup Championship by taking off her shirt to be in poor taste. It was every crotch-scratching, coach potato's dream: dirt, sports, women, boobs. I can't tell you how many men I have met who say that this sort of fantasy is what inspires them to watch women's sports in the first place—the thought that at any moment, the female players may rip off their clothing and jump all over each other. So much for an appreciation of athleticism. But what do we expect when the women who work their way into the spotlight parading around as cheerleaders at major sporting events are doing so in their underwear? How could this possibly be an ennobling role? And only a society with an utter lack of modesty and respect for the female form would think nothing of a woman whipping off her shirt on national television as Chastain did.

Sporting Events Attended by Women Are More Civil

Despite the sexualized position that women have been given within the world of sports, it is fascinating to observe the influence women can have on those who attend sporting events. In fact, sports arenas are an ideal case to illustrate how the very presence of women can affect the surrounding environment. After all, look at the behavior of men who attend English football (soccer) matches. They are notoriously violent. There have been tragic stories about the crowds getting out of hand and about rival fans brutally assaulting one another. Additionally, if you have never been to a match, let me warn you that if you ever attend one you had better brace yourself for an earful of outrageous screaming that even the crassest NFL fan might find blushworthy! When you go to a British soccer game, you run the risk of being trampled to death by the usual army of drunken armpit-sniffers and crotch-scratchers. And why are they such embarrassing brutes? Search the stands the next time you watch British football on TV and you will scarcely ever find a woman. (Assuming you can stay awake for the predictable nil-nil final score. International soccer seems to be the one exception to the rule that men are goal-oriented.)

Some might propose that this riotous behavior is a product of socioeconomic factors. English football tickets are relatively cheap, which means that the men in attendance are often working class or out of work altogether. I do not doubt that these factors affect the behavior one sees at an English football match, but how does that explain the crowds at American football matches? Tickets to an NFL game are not inexpensive—which means that we are not dealing with a crowd of aggressive and frustrated out-of-work men who need to let off a bit of steam. Yet at Oakland Raider games alone, there have been incidents that have escalated as far as stabbings. It is not even a matter of rival fans getting out of control since, according to Gary Schellenberg of the Alameda County Sheriff's Department, 95 percent of the violent outbreaks at Raider games are Raider fan against Raider fan.

Apart from crazed Raider fans, however, most American football fans only run the risk of having their eardrums burst by earthquakelike belches from bare-chested brutes on a Heineken drip. Still, where are male fans the best behaved? At tennis matches and basketball games. Why? Well, it doesn't strike me as a coincidence that tennis and basketball are the professional sports that draw the highest percentage of female fans to the stands. I recognize that the November 2004 NBA brawl between the Detroit Pistons and the Indiana Pacers, and the Pistons' disgustingly drunk fans would seem to contradict this. Still, such brawls are much less common at basketball games, compared with other professional sports. And at tennis games, we hardly see them at all. Tennis is arguably the only sport where there is true parity in the sexes, insofar as celebrity draw is concerned. In the stands the sexes are also equally represented. This fact is reflected in their far more decorous behavior.

Even today, men are slightly more civilized around women. Just think about it: Even in this very masculine world of sports, even when there are scantily clad women to cater to the lascivious nature of men, the presence of women in the stands can at least curb the more animalistic nature of man—the violent, aggressive traits that are said to have helped men survive before civilization developed. If women can exert a positive influence in this very masculine arena (and with scantily clad woman bouncing around as cheerleaders), think what they might be able to accomplish if they were to ban together and insist on getting the respect they deserve.

15

∽

A WORLD OF
VEILED WOMEN—ISLAM

Looking at the world of sports offers a glimpse into the ameliorating powers of a womanly presence to soothe and tame male aggression. Still, when we are talking about the dearth of women at
a recreational event, we are merely looking at a few hours of uncouth, loutish, and hostile behavior that, with few exceptions, has
no serious or sustainable repercussions. But the absence or marginalization of a feminine influence in the wider world has had an
exceedingly grave effect on human society as a whole. There are,
undoubtedly, tragic consequences to the denigration of women.
Foremost among them is the coarser, harsher, ruder world that has
developed as the result of cultures not only marginalizing, but cor-
rupting women's principal nurturing presence. Evidence of this
new brutishness is apparent everywhere.

Another significant example of this experience is the increasing militancy in the Islamic world. The days since September 11,
2001, have led to a passionate debate over whether the Islamic
faith is intrinsically militant or peaceful. The debate is silly insofar as it ignores that for many hundreds of years, the Islamic world
was much more civilized, developed, and peaceful than the Christian world. Richard Rubenstein's book, *Aristotle's Children* (Har-
court, 2003), chronicles the well-known historical fact of how

Muslims saved the Western classical tradition from extinction by preserving the writings of Aristotle and other leading Greek thinkers. Rubenstein describes the shock of Christian conquerors after their invasion of Muslim-controlled Spain in the fourteenth century: "Not only were cities like Toledo and Cordoba clean and well-ordered (unlike European Christian cities); not only was life softened and beautified by fountains, flowers, music, and an architecture as imaginative as Europe's was stolid; not only did Arabs live at peace with a bewildering assortment of minority communities, but scholarship flourished as in some dream of ancient Athens or Alexandria" (page 14). This depiction would hardly fit many cities in today's Muslim countries, which are depressed slums that serve as seedbeds of radical hatred fueled by growing desperation and antiquation.

But the ancient Arabs were a proud, advanced, and glorious civilization. Already in the ninth century, Muslim rulers were prioritizing general education. Al-Mamun (Caliph of the Abbasid dynasty) established state-funded places of study, focusing on translations of Greek and other works of antiquity, and his efforts predated the first European universities by more than three hundred years. Moreover, the Abbasid Muslim Empire had an agricultural revolution in the eighth century that produced technological innovations the likes of which would not be seen in the West until at least 1180. In the area of medical advancement, the tenth-century Al-Razi of Baghdad wrote numerous medical books, including groundbreaking health treatments that Western medicine would not match until the eighteenth century. As for leadership, in the sixteenth century, the Mughal emperor Akbar of India was known for his cross-cultural appointments to office and his enactment of laws embracing religious toleration and protection of women and children. He was also one of the first commanders to insist on the proper treatment of captured enemy troops.

Although the exact causes for the decline of the Islamic world are well beyond the scope of this book, the history of this culture provides further evidence that the neutralization of women in any society leads to a more militant, coarse, and unsympathetic civilization, and this is especially true of the Islamic world where women have few or no rights.

The era ushered in by the massacre of September 11 has largely focused on the troubles within the Islamic world. When I served as rabbi at Oxford, I had many close Muslim friends, including sons and daughters of some of the world's leading Arab families, and I have many devoted Muslim listeners on my daily radio show; I lament the debasing of a great world faith. Islam today is becoming increasingly synonymous with rage, murder, and blood. By one estimate, about 98 percent of all the world's conflicts today are inspired by militant Islam, a tragedy for Muslims and, even more so, for the victims of this terror.

The fall of large tracts of the Islamic world into the hands of spiteful zealots has also focused attention on their treatment of women. The contrast in the public's near complete support for the United States' war against the Afghani Taliban versus the much more vociferous opposition to the war in Iraq can largely be traced to the horror Americans felt at the Taliban's treatment of women. Few could stomach women being beaten in the streets with leather whips for the crime of going out without a face covering. Americans were similarly moved by the incomprehensible death sentence meted out by an Islamic Nigerian court against an impoverished woman, who had a baby with a man who was not her husband. And who could forget the Saudi's religious police locking the gate of a burning women's high school so that the teenage girls would be trapped inside, rather than escape the conflagration without their face coverings. The action resulted in more than fifteen innocent young women burning to death, including some girls who had actually escaped the blaze but were pushed back in by the *mutaween*, the Saudi purity police, because they were dressed immodestly.

As mentioned, the identifying characteristics of a feminine society include traits of confidence and nurturing. The feminine force, unlike the male force, is self-assured and therefore can be inclusive, and allow others to shine and succeed. That is part of its great strength. At the same time, this female energy is not about power mongering or physical strength. It depends on the male energy to provide these complementary characteristics. In the Islamic world, however, the actual voices of women have been all but silenced, and the result is a rampant competitiveness with deadly consequences.

The Islamic Cry of "Humiliation" Smacks of Wounded Male Pride

Much of the rage that has instigated Islamic terrorism seems to be founded on a blind insistence on supremacy. We hear over and again of the need for Islamic pride, which seems—in the minds of the radical zealots—to have been compromised by the success and proliferation of the Western world and its ideals. In April 2003, at the Special Session of the Islamic Conference of Foreign Ministers on Terrorism in Kuala Lumpur, Mahathir Mohammad, the former Malaysian prime minister, spoke about the humiliation and embarrassment that the Muslim nations were feeling at the hands of Western society. The humiliation of Islam at the hands of the West was his primary theme, and it generated huge applause among Islamic leaders everywhere. It has become commonplace for radical Islamic leaders to incite violence based on this sense of wounded pride and anger over a perceived humiliation. This terminology is distinctly masculine and this message has come to permeate too much of the Muslim world.

This indicates a shunning of the feminine spirit, with its communal acceptance, in favor of the dogged individualism and aggression of the masculine energy. When Iran suffered a deadly earthquake in the city of Bam in December 2003, killing nearly 30,000 people, the state of Israel offered life-saving aid. Unlike a mother whose natural instinct would drive her to the door of her greatest enemy if such an action had even the slightest potential to save her child, the Iranian government showed its harsh, patriarchal ethos and refused any help from the Jewish state, despite the consequences such a move had on its own afflicted citizenry. This, too, was a distinctly masculine decision, placing pride above all else. It was a wholesale rejection of any feminine influence.

Shamefully, Sri Lanka did the same thing in December 2004, refusing Israeli medical and humanitarian assistance for hard-pressed victims of the tsunami.

This rejection of the feminine has become a dangerously ubiquitous aspect of present-day Islamic society. In fact, when the Starbucks coffee chain opened in Riyadh, the Muslim clerics banned the mermaid logo, based supposedly on the complaint that the image was mythological. We must wonder, however, if the real issue was a denunciation of a mythological creature or a rebuff of a distinctly womanly, often seductive image. In essence, the Saudis believe that women are the source of all corruption. Is it any wonder that Islamic society oppresses its female members—refusing in Wahhabi Saudi Arabia to even allow them to drive a car—and largely discounts their potential contributions? With this in mind, it also becomes less of a surprise to find that the women in these societies have, themselves, lost much of their natural instinct for nurturing energy. Many of them have embraced the destructive idea that they must naturally inhibit their femininity and not allow it to leak out, lest it corrupt the virtuous males who surround them. And many, sadly, have gone much further and made traditional male hate and aggression the very cornerstone of their existence.

Rise of the Female Suicide Bomber

Nowhere in the world are women more oppressed and marginalized then in the modern Islamic world. The abuse of the female sex in Islamic society is hitting new lows with the increasing encouragement of young women to become suicide bombers—such as Hanadi Tayseer Jaradat, the woman who killed eighteen adults and three children in Haifa in October 2003. Reactions to Jaradat's activities, as reported on October 5, 2003 in the *Globe and Mail*, a Canadian newspaper, included the following remarks: "Everyone was happy and proud of her," said a neighbor in Jenin, the explosive refugee camp where she lived. "We are receiving congratulations from people," said her fifteen-year-old brother, Thaher.

"Why should we cry? It is like her wedding today, the happiest day for her." This very conceptualization of such violent activity being akin to the hopefulness and happiness of a bride entering marriage is chilling. In fact, the article goes on to say that several months prior to Jaradat's horrific bombing, the director of a Palestinian children's aid association gave a television interview in which she explained that part of their education policy has been to teach children to aspire to death for Allah. One of the most unnerving television moments featured two eleven-year-old girls being interviewed on a news set in 2003. They were talking about wanting to die in the same way that girls in the West talk about wanting to be teachers, doctors, or mothers.

This perverse replacement of positive female goals with a bloodthirsty desire for self-sacrifice is not limited to Muslims in the Middle East. Indeed, Islamic Chechnya has also embraced the sacrifice of women to achieve its goals. Recall the horrific events of October 2002, when twenty-two Chechen men and nineteen women, under the leadership of Movsar Barayev, took over a Moscow theater and held its evening audience hostage. The terrorists asserted that if their demand for the immediate withdrawal of all the Russian troops from Chechnya was not met, the order would be given for the *women* to detonate themselves, obliterating the theater and all of those inside it. These masked Chechen women were clad in black robes and guarded the hostages with 2kg bomb-belts strapped to their bodies. They had essentially turned themselves into human bombs, each outfitted with a grenade and pistol as well.

According to the *New York Times*, between April and early August 2003, more than 160 people were killed during the course of seven suicide attacks. Women carried out all but one of these attacks. The *Times* believed this pattern of using women as human bombs set in motion a new dynamic in the war against Chechen secessionists. The Russian news media dubbed the perpetrators "Black Widows." The Black Widows were women who were prepared to kill others and to die themselves to avenge the deaths of fathers, husbands, brothers, and sons who had died at the hands of

Russian troops in the current war, or during the war that took place in the 1990s.

Then there was the equally horrific story of the hundreds of Russian parents and children killed in an Islamic terror attack in the Russian city of Beslan in September 2004. While the families sat as hostages, without even water for more than three days, several veiled Islamic female Black Widow suicide bombers walked around with bombs strapped to their bodies, intimidating and terrorizing the families. As soon as the Russian troops moved in, these women were the first to blow themselves up in the crowded room, taking as many lives with them as they possibly could.

When in history were women known to avenge grievous wrongs by murdering innocent people? Even Nazi Germany, the most monstrous government of all time, never thought to subvert the maternal and nurturing instinct within women by making them killers. The most depraved Islamic extremists would have to admit that women were never meant to blow themselves up for the faith. If they were, Sura 55 of the Koran, which promises seventy-two wide-eyed virgins for martyrs, would have to be understood as promoting the wild lesbianism seen in the likes of the *Girls Gone Wild* videos.

Here is the point that I am asking you to think about for a moment. If even the women, who are traditionally more attuned to the value of human life than men, become killers, who will rescue the men from becoming murderers? If you neutralize the feminine voices that call on men to grow up and solve their differences with means other than war, who will ever bring peace? Many times, right after a Palestinian suicide bomber in Israel blows himself up killing many innocent, men, women, and children, the very next day the newspapers will carry an interview with the mother of the bomber in which she invariably says something like, "I'm so proud of my son becoming a martyr. Would it that all my sons would blow themselves up, too."

This fevered thirst for violence, even among women and mothers who seem perversely eager to sacrifice their children, was the reality that *New York Times Magazine* journalist Joseph

Lelyveld encountered when he conducted interviews in Gaza in 2001. Lelyveld writes:

> [In the home of a suicide bomber,] you might expect to see some small hint of demurral, and occasionally, I'm pleased to report, you do. But I could detect nothing of the kind at the spanking new apartment of a solemnly prideful Bashir al-Masawabi, whose twenty-three-year-old son, Ismail, had blown himself to bits along with two Israeli Army sergeants on June 22, several days before his scheduled graduation from a local university. . . . His father, a glazier, had a haunted look as he told how the community had turned out to congratulate him on his son's advent in paradise. His wife, completely covered except for her hands and her resolutely cheerful countenance, betrayed not a hint of sadness as she spoke of her departed son. "I was very happy when I heard," she said. "To be a martyr, that's something. Very few people can do it. I prayed to thank God. In the Koran it's said that a martyr does not die. I know my son is close to me. It is our belief. . . ." "I hope," said Ismail's mother, "my other children do the same." (*New York Times*, October 28, 2001)

In fact, rather than being seen as monstrous or lacking womanly and maternal instinct, mothers who send their sons off to perpetrate such acts gain recognition from organizations like Hamas, which give them the title *Hanas*—women who have attained a sacred level in Islam (in the time of Mohammad the prophet) after having sent four children to fight the infidels until death. Hamas uses these women in television interviews and in Internet discussion forums to encourage other mothers to send their sons to perpetrate suicide attacks. In an article in the *New Yorker* entitled, "An Arsenal of Believers, Talking to the 'Human Bombs,'" the writer, Nasra Hassan, describes the scene in the homes of martyrs shortly after their deadly operation. The author writes, "Often the mother will ululate in joy at the honor that Allah has bestowed upon her family" (November 19, 2001).

Yassir Arafat's wife Suha, from the comfort of her Parisian condominium where she is sitting out the intifada, even lamented that she only has a daughter. According to a summation by NewsMax.com of Tuesday, April 16, 2002, Suha said that she'd gladly see her son become a suicide bomber in the intifada against Israel. In fact, according to numerous published reports, Mrs. Arafat said "there would be no greater honor" than having her son blow himself to smithereens while strapped to a high explosive. Alas, Suha Arafat doesn't have a son so, pity, she will not have the limitless joy of watching him detonate himself and decapitate pregnant women and babies. With rhetoric like this, is it at all surprising that all too many Arabs are increasingly militant and hate-filled? Who is going to temper their rage? Once it would have been the women. It would have been mothers dissuading their sons from becoming killers with the kind of influence that only mothers have. But today, these women have chosen to become rage-filled men themselves. Bereft of any trace of feminine compassion, they rejoice when innocent babies, children, and civilians are mercilessly destroyed by human bombs.

Given these societal mores, the awarding of the 2003 Nobel Peace Prize to Shirin Ebadi, the Iranian judge and women's rights activist, was remarkably prescient and courageous. The judges, who wanted to use the prize to promote democracy in the Islamic world, could easily have given the prize to a male human rights activist. But giving it to a woman sent a double message: Democracy is essential in the Islamic world, and women are even more capable of promoting it than men, by tempering the society's aggression. The startling and unexpected awarding of the 2003 Nobel Prize to Shirin Ebadi sent a strong message that those who award this most prestigious of all prizes believe that the key to softening the hardline stance of the mullahs of Iran is the empowerment of women.

16

∞

WOMEN AS NATURE'S
SYSTEM OF
CHECKS AND BALANCES

While the trouble brewing within the Islamic world largely dominates our airwaves, there are more examples from recent history that illustrate how marginalizing women can impact the ethos of an entire society. Women and the feminine energy are meant to serve as a counter to the aggressive male force. Any civilization that denies this natural balancing act will suffer the consequences for ignoring this most basic need, and this neglect becomes evident in the society it produces.

The great political thinker Montesquieu, who became a judge in France and president of the *parlement* in Bordeaux, was the first to argue for a system of checks and balances in government. He was most famous for his work *The Spirit of the Laws*, which was published in 1748, and his seemingly radical idea of distributing power to avoid corruption had a profound influence on the founding fathers of the United States, particularly James Madison. This idea was incorporated into the American system of government and forms the cornerstone of our constitution. One of the manifestations of Montesquieu's theory is that the president of the United States is not granted absolute power. Congress can override the president's vetoes and must approve his judicial and executive appointments. Only in this manner can there be any guarantee that a president will not become a tyrant.

I bring up Montesquieu to illustrate that what is true of one man is true of all men, not just power-hungry presidents whose desires for greater supremacy might necessitate serious safeguards to limit his authority. Montesquieu understood that it was in the nature of men to crave power and strive for supremacy. Not all men, of course, but enough men to make checks and balances a necessary component of good government. The fact that all men carry the possibility for excessiveness is the reason God instituted checks and balances at the heart of nature when he created the world. In a literal sense, men are powerful, and their power can be a necessary force in creating a just and flourishing society. Men are powerful enough to dig wells and till the land, powerful enough to hunt large game and feed their families, strong enough to offer defense against an attack and protect innocent members of their communities. But what guarantees that all that power will not be used to impose a tyranny? The check that God put on the aggressive, male power in the world was woman, a higher, more subtle authority, capable of raising men to an elevated understanding of how their own power could be used to create harmony rather than war.

A true woman does not emasculate a man. She does not seek to make him weak. Rather, she seeks to direct his energy into the productive, the romantic, and the useful and away from the destructive, the lecherous, and the selfish. Women are the light. Possessed of an innately more spiritual consciousness, they direct men to do what is right. Where femininity is undermined, subverted, corrupted, or marginalized, societies decay and often become scary places to live.

If we look at Nazi Germany, we see that there were no women in positions of power in the Third Reich. In terms of high-ranking Nazi officials who were women, the highest one to whom we might point would be the recently deceased Leni Riefenstahl. She served as a filmmaker and propagandist, but had no authority or influence in the making of policy. Besides her, there were no high-profile women in Nazi Germany. Like today's militant Islamic nations, Nazi Germany was a world dominated by men with a decided exclusion of women. As far as the regime was concerned, the sole purpose of good, Aryan Nazi women was to serve as baby-making machines, supplying Hitler's army with sturdy, fierce soldiers. That was the purpose behind the Lebensborn programs, where robust Nazi women were inseminated by Aryan-looking SS men to give Hitler the troops he needed to conquer Europe. Apart from this purely physical role, there was no concept that women had anything to contribute, nor was there any thought of allowing them to exert influence on the nation at large.

You might argue that it was the 1930s, and women had no more power in Allied countries than they did in Axis countries. But there is a key difference between the two. Franklin Roosevelt was strongly influenced by his wife, Eleanor, as was Winston Churchill by his beloved wife Clementine. Hitler, on the other hand, intentionally isolated himself from the softening feminine influences of women and did not know how to accept or offer any sort of nurturing love. At one point, he seems to have made his own niece, Geli Raubel, his mistress and so controlled her life that she committed suicide in 1931 at the age of twenty-three. He then chose the wholly unremarkable Eva Braun as his mistress. She exerted so little influence over Hitler that she could only persuade him to marry her a few hours before they both killed themselves.

The same disdain of any feminine influence was felt by the second most evil man in the Third Reich, Joseph Goebbels. He was married, but to a woman who had lost any womanly or maternal instincts. Indeed, Magda Goebbels was akin to the present-day mothers of Palestinian suicide bombers. When Hitler decided to kill himself in the bunker in April 1945, she insisted on killing all her five children, along with herself and her husband. So dead was any real maternal instinct inside her that she could somehow muster the resolve to poison her own babies.

Women such as Magda Goebbels and the Black Widows (the Chechen female terrorists) have had their very natures altered by immersion into hateful and sadistic cultures. These cultures assail any and all ideals of pity, compassion, generosity, or humanity; ingesting this poison distorts women's emotional constitution.

The More Isolated Men Are from Women, the More Violent They Become

This is always the rule. The more isolated men are from women, the more violent they become. Contrast the former Soviet Union and Arab society with Scandinavia in general, and Norway in particular, and you see a huge difference. Scandinavia is one of the most peaceful regions in the world and Norway is famous for involving itself in numerous international efforts at peace, most notably in the Middle East and Sri Lanka. Norway is also the country that annually awards the Nobel Peace Prize. But should we really be surprised that Scandinavia is a denizen of peace? After all, they have the highest percentage of women in government in the world, and Norway has already had several female prime ministers. Norway also passed a law in 2002 mandating that at least 40 percent of all corporate boards consist of women. Scandinavia is a region where women have an elevated role and influence, which results directly in the society being more peaceful and productive.

PART
FOUR

THE TYRANNY OF
THE BEAUTIFUL

17

∾

THE ASSAULT ON
UGLY AND FAT WOMEN

Our society's obsession with fame and trends has impacted the culture in a most disturbing manner. It began long ago with celebrity endorsements. Become a movie star, and suddenly you are an expert on motor oil and toothache pain relief. And we—the suckers who stand in awe of fame—buy the product based on the empty endorsement of someone who looks great but may not be able to stay married, stay off drugs, or raise well-adjusted children. Now our appetite for fame has moved us down the food chain to snack on a group that psychologist Warren Farrell refers to as "genetic celebrities"—those who, through no effort of their own, boast a pretty face or figure.

The aristocracy of the beautiful is becoming increasingly pronounced in the United States, with looks and figure trumping talent and effort in the professional marketplace. Even in such serious professions as broadcast journalism, appearance has become more important than substance. Just try to find a new female television anchor who isn't blonde-haired and blue-eyed. In fact, they are all beginning to look exactly alike.

When we were kids, our parents told us we were beautiful, even if the world did not agree. Our parents were not lying. Rather, their emotions colored their appraisal. Their affection dressed us up so that in their eyes we were, in fact, gorgeous. That is what love is: the inability to be objective about the object of your love. Love is where your beloved is always comely. To be in love is to be rendered incapable of rendering a rational evaluation. If you love your house, then you prefer it to a palace. If you love yourself, then you would not be dressing up to look like someone else. But I know very few women today who are in love with themselves and who would not radically reconstruct their faces and bodies with plastic surgery if they had the money. Just tune into the reality hit *Extreme Makeover* to witness how this kind of transformation has become a fairy tale dream for many Americans with faltering self-esteem. Each week, the show focuses on two people who are so distraught with their looks that they undergo radical plastic surgery. It should be no surprise that the vast majority of those who appear on the show are women who have embraced the societal notion that they are not good unless they look "perfect," their idea of perfection deriving primarily from the plastic Barbie dolls they played with as children.

Once upon a time when a man fell in love with a woman, he was supposed to stop comparing her to all the other women he could potentially date. He was to become *subjective* in his appraisal of her. Even as they aged together and the world saw her wrinkles, he would still remain fixated on her sparkling eyes.

But the constant bombardment of beautiful faces, and the portrayal of women as the lewd man's plaything through every conceivable medium, has rendered us incapable of being subjective about beauty. We have all become experts in objective standards of attractiveness—those five or six models of beauty that have become the only acceptable images that we are supposed to try and squeeze ourselves into. For women, it usually means a round face, blue eyes, blonde hair, and boniness like a scarecrow whose purpose is usually scaring off buzzards.

Forget that Marilyn Monroe was a size 14, or that the great art masters never painted a single skinny woman. Television and glossy magazines have changed all that. Visual media caters to the eye's need to reduce everything to a series of lines, and hence, stick figures reign. A hundred years ago, people made love with their hands and "meat was neat." Today, they make love, much less artfully, with their eyes, and "thin is in."

I have to applaud the Chicago reporter who wrote a mock graduation speech that director Baz Luhrmann, of *Moulin Rouge* fame, made into a top-ten pop song. In the list of dos and don'ts for a happy life, the lyrics prescribe, "Don't read beauty magazines, they will only make you feel ugly." In fact, even supermodels have admitted that they hate to see themselves in magazines, because they are discouraged by all the airbrushing they can identify on their images. If *they* need so much help to make it onto the cover of *Cosmo*, can they really be that gorgeous? Our obsessive, perfectionist media has managed to make even the elite beauties feel unattractive. What is truly damning is that in emphasizing a singular look, and in promoting celebrity above all other traits, we as a society have undermined our ability to appreciate a feminine woman no matter what her size, shape, or style of beauty.

Are Ugly Women Allowed to Report the News on TV?

Whenever I appear as a guest on a TV news show, I'm struck by the fact that all the female legal experts retained by the network are blonde and beautiful. Forget the anchors—who, of course, have to be gorgeous. Even the pundits need to look like Nordic goddesses. But it is clear that a heavy, plain woman would find it nearly impossible to get airtime, even when the subject requires an agile brain rather than merely a copious bust. The practice of valuing a woman based on her high cheekbones instead of her intelligence reached its zenith when CNN advertised its new anchor, Paula Zahn as, "just a little bit sexy."

Why shouldn't reading the news be like playing sports? Shouldn't it be the best qualified, instead of the best looking? But newswomen are not *primarily* valued for their minds and the intellectual contributions they can make, but for the images they project.

George Stephanopoulos impressed me back in the days when he was Bill Clinton's genius boy wonder. Now, he has one of the most important Sunday morning political talk shows on TV. He and I have met on several occasions, and he is always a friendly and gracious gentleman. His wife, Ali Wentworth, who had her own morning talk show on CBS, has cultivated a very different image from that of her husband. Here are a couple of snippets from an article about Wentworth from *W Magazine*, written on the launch of her TV show:

> When the *New York Post* ran a segment in July suggesting that Wentworth's rising star was straining her marriage, she defended their relationship by bragging about their sex life. . . . "George was horrified," Wentworth says. "I kept saying to him, 'Okay, so I told people we have sex twice a day. It's not that bad for you, honey. . . .'" According to executive producer Bruce McCay . . . , "We gave her a legitimate story about a singing gynecologist, and there was only one place she would go with it. She set a record for TV for saying 'vagina' the most times in two minutes."

This was a morning show, not a late-night show, and this is the wife of one of the leading television political commentators in America. Now I realize that just because a husband regularly interviews senators and congressmen does not mean that a wife has to be cultured or dignified. But must she talk like Sharon Osbourne? Must she use the lowest shock tactics on network TV to get ratings? Is garnering an audience at the expense of your dignity worth the price? Classiness should be worth a couple of ratings points, too, no?

Wentworth ended the interview with this important insight: "I don't think George could have married me if I was a Republican. No matter how big my boobs were." This is a free country and she can say whatever she wants, but coming from an ambitious woman with the opportunity to make an impact through her own show, it is all pretty disheartening. So why does she do it? My guess is that she wanted to be on television and she knew that she was not going to get an audience unless she catered to what has become the stereotype of outrageous, sleazy, blonde women.

Silly, Simpleminded Playthings

Many will argue that there are plenty of serious, formidable women in power. I don't disagree. That Condoleezza Rice, an African American woman, is the second most powerful person in the world today is truly astonishing. As a woman of high intelligence, vast erudition, and quiet dignity, she deserves the exalted post she's been given. But my point is that the depiction of women as silly, simpleminded playthings is so pervasive in our popular culture that it is almost impossible for a powerful female figure to find the respect she deserves. When I did my morning radio show on WWRL, the oldest black radio station in the United States, with my dear friend but political antagonist Peter Noel, the celebrated journalist, we would often talk about Condoleezza Rice. I was the conservative on the show and would speak of Condi as a woman of unshakable principle, high intelligence, and noble spirit. Peter would say, "I hate her politics. She's an Aunt Jemima, a traitor to her people. But I would sure like to *do* her. She's got the most amazing legs." This would all happen on the air; Peter, of course, was trying to be provocative and funny. I would take umbrage at this and tell Peter that he should not reduce her to a sex object; she had worked damn hard to make a serious place for herself in politics. Despite her obvious accomplishments, he would still come right back at me with, "I want to *do* her." Peter is one of the people I respect most in the world and is a thinking, fair-minded, respectful individual. Yet even he had fallen prey to this disturbing trend in the assessment of women.

The Disenfranchisement of the Non-Bombshell

Yes, hundreds of millions of men in Western society have succumbed to the image factor. In other words, the expectation that

Paula Zahn should be a little bit sexy before she can read them the news. Undoubtedly, the beautiful people get ahead faster, and this is a long standing reality. But today, that preference for good-looking individuals has given way to an all-out assault on those who are not considered beautiful. When it comes to women, this demand for the stereotypical good looks helps build the notion that a woman is little more than an object of attraction and arousal. Only in such a milieu could a political power like Condoleezza Rice be assessed for her hot legs instead of her formidable intelligence. The irony is that the men who are objectifying women are not even aware that they, too, are suffering from a reciprocated kind of judgment.

I have had plenty of personal experience watching this scenario up close. A few years ago, at the height of the Internet boom, I agreed to serve as Matchmaker-in-Chief for a leading Internet dating firm. One of my responsibilities was to lead singles cruises to places like Alaska and hold seminars for the men and women who were our passengers. I thought to myself, "Man, what a great perk." Little did I realize that my first voyage to Alaska was going to be on the "singles *Titanic*." As the women on that cruise embarked, they had no idea that they were going to suffer the indignity of being ignored by most of the men onboard, who overlooked them because they were not deemed pretty enough.

Ostensibly, every person who came on the cruise was there to meet someone for the purpose of a long-term relationship and marriage. Approximately one hundred singles made up our group, certainly numbers that seemingly would have assured a positive outcome for some. In reality, not only was it a waste of time, it was also painful to watch.

At the very first meeting on board, where I gave a lecture about the essentials of attraction, I asked the men to raise their hand if they found twenty-five of the fifty women present attractive. No hands went up. "Okay," I said, "how about *fifteen* women out of a fifty?" Three hands went up. (As a side note, you should be aware that most of the guys raising their hands were in their forties and bald.) "Okay, how about ten women out of fifty?" About five hands went up. "Five out of a fifty?" Fifteen hands went up. "How about two? Are there two really attractive women out of the fifty?" I queried. Nearly all the hands went up. And what do you know? Over the next week, it was these two women, considered attractive by a consensus among the men, who became the objects of all the male attention onboard. The ship had a small disco floor. It was sickening to watch how these two women would be asked by one guy after another to dance while nearly all the other women looked on from the sidelines. The men had no idea of how stupid and foolish they looked as they competed against one another for the trophy girlfriend. The rest of the women could not wait to get off the ship.

I spent the next week presenting two daily seminars in an effort to educate the men about the real principles of attraction and eroticism, among which the physical should account for no more than 20 percent (I discuss this in my book *Kosher Adultery: Seduce and Sin with your Spouse*). After all, look at the longevity in the public eye of women like Katharine Hepburn or Barbra Streisand, although there have been many women who were considered to be much more beautiful. But in Streisand, all the other ingredients of attraction are present, including a keen sense of humor, dynamic personality, sultry demeanor, ultrafeminine voice, and a razor-sharp mind. Had Barbra Streisand been 80 percent looks and 20 percent personality, she would have been forgotten like the starlets who get their fifteen minutes of fame and retreat to the obscurity whence they came.

I said to the men, "If over the next week I can get you guys to look at these same fifty women and see half of them as beautiful, then I have succeeded on this voyage." And I did succeed with a few of the men and there were even three couples who are still together a few years later. Nevertheless, this remains an embarrassingly low success rate.

Abercrombie & Fitch Won't Hire "Ugly People"

What I find so overwhelming about this confined image of beauty is that it is so readily acceptable for society to present a uniform standard of attractiveness that we are hardly aware of this incendiary message. What would be the repercussions for a retail clothing company if it were to announce that it only hires white women? Would any business get away with such racism? But trendsetting Abercrombie & Fitch is basically outed in the *New York Times* as hiring only pretty women. (And yes, they only hire handsome, well-chiseled men as well, but it's primarily the pretty women that drive the customers in, not the men. In college sports, there are great-looking guys who are cheerleaders. But if you think that is what the fans are looking at, think again.)

Discriminating against heavy women, short women, small-eyed women, or any other characterization that is today labeled as ugly is entirely acceptable in our misogynistic culture. I assume they would not hire dark-skinned black women either, since commercials and print ads would seem to indicate that only light-skinned African American women are beautiful. Don't believe me? Try and find even one *black* magazine that regularly features dark-skinned black girls on its covers. When I cohosted my morning radio show with Peter Noel, I put it to my African American listeners that this was the case, and there was no serious opposition.

In the landmark Supreme Court ruling on affirmative action in the summer of 2003, Justice Clarence Thomas declared in his dissent that he objects to affirmative action first and foremost because it degrades its recipients, making them beneficiaries of someone else's largesse instead of being capable people who advance on their own merit. If so, let us all shed a tear for the employees of Abercrombie & Fitch who, the company acknowledges, are chosen for their high cheekbones rather than their high standards, for hard chests rather than hard work.

It seems that A&F is one of those savvy employers who practice affirmative action for a decidedly tiny American minority—those who look better than you and me. Antonio Serrano, a former Abercrombie assistant store manager, explained the policy in the *New York Times:* "If someone came in with a pretty face, we were told to approach them and ask them if they wanted a job.

They thought if we had the best-looking college kids working in our store, everyone will want to shop there." Likewise, Tom Lennox, Abercrombie's communications director, acknowledged that the company targets sales assistants who "look great." Now there's real affirmative action. Action for people with especially firm bodies.

Beautiful people have a miraculous ability to part us from our money. In a misogynistic culture where women are trained to disparage themselves and look up to supermodels as examples of women who are really blessed, it becomes a privilege to hand our credit card over to someone we wish we could look like. Abercrombie has learned that the beautiful people can motivate "regular" people to try to impress them. We humans like to be charitable and bighearted, but we prefer to show our generosity toward the big-breasted or the long-legged. While normally being loath to pick up a hitchhiker, we somehow manage to overcome our caution if a beautiful blonde or a stubble-faced stud sticks out a thumb. Studies have shown that good-looking men or women who have lost a wallet with their picture inside stand a far greater chance of having it returned to them—even through the mail—than someone ugly. Now there's altruism for you. Yes, it is pathetic to think that we would buy a pair of jeans more readily when a bodybuilder with six-pack abs tells us those jeans look great on our flabby bodies. But it works. People love feeling validated by sexy, hot people. They love getting compliments from them. And they love looking like them, all facts that Abercrombie has shamelessly exploited. And Abercrombie is capitalizing on its customers' natural desire to put aside reason and believe that an article of clothing, a purchase, will somehow lift them into the ranks of the beautiful people.

Once this kind of behavior is accepted, it is no surprise to find that any woman who is considered to be ugly by these strict standards is veritably finished. She can look forward to a life of dating where the guy rarely ever calls back, unless he has just broken up with a girlfriend and wants some uncomplicated sex with a person whom he considers desperate.

Hatred for Fat Women

The assault on overweight women in our culture is especially insidious. It's gotten so bad that in February 2005 one of Atlantic City's leading casino resorts, The Borgata, announced that it had warned its female servers, known respectfully as "Borgata Babes," that they could be fired from their jobs if they gained more than 7 percent of their body weight from the time of their hiring. When Borgata spokesman Michael Facenda was asked by CNN (February 21, 2005) how they could justify such a discriminatory policy, he replied, "We find this policy to be legal and fair, because the job is defined as a 'performing art.'" Yup, women are permanently performing. They are placed on God's green earth to perform for men, even when they're just serving men drinks. And they better be damn skinny, or they'll be fired. Because being fat, by today's standards, is a serious offense—on par with stealing or not turning up to work.

Now, I don't believe that men or women should allow themselves to grow overweight, mostly because it is unhealthy and it constrains one's freedom in life. Rousseau postulated, "Man is born free but everywhere he is in chains." He was talking about political servitude, but being overweight is a kind of shackle. I have overweight friends who can not take long walks or climb hills to see beautiful sunsets. I'm not being judgmental, because I am somewhat on the overweight side myself, and I find it constricting.

The problem is that when men describe women as overweight and dismiss them as ugly, they are not talking about obese women. They are often talking about women who carry a mere five to ten extra pounds! Beautiful today is a woman who looks like an emaciated scarecrow. She looks as if she belongs in a field, scaring off buzzards, but instead, she is placed on a catwalk because of her long angular figure. Voluptuous used to be the ideal, and it was synonymous with sensual. But sensuality is out, and malnourishment is in.

During the 2004 presidential race, when John Edwards was chosen as John Kerry's running mate, I predicted that the television cameras just might decide to skip Elizabeth Edwards. Indeed, my prediction came true. Right after introducing her husband at the Democratic convention in Boston, she all but disappeared, despite being arguably the best thing the Democratic ticket had going for it. An intelligent and accomplished professional woman who exuded genuine, down-to-earth warmth, Elizabeth Edwards also earned the respect of traditional-minded Americans by courageously deciding to have two young children in midlife after losing her eldest child in a car crash. A woman of quiet dignity, refinement, and grace, she was the perfect antidote to the arrogant condescension of the opinionated Teresa Heinz Kerry.

So why didn't you see a lot of Elizabeth Edwards on TV? Because the United States has a silent contempt for heavy women. It hides them away. They are seen as unattractive and are endlessly analyzed by armchair psychologists, who seek to unravel the mystery of why they would have allowed themselves to become repellent.

This is especially true of women who, like Elizabeth Edwards, were once thin. The women who have always been heavy may elicit the public's sympathy. "Maybe it's genetic," they think inwardly. But women who were once thin and attractive, like Elizabeth Edwards, but who dare to put on weight—even after suffering a horrific personal tragedy like the loss of a child—are treated as if they have violated some sacred commandment: Thou shalt always look pleasing for thine menfolk. And by menfolk, we mean here not only the husband of Elizabeth Edwards but all American men who have a right to look at a young candidate's wife and see someone who pleases the eye, like Jackie Kennedy. After all, he's good looking, right? So shouldn't his wife be, too?

There was endless "political commentary" about how handsome and vibrant John Edwards is and how he nicely complemented the long-faced taciturnity of John Kerry. Even Kerry himself praised his good-looking vice presidential candidate for having "great hair." But those same commentators are utterly silent on the looks of Elizabeth Edwards because to them, as to the rest of America, the fact that she is overweight means that she is unpleasant.

For the longest time, the United States has been waging a holy war against women who dare to be fat. For months, the American tabloids have shown us pictures of the "obese" actress Kirstie Alley. The pictures of her at three hundred pounds are invariably contrasted with photos of how she looked when she was thin and pretty on TV's *Cheers*. She is depicted as a circus elephant, replete in tentlike clothes. The implication is that she is the victim of some grave mental illness—why else would she have allowed herself to mushroom to such proportions? Fortunately for her, she finally redeemed herself in the public eye by becoming the spokesperson for *Jennie Craig*, the perfect role for a fat person. At least now she fits in.

I do not deny that shedding extra pounds can make us healthier, improve the quality of our lives, and enhance the self-esteem of both men and women. But do we really want our daughters to be numskulls like Paris Hilton and Britney Spears, who have perfect bodies but rotting brains?

Just think about the message that American girls get when large women are unjustly treated as repulsive. They learn that personality, education, virtue, and motherhood (pregnancy often causes women to put on and retain extra weight) counts for nothing in the eyes of men. Spend all your time in a gym burning off fat, rather than being idle in a library and reading a book, advancing causes you care deeply about, working hard at your career, or striving to raise a healthy family. This will keep you in the good graces of our society at large.

Even the American TV networks these days seem to hire only thin, beautiful women to read the news. Just try and find a *new* female news talent on TV who is either heavy or over forty. I bet you can't think of even one. You are more likely to see a space alien on your rooftop than a heavyset woman on your TV screen.

This is also part of an ugly double standard. Weight is not an impediment to power and success among men. Just look at Michael Moore and Harvey Weinstein. But the only women who are allowed to be heavy in America are funny women, like Starr Jones.

Thinness may have become synonymous with beauty in the United States, but it is decimating the erotic life of marriage. In multiple sexual surveys, one of the biggest complaints that husbands voice about their wives is that they rarely initiate sex and are far too reserved in the bedroom. But can we really expect the American wife to be sexually adventurous when she is permanently self-conscious about her weight? It makes sense that women who feel unattractive will choose to hide under the covers.

Dr. James Watson, the Nobel prize–winning geneticist who was jointly responsible for discovering the structure of DNA, maintained that plumper women were more likely to enjoy a better sex life than their thin counterparts. He told an audience at University College London that extra pounds had the biological effect of making a woman well rounded in character and better in bed. "Thinness is never associated with sexuality," he noted.

He explained that extra fat had the effect of boosting endorphins, the natural mood-enhancing chemical that is also linked to sexual desire. "Kate Moss is probably the most famous thin person in the world, and she's looking particularly sad. Who has ever heard of a happy supermodel?" Watson asked.

He also argued that leptin, which is produced in fat tissue, boosts the chemical MSH, which enhances sexual desire. "Your mood is controlled by endorphins, and you make more of these when you are fat; hence, nobody has ever drawn Santa Claus thin. Thin people are discontented." And the obsessive American war on fat is also taxing the American family, with more women growing afraid to "disfigure" their bodies with pregnancies and postpartum pounds.

The Loss of Reverence for Women Begets the Loss of Girlhood

Our society's failure to nurture the feminine spirit with all its complexities, coupled with our obsession with Hollywood ideals, is having a tremendously powerful influence on young girls. After all, who is it that little girls are looking up to? The tawdry and depraved trio of Britney, Madonna, and Christina? Their proclivity to expose their bodies in undignified and sleazy ways not only depicts a lack of self-respect, but it also presents an image of the female figure that brooks few alternatives. The insistence on a stereotypical female form has long been problematic, right back to the time when the Barbie doll was created with her unattainable figure. The need to be beautiful, to get ahead, even in reputable professions, is problematic in and of itself. What the "Musical Axis of Evil" adds to this image is even more distressing. The example of a Britney Spears not only teaches young girls that they must hate themselves if they are not perfectly built, but it also pushes them to grow up quickly, to embrace the imagery of women developed by our pop culture—a vision that leaves them few alternatives but to personify, in some way, the role of the sex kitten. Why do you think that so many women go to the gym at night instead of the library? Why do they go jogging instead of to a night class? They realize that the real rewards in society come from looking great rather than having a lot of knowledge. I recognize that society has always glorified beautiful women and held them out as models to be emulated. But the difference is that beauty used to be more holistic. It encompassed not only a human's figure but her feminine demeanor, her heart and mind, and her grace. Beauty once was a total statement of a woman's appeal, whereas today it means her physical appearance exclusively.

Accelerated Adolescence

Psychologists and sociologists have noted in recent years that the youth in our country are experiencing an accelerated adolescence. This phenomenon was illuminated by a *Time* magazine story (October 6, 2003) detailing how 40 percent of all female high school students wear thongs with one of the straps showing above their pants. Moreover, the research indicated that girls as young as age seven have begun to choose these undergarments and the thong market in 2002 for girls under age twelve was a staggering $120 million (up from just $400,000 in 2000).

Could anyone have imagined twenty years ago that little girls would be insisting on wearing this overtly sexual lingerie? How did they go from being made of "sugar and spice and everything nice" to being desperate for heavy makeup, high heels, and birth control? How did we wind up with girls who worry about developing their bodies and learning how to shake their bottoms—but don't give a thought to cultivating their spirits, their minds, and their characters? Wasn't the feminist movement supposed to teach little girls that they could be nuclear physicists? When did they abandon these dreams in order to strive toward becoming a conglomeration of nothing more than their perfected body parts? What has changed today is that the culture has made women pedestrian. No one cares whether Natalie Portman goes to Harvard, or Julia Stiles attends Columbia, or whether they are respectful daughters or socially conscious individuals. All the public wants to know is when these young celebrities are going to graduate to nude scenes in films, take it all off for *Playboy*, or at the very least, do some steamy love scene with Leonardo DiCaprio. A woman in and of herself is only valued for the hormonal excitement she can inspire, not the intellectual contributions she can make, nor the emotional and spiritual healing she can offer.

That little girls are losing their girlhood is even being evidenced physically. Doctors are at a loss to explain why the age of puberty for girls continues to go down, with white girls getting their period these days at about age eleven, and African American girls beginning at the startling age of nine. Menstruation used to begin in the early teen years. Some doctors, including those with wide experience with teenagers, such as Dr. Drew Pinsky, surmise that the phenomenon is akin to that of Pavlov's dogs. These girls are watching so much explicit material on television and the like, and being sexualized at such an early age, that their bodies are actually responding. They are becoming women when in fact they are only vulnerable girls.

The dELiA's Catalog of Pornography for Teens

My sixteen-year-old daughter, with whom I am in constant discussion about this book, came over to me the other night and handed me a copy of dELiA's, the mail-order catalog for teenage girls. What a shame it is that I cannot reproduce some of the pictures that appear in this booklet. I can't because they are disgusting and would shock you to no end. We all know that child pornography is supposed to be illegal, but you would never think so if you saw this catalog. It has pictures of fourteen- and fifteen-year-old models wearing lingerie. I know that this is not shocking anymore, particularly given the statistics on how many French teens buy thongs or how many American teenage girls are wearing thongs to high school, so I am going to repeat myself to be sure the message gets across. *There are fourteen- and fifteen-year-old girls in lacy underwear, modeling the skimpiest undergarments in the hopes of inspiring other fourteen- and fifteen-year-olds to buy and wear the same. Corporate America is sexually exploiting fourteen-year-old girls for money. Does anyone give a damn? Or has that too passed silently into the realm of acceptance?*

And then there was this report from CNN on May 28, 2002: "Abercrombie & Fitch, the retailer that has been criticized for sexually and racially provocative catalogs and designs, is under fire—again. Several consumer advocacy groups said they have sent e-mails to A&F to protest the chain's latest offering of thong underwear in children's sizes, with the words 'eye candy' and 'wink wink,' printed on the front. . . . Last year, the youth-oriented clothing retailer angered many consumer advocacy groups with its summer and Christmas catalogs showing sexually provocative teenage-looking models apparently in the nude."

It is one thing when, say, Victoria's Secret models make themselves look seductive. That too has become pornographic and problematic, but at least these are adult women. Who, pray tell, is supposed to enjoy leering at these young girls in their lingerie? Who is supposed to be stimulated by seeing them nude in these catalogs? Well, it is unlikely to be their fathers or their brothers, so what is the message here? You are fourteen, and even then you should be wearing provocative underwear, or going naked for your boyfriend? Or wearing underwear that says "Eye Candy" on your crotch?

Wait, it gets better. Not only should your boyfriend be seeing you in your lingerie, even though you are only in ninth grade, but all the other boys in the classroom should also know that you wear sexy underwear. To that end, the dELiA's catalog is selling thongs with a butterfly clasp that is designed to be worn outside the girl's pants, about two inches above the belt line. So the underwear's waistband is worn completely outside the trousers. The bottom line is that these girls are being told to wear their underwear in a way that makes it visible to all—at school. It is like wearing a sandwich board that says, "I'm fourteen, and I'm wearing a thong. Here, have a look. And, by the way, if I'm willing to let you see this private part of my attire, who knows what else I'm prepared to show you." In general, the depiction of women in their underwear is so common that we have grown almost bored with it—even if we are not talking about women but merely girls.

What trends like this have done is take the coquettish, tawdry persona of the Playboy Bunny and paint every young girl and woman out there with the same qualities. There is no mystery anymore, no protection of the private and sacred. Now we are conditioned to see the girl next door as a sex toy. Forget the girl, we are even permitted and encouraged to imagine her mom in one of Victoria's slinky teddies. The hit song by the group Fountains of Wayne, "Stacey's Mom," is all about a young boy lusting after his friend's mother. The video that accompanied this particularly offensive, popular song does not even portray the boy as an older teen at the cusp of manhood, nurturing lecherous thoughts about an older woman. No, instead the male star of the video is a very young, preteen boy who is fantasizing about the woman next door. I would have been horrified if some friend of mine had thought of my mother in such a tawdry way. I would be horrified for my sons to cultivate such inappropriate, libidinous thoughts. I would have been a much different man today if I had not been raised in an age that revered women and by a woman who had respect for herself. (And yes, I know that Dustin Hoffman's character has an affair with Mrs. Robinson. But remember, in the movie, while younger, he is already an adult.)

Our society has lost its reverence for women. It has become commonplace to see body parts put out for display, critiqued, criticized, and deemed wanting. But in desensitizing ourselves to modesty, to sanctity, and to the mystique of femininity, we have become bigots who embrace a slutty Madonna while making dignified women, who prefer to develop their brains, feel ordinary. The repercussions are terrifying for a society that does not honor its women and does not value time-honored feminine traits. Harshness will triumph over subtlety, commerce over the environment, and ruthlessness over ethics.

18

∽

A CRISIS IN MANHOOD

What is at risk here is more than just the disenfranchisement of nonbeautiful women and the early maturation and psychological marring of girls. As if all this were not bad enough, we are also witnessing a crisis in manhood. Most men today have little clue how to be gentlemen, which means they do not know how to act in a refined and dignified manner. They certainly have little idea how to treat a woman. But, even worse than these behavioral deficits, at a visceral and automatic level, the attraction men have for women is faltering as well.

Men today are attracted not to *womankind*, but to *a kind of woman*, a reflection of the diminishment of their masculinity. It is as if the magnetism of polar opposites that once drew the sexes together has largely ceased to function, and men's energy is weakened as a result. The very definition of a heterosexual man is one who is attracted to women. So if a man is attracted to only 5 percent of women, does that not mean that he has been compromised as a man? Let's stop blaming the women. It's not that they aren't "hot" enough. It is the men who have changed, and they are strangely unattracted to the majority of women. As a result, men are losing their appetite for women. Like a man who slowly loses his appetite for food and can only feel hungry when around the most expensive and succulent dishes, men are so overexposed to women that to take notice of one, they need "an offer they can't refuse." That is why super-models have such dominance today. They represent that tiny sliver of the female population to whom most men are still attracted. Hence, the bar keeps on going up and up. The women have to be ridiculously gorgeous just to attract men's interest.

After creating Adam and witnessing his loneliness, God created Eve from Adam's rib and brought her to him as a companion. The miracle was that Adam liked her as soon as he laid eyes on her, and they spent the next few hundred years happily married to one another. This means not only that Adam found Eve adequate, but that all his impulses as a man actually worked. His attraction to Eve, the archetypal woman, was strong. Could anyone imagine that happening today? If the story were a modern one, God would bring Eve to Adam; he would look at her and then complain, "Why couldn't the Garden of Eden have been in Scandinavia? And God, do you have silicone in this garden?"

Men today have been conditioned to be attracted to a single stereotype of beauty: blonde hair, blue eyes, small tush, big boobs. Oh, I forgot the long legs. Sorry. In a pinch, they will take a brunette, if their compromise on the hair color is compensated by a few more inches in height.

I mentioned earlier that light skin is another prerequisite for beauty. Even in the black community, people with light skin are generally considered to be more beautiful than people with dark skin. My wife and I traveled to Dakar in Senegal, sub-Saharan Africa, one of the poorest countries in the world, and were absolutely gob-smacked to see giant billboards advertising skin bleach. The imposition of a single standard of beauty is so overwhelming that women who don't measure up feel so ugly that they use food money to change.

This emphasis on physical appearance not only affects female esteem, but also impacts on the male psyche and ability to relate. What this all comes down to is an inability of men and women to relate to one another and build lasting relationships.

The Sensual versus the Sexual

This skewed emphasis on the physical image is certainly affecting the quality of sex in relationships. Stated simply, sensuality is being lost from sex. Lovemaking is meant to be sensual rather than sexual. Sex is an act of congress between two people who want to share humanity's most intimate connection. The question then becomes, "How do these two people become one flesh when they are in two separate bodies?" The answer is that sex provides five connecting points, five adhesive connectors through which men and women conjoin to become bone of one bone and flesh of one flesh. These five connecting points are the five senses. You are meant to make love with your hands, your eyes, your nose, your ears, and your mouth. Couples are meant to enjoy the touch, sight, scent, sound, and taste of sex. In this age of television and spotlight, the problem is that we only make love with our eyes. Attraction has become an entirely visual experience. Woman's attractiveness to men has become unidimensional. The sexual has triumphed over the sensual. The result is that we are firing on only one cylinder, we are connecting through only one sense. And how strong is that connection going to be? An entire generation, suffering from a profoundly diminished sense of sensuality, is having really bad sex.

The emphasis today on the aesthetic is pronounced and profound. Men and women work out at gyms to make their bodies ever more attractive to the exclusion of virtually anything else. If you were to look at erotic French literature of the eighteenth century, you would see that there was much greater emphasis on a woman's natural fragrance, her *casserole*, than her looks. Back then, the words "scent of a woman" brought more to mind than an Al Pacino movie. Napoleon writes to Josephine, just after the Italian campaign and the battle of Marengo, "I'll be home in three days, don't bathe." Reading this today, most of us would probably shake our heads in disgust, "Uucchh!" Don't bathe? But to men of an earlier generation, the natural scent of a woman was the most intoxicating aphrodisiac and drove them wild with desire. So today, women have learned to sanitize themselves with artificial scents with names like "Passion" and "Desire."

In my first appearance on the popular national radio show *Loveline*, a fifteen-year-old boy called up and said, "I'm having sex with my girlfriend and I like going down on her. But she has this smell in her vagina that is really off-putting." The advice he was given by guest Doctor Bruce was to encourage her to go to a doctor to do something about the odor. What no one told this boy— forget young man, he was a boy—was that his immaturity was evident in everything he was saying, and that he clearly wasn't ready for sex yet. What did he think a woman was? A Barbie doll whose only scent was that of shrink-wrap? Indeed, this is one of the strongest arguments—aside from the obvious moral ones— against adolescent sex. The human body is not built to share such powerful experiences with such underdeveloped senses, and the sex turns out to be so inadequate that it leaves permanent scars. But that aside, because even grown men no longer make love with their noses, women have quickly run to conceal every natural scent with far more alluring artificial ones like Chanel No. 5 and Coco (and the guys follow suit by dabbing on alluring aftershaves with manly names like "Seven Nights in the Stable. . . . Because a Real Man Smells Like His Horse"). All our human senses have been drowned out in a din of light. We are so unaware of a woman's natural sexual scent that today we have to be reminded of it by scientists. It is called *pheromones*. And pheromones play a central role in the science of attraction.

The same thing is true with the sense of touch in lovemaking. The great masters like Rubens nearly always painted plump women, literally women of substance. To them, women who had a bit of flesh were always more attractive, because it meant that they were softer and more pleasurable to make love to. After all, what feels better? To make love to a bag of bones and a rib cage, or to tender, supple flesh?

In an age where men and women make love only with their eyes, women are starving themselves to remain attractive to men. During the 1950s, the dawn of the television and glossy magazine era, there were only a few hundred cases of anorexia in the United States. Today there are hundreds of thousands.

And the consciousness about weight starts so young. According to the September 2003 issue of *Pediatrics*, a shocking 40 percent of nine- and ten-year-old girls are trying to lose weight. And on December 19, 2001, ABC News made this report: "Eating disorder experts say that prepubescent girls are developing eating disorders as young as five and six years old, and they may be acquiring their new obsession from parents who are preoccupied with their own body images, and media images of skinny pop stars. Experts say the problem among children is growing. . . . Justine Gallagher was five years old when she started eating paper in order to lose weight. She ate up to ten pieces of paper a day, believing that filling up on paper—rather than food—would help her lose weight. The boys at school were telling Justine that she was fat. Meanwhile, her teachers noticed that parts of her books were missing." This is how extreme women's obsession with their weight has become.

From the earliest age, women think that if they just shed a few pounds they'll attract the immediate stares of guys. And they may be right. But something essential is lost in the process. And the millions of husbands all across the United States who daily make their wives feel too heavy, and thus unattractive, should take note and mend their ways. (This is aside from the well-known reason that married women are always heavier than single women. The single woman comes home, checks what's in the fridge, and then goes to bed. But the married woman comes home, checks what's in the bed, and then goes to the fridge.)

I'm convinced that one of the reasons that Bill Clinton is so attractive to women is that he is one of the last sensual men around. I am not condoning his inexcusable extramarital proclivities that ought rightly be utterly condemned (I was one of his biggest critics). Okay, his power and stature in the world, of course, goes some way toward explaining his attractiveness to the feminine gender. Power is, after all, the ultimate aphrodisiac. But Richard Nixon and Jimmy Carter also occupied the same seat, and we didn't hear of White House interns showing off their thongs to either of them. Bill Clinton is a sensual man, and was described as such several times by Monica Lewinsky. By sensual, I mean that he takes in a woman in her entirety, he swallows her with all of his five senses, and not just his eyes. The standard description for women who have met Clinton, including a highly intelligent female reporter who went to interview him, is that they get weak at the knees on meeting him. And he instantly makes them feel so incredibly desirable—something that women want most from a man—that they find themselves unable to resist. In political circles they say that while George W. Bush is a *man's* man, Clinton is a *ladies'* man.

One of the biggest criticisms about Clinton's affairs was this: If you're going to have an illicit affair anyway, then why not have it with some really attractive woman, a famous model, instead of Monica Lewinsky or Paula Jones? Why a fat woman and a woman with a big nose? Why not just go for leggy model types, like JFK did? But that is Clinton's secret. He finds a woman attractive in her entirety, and not just her physical appearance. Women who seem unattractive to most men appeal to Clinton because he has four other barometers of attraction to respond to. And that kind of attraction—the kind that doesn't merely reduce women to a collection of body parts—is what every woman dreams of. Every woman wants to be loved in her totality, not just her skin texture or her curves. (Now, if only Clinton could transfer that kind of attention exclusively onto his wife!)

19

∞

HUSBANDS HAVE LOST
AWE AND REVERENCE
FOR THEIR WIVES

There is another important reason sex has become so unfulfilling. We are having bad sex today not only because of diminished
sensuality, but because of diminished commitment. Sex is beautiful
specifically because it allows us to let go. Sex is the ultimate act of
freedom, the highest form of liberation. Great sex makes you feel
like you can soar. Sex is about the total submission of humans to
raw instinct. But how can you let go and achieve that level of freedom in sex when you are making love to a stranger? Won't you be
inhibited and self-conscious? The only time you *can* let go in sex is
when the two of you are committed to each other and there is total
trust. Only when there is commitment, can you both kindle a
wildfire that you will allow to burn out of control, consuming both
of you in its entirety, because you are not afraid of where you will
end up together. And that is why the best kind of sex is found between a man and a woman who have become husband and wife.

Of course, it is not enough for a couple simply to commit to
one another to ensure a healthy and satisfying sex life. The fact
that men are no longer overcome by a reverence for womankind has
led to a complete decline in chivalry. Simply stated, if husbands

don't believe that their wives are special, they will make far less of an effort to romance them. Once upon a time, a man was motivated to be a gentleman to woo and win a lady, to make that lady his wife. So many women dream of converting the "bad boy." They long to tame a man like Jack Nicholson, who in his profound words in the Academy Award–winning film *As Good As It Gets*, finally meets a woman to whom he can honestly say, "You make me want to be a better man." Only in the presence of a lady do men feel the compunction to offer greater decorum: to be, in fact, better. I doubt many men would refrain from belching in front of Britney Spears. I bet she could eek out a good one with the old boys. But would the same pigs behave this way in front of, say, Laura Bush? Whatever your politics may be, you must admit that Mrs. Bush is a lady. Would you burp in front of a lady without dying of embarrassment? Of course not. You would find a way to live up to what is expected of you.

As old-fashioned as it sounds, it still holds true that a lady inspires a man. Such inspiration can have a profound effect on how and what one accomplishes. While it is entirely possible to pray at any time and any place, being inside a church, temple, or mosque encourages us. This same rationale helps us to understand why ladies arouse an awe in men that hones gentlemanly conduct. If women put up with juvenile, crass behavior and allow themselves to be won over despite this loutishness, how can they hope to be surrounded by decent men? Men, after all, are motivated by necessity alone, which is why they—so much more so than women—are in need of discipline. This is the reason that in traditional Jewish practices, it is the man who needs the physical head covering—the yarmulke—to remind him of God's overriding presence. It is the man who needs a barrage of physical and time-bound duties to cultivate his spirituality. Women, by contrast, must fulfill far fewer requirements, for it is understood that they are more naturally in tune with the spiritual world.

In terms of relationships between men and women, there are really only two choices. A woman can impose artificial rules on her husband, such as if you are a pig, if you cheat, I leave. Or she can be a lady herself and, with her unswerving example, give her man an image to which he must live up. In my own experience, I have to admit that being married to a true lady has out-and-out embarrassed me into being more of a gentleman. My wife is naturally a nurturer and she is very feminine. She seldom loses her temper, and she has never chided me with imposed, motherly rules. Just being around her, watching her, has motivated me to want to make myself deserving of her. When I think of the early days of our marriage, I am ashamed of how careless I used to be in not always knowing how to treat a woman, and I admire my wife all the more. It was her consistency, her unwavering feminine charm that inspired me in a million different ways. She is the most important inspiration behind this book. But there are all too few ladies in today's society. Too many women, rather than becoming the nurturing female facilitator, become enablers and facilitators of bad behavior from the men in their lives. They are prepared to tolerate the intolerable.

In the course of counseling many married couples, I hear two common refrains from the wives. The first is, "He never helps around the house. I work, too, you know. But I come home and he leaves everything lying around for me to clean up after him." The second refrain is, "We have such bad sex. He watches TV until it's really late and then expects me to be in the mood when he rolls over and wants it. I'm too tired. I work hard during the day. Then I come home to the kids and have to help with their homework and make dinner. When I put my head on the pillow I'm immediately asleep. And it's not as if he does anything particularly romantic. He just wants sex on demand."

The two complaints are related. When men stand in awe and wonder of their wives, they would never leave a mess for them to clean up. On the contrary, they would feel they were defiling something special. They would also be ashamed to have someone whom they so highly regard think ill of them. If the president of the United States visited your home, would you want him to find it looking like a tornado had just hit? But many husbands do not consider their wives to be worthy of this kind of respect and consideration. Rather than feeling awe, they feel boredom, or worse, contempt.

20

~

TURNING YOUR WIFE
INTO THE CLEANER

Of all the contemptuous things that men do to their wives, making them into the cleaner is perhaps the most contemptuous of all. Nobody truly respects their cleaner. They may say hello and goodbye, thank the person for good work and hand over a paycheck. They may even feel sorry for the person, but they take no real interest in the cleaner's life. On the contrary, the cleaner is there to serve them.

If a man demotes his wife to the level of a housekeeper, he has certainly lost any awe for her. The mystery, and thus the attraction (which is all about mystery), is utterly gone. This loss of awe evidences itself in terrible or nonexistent sex. Imagine for a moment that a man was truly in awe of the sexual delights that he could share with his wife. Imagine if even seeing her naked body was like the skies opening up to reveal a host of angels. Imagine that rather than merely lusting after his wife—and lust in marriage is both good and important, as there is precious too little of it already—he looked at her body in wonder.

I remember once that the actor Michael Caine was asked why he never does nude scenes. His answer went something along the lines of, "Have you ever seen a naked man run? How ridiculous it looks? How everything is flopping around? That's why." Yet, when women run around naked, even though there is a lot more flopping around, men find this sexy and erotic. That is because a woman's body is so much more naturally graceful than a man's, so much more magnificent and exquisite. Imagine that a man actually saw and appreciated the potency of a woman preparing to share her body with him. Moved by the wonders of the pleasures she could offer him, he would never just give her a meaningless peck on the check as foreplay, have five minutes of sex, and fall asleep. He could never treat a goddess so contemptuously as that. But in his interactions with the cleaner, he would more likely be dismissive. Indeed, if he was forced to make love to the cleaner, especially night after night, he would probably fantasize about other women while doing so, and use the cleaning lady's body for nothing more than masturbatory friction.

During an interview once on the Steve Cochran show in Chicago, the host said to me, "What's wrong with women choosing to model naked for money? Okay, so porn is degrading. But if women want to do that, it's their choice. If Tim Russert wants to interview people for a living, that's his choice."

"Yes," I said. "And I'm not arguing for censorship. But the difference with Tim Russert is that when he interviews people, we end up respecting him. But when women take off their clothes for money, it affects our opinion of *all* women and we end up calling them bitches, sluts, and whores. It makes us contemptuous of women as our undignified plaything."

The same thing happens, albeit to a lesser extent, when husbands reduce their wives to the household help. I have heard an endless number of women complain to me that their husbands never assist with the kids, never pick up a plate, and never even have the decency to put their dirty clothes in a laundry hamper. Men are excited by women whom they see as their equals, or even their superiors. When a woman is beneath you—and every woman who is designed merely to clean up after you is beneath you—you are not drawn to her and end up pitying her instead. This is compounded by the wife looking and feeling tired and haggard, frizzled and frazzled. She simply does not look her best. Yet, these same husbands will then blame their wives for the loss of attraction in the marriage. "You've let yourself go," he'll tell her. "You never exercise. You don't put on makeup." Yet, all the while, he is the one responsible. When is the last time the cleaning woman went to the hairdresser before she came to vacuum your carpets?

The cleaning-woman mentality leads directly to husbands having empty sex with their wives, with no sense of reverence and with no sense of awe. When a man makes love to his wife but thinks about another woman, then climaxes and climbs off of his wife, he has treated her like an available whore who is there to satisfy his needs. There is no way that this physical intimacy could ever cultivate a sense of wonder or awe in the relationship. Neither can the wives be fooled into believing that their husbands are thinking about them, when really the men are fantasizing about someone else. This, too, is an unfortunate consequence of the explicit nudity on TV and the Internet. It is leading husbands to get excited by smut, and then to use their wives as a form of masturbation. Hence, sex is failing to draw husbands and wives closer, a phenomenon I dealt with in my book, *Kosher Sex*.

In the follow-up book, *Kosher Adultery*, I argued that one of the best ways husbands who feel bored with their wives might reinvigorate the eroticism of their relationship is by following the ancient biblical proscription of never having sex with your wife without her climaxing first. Aside from the obvious chivalric and gentlemanly dimension of having her enjoy, rather than endure, the experience, the more important reason is there is nothing so wondrous as to watch a woman in the throes of pleasure. A woman is spirituality incarnate. And like a nuclear bomb whose energy is created by the transformation of matter into energy, a man who serves as the detonator, releasing all that energy and witnessing the raw, erotic spirituality of his wife converted to explosive passion, cannot help but be overcome with wonder and awe. And it makes him desire his wife anew.

Unfortunately, studies show that whereas husbands climax in marital sex about 85 percent of the time, for the wife it is less than 20 percent. Men feel entitled to their sexual satisfaction, even if they are not sharing it with their wives. Certainly they see this often enough. Notice how in pornography the focus is almost always on the man's climax. It is rarely about the woman. And it is always about the man climaxing in the most degrading way for the woman. That is why so many spam e-mails say, "See him cum all over her face." It is about treating the woman contemptuously. She is there to excite the man and get him off no matter how it lands up for her. To be sure, some porn videos try and show a woman climaxing, but usually this is done in the most counterfeit and hysterical way, so she winds up shrieking wildly even though she looks like she's thinking about the laundry. You can see that, in the midst of "ecstasy," what she is really thinking is, "Okay, the director said I get an extra hundred bucks if I do a convincing orgasm." And so there is no awe for womankind and the degradation of women continues.

Men's Sense of Entitlement Often Leads to Violence

Rather than feeling awed by the wonder of a woman, many men today have been conditioned to look on a woman as something akin to a possession, to be used for their pleasure *so long as she is bringing pleasure*, after which she may be discarded. The portrayal of women as a means to an end is the misogyny of our time, and it comes to men all too readily. It also leads to tragic and horrific consequences. Naturally, these degrading notions of women have a direct impact on the manner with which men view and treat women. In some cases, when misogyny is brought into contact with an already shaky psyche, the consequences can be deadly.

On November 5, 2003, in Seattle, Washington, Gary L. Ridgway, a fifty-four-year-old former truck painter, stood before a courtroom packed with weeping relatives of his victims and uttered the world "guilty" forty-eight times. In a horrible closing to what became known as the "Green River" killings of the 1980s, Ridgway admitted to strangling an unthinkable number of women, mostly prostitutes and runaways, in his home or in his pickup truck while having sex with them, then dumping their bodies around the Seattle area. Ridgway is the most lethal serial killer in American history.

During the court hearing, the lead prosecutor Jeffrey B. Baird, of the King County Prosecuting Attorney's Office, read from a statement by Mr. Ridgway, explaining how and why he had conducted his murderous rampage. Ridgway said in his confession, "In most cases, when I murdered these women I did not know their names. Most of the time I killed them the first time I met them, and I did not have a good memory for their faces. I killed so many women, I have a hard time keeping them straight."

As he read, the prosecutor paused, turned to Ridgway, and said, "Is that true?"

"Yes, it is," Ridgway replied stoically.

The statement continued: "I placed most of the bodies in groups which I called clusters. I did this because I wanted to keep track of all the women I killed. I liked to drive by the clusters around the county and think about the women I placed there."

Sheriff Reichert, who started investigating the murders as a detective back in 1982, described Ridgway as a ruthless and remorseless killer who barely flinched when telling investigators about what he called his "patrolling" for prostitutes. As the *New York Times* reported, "He said that he hated them and that it would be easy to get away with killing them." In court documents, prosecutors said Mr. Ridgway appeared "indifferent to the race of his victims," telling them, "I'd much rather have white, but black was fine. It's just, just garbage." Each woman, he said, was "just something" to have sex with before he would "kill her and dump her."

After the hearing, in one of the most memorable lines of the case, Ridgway's chief lawyer, Anthony Savage, said: "Gary breaks the mold in a lot of different directions. The man is obviously off the rails, around the bend, down the river, whatever you want to call it. I don't think we'll ever know what fueled his anger."

Hmm. Interesting. We will never know what fueled his anger? Well, let me venture a guess. I have seen many loners and losers who hate women. They speak of them in the most derogatory way and often threaten them with violence. While I, in no

way excuse the personal accountability of monsters like Ridgway—and indeed I think he should have gotten the death penalty
instead of the plea bargain he received—I believe there is a link
between the hatred that the Ridgways of this world display toward women and the culture in which they are brought up. Here
is how it works.

The principal portrayal of women in modern society is that of
a creature put on the earth to satisfy men. Men get hundreds of
e-mails per week telling them that if they click their mouse, thousands of slutty whores will be at their fingertips to titillate them.
When they turn off the computer and turn on the TV, they see
that the networks have a special treat for them that day: the Victoria's Secret Fashion Show, or *Desperate Housewives*, or *Wifeswap*.
One way or another, some woman is being made available in some
situation to entertain men. While the models go prancing around
in their skimpy underwear, the men sit salivating. It is sheer bliss
in prime time. The guys think this is what life is all about. This is
what women are for; they are created for men's pleasure and enjoy-
ment. When the television show is over, the guys can stroll off to
strip clubs where they pay a few bucks and then even the underwear comes off. "Take it off bitch!" they yell, and the women,
smilingly, seem happy to oblige.

Now fast forward a week, and a psychopath like Ridgway goes
out for some relaxation. There is an attractive woman at the bar.
He walks up to her. "Can I buy you a drink?" She looks at him,
sees that he is dressed shoddily and notes immediately that he is a
loner, and probably a loser. She politely declines. He persists.
"Come on, it's just a little drink." She gets angry. "Look, I said no
thanks. Okay?" The barman walks over. "Come on mister," he
tells Ridgway. "She said no. Now move on."

Ridgway leaves the bar. He is steaming. By the time he arrives
home, he is full of rage. He is not angry that the woman rejected
him or humiliated him. No, it is much worse. *She is a woman who
does not know her place.* The bitch does not know her place. He has
a sense of entitlement. He is a man. She is supposed to be there
for him. She's supposed to cater to him. She is supposed to put

out for him. Everything around him tells him that women are beneath him and are created to serve him. They are just stupid sluts who want to hook up with a guy as long as he gives them something, a drink, some cash, any sort of trifle. But this woman, and in fact all the pretty ones, why, they think that they are better than him. He has noticed that it is particularly the better-looking ones that get all hoity-toity with him. They act aloof and condescending. *It is time for her to learn her place.* "I'll show her," he thinks. "We'll just see what happens when she thinks she can treat me like dirt. We'll see just how highfalutin she is when I break her neck."

The Gary Ridgway phenomenon is akin to a white supremacist in the Deep South during segregation. The white racists would terrorize black people that the whites determined were becoming too uppity and didn't know their place. The hatred was based on the idea of an inferior challenging his superiors. Imagine that a white supremacist tells a black man or woman, sometime in the early 1960s, to move to the back of the bus, but is greeted with a stubborn refusal to do so. The Klan guy walks away thinking, "This nigger is too uppity," and he goes back to his home and plans a way to teach this black man to know his place.

And that is what the Ridgways of this world are thinking. They treat independent women the same way independent Southern blacks were treated during the civil rights movement. We can see how the Ridgways of our society who harm, rape, and murder women come to speak of their female victims in the ways that they do, as "human filth" and "garbage." The anger they vent toward these women is rationalized as a response to the arrogance they believe their victim has shown them. Bang. Bang. "Now I've taught the bitch a lesson. Just try and be uppity and forget your place now that you're dead."

To say that there is no connection between the Ridgways of the world and the culture of misogyny in which they were raised is as naive as believing that there is no connection between white violence against blacks in the South and the culture in which those whites were raised.

The Demise of the Gentleman
and the Rise of the Crotch-Scratcher

The horrors of a Gary Ridgway are, mercifully, an extreme. But I stand by my conviction that when a depraved nature combines with an environment that nurtures amorality, disaster is imminent. Extreme examples aside, let's have a look at the men that we are raising today. Just as Ridgway was, in part, a product of his environment, your guy next door is a product of his. As the self-esteem of the girl next door plummets, the men around her devolve as well. Men, more so than women, need a counterbalance. If they are surrounded by positive female influences and images, they will ascend to be worthy of their surroundings. Alternatively, if they are bombarded with negative images and cheapened estimations of their female counterparts, they will in turn, be debased as well. The rule of thumb is that in a world without ladies, there can be no gentlemen.

I recently heard a line that summed up this idea in its entirety. The television show *Elimidate* is part of the reality TV genre. In this classy example of great television production, one person, most often a man, is set up with four members of the opposite sex. The object of the show is for the chosen one to eliminate three of the four competing dates until only one remains. How does this happen? The group of five go out barhopping, and the entertainment value of the show is watching the women scratch each other's eyes out vying for the lone man's attention. In the end, it is inevitably the loosest, sluttiest of the lot who goes home with the guy. On one episode, the final two women were slugging it out with each other in an effort to emerge as the winner, each sinking to a lower level of trampiness to gain attention. The man in question offered a classic summation of how such behavior affects the general male population when he said: "Look, I don't mean to be a pig but if you're going to show me your boobs and lick my stomach, well, all I have to say is 'oink, oink!'"

And the degradation infects every area of society. The *New York Times* reported in October 2004 that Andre Agassi complained about a bizarre twist in the Spanish tennis championships in Madrid. The tournament decided to get rid of ball boys—the youth who run around the court picking up the tennis balls—and replace them with scantily clad models instead. They thought this would greatly increase interest in the tournament. How charming: the sight of nearly naked women running around after a man's "balls." And this wasn't mud wrestling, it was tennis, once the most refined of all sports. I suppose the rationale was that if football can get a boost out of women bouncing up and down in Lycra, why shouldn't tennis cash in as well? It is to the credit of Andre Agassi that he protested against this because he wants himself, and his sport, to be taken seriously, and he understands that the moment a woman is behind him on the court in her underwear, the focus will not be on him or the tennis match.

21

~

FAT WIVES HAVE THEIR
HUSBANDS TO BLAME

When I think about the stereotypical husband today, the main issues that jump out are that they spend far more time in the office, or at home watching football and drooling over the cheerleaders, than they do watching their wives. I think I can best sum up the uninterested husband syndrome with one of the most common complaints that I hear from the married men who contact me. If I had a dollar for every e-mail I have received over the past few months from husbands who complain that their wives are too fat—and they have no idea how to tell them diplomatically that they should lose a ton or two—I would have a Warren Buffett–size fortune.

These husbands write to me to contest my assertion—made principally in my book *Kosher Adultery: Seduce and Sin with Your Spouse*, but repeated in many of my essays—that their loss of attraction to their wives has little to do with their wives' appearance, and everything to do with laziness on the part of husbands who do not strive to bring erotic playfulness to their marriage.

"Oh yeah," said one writer, "nothing would make me happier than for me and my wife to have a passionate sex life again. But let's get real. When we married, she was a size 6. Now she has trouble squeezing into a size 18." Another husband echoed the sentiment: "Being married to my wife, I feel like a polygamist. She's so large, it's like I'm married to two women. She was half this size a few years ago."

There are other comedians out there like Stan, who wrote to me: "Don't lecture me, Shmuley, about how *I* am to blame for not feeling attracted to my wife. While some guys get to see their wives in bikinis, I am afraid to take my wife to the beach for fear that she'll be harpooned."

Other husbands write to me with a more reflective approach:

> I partially agree with you, Shmuley, that the lack of passion in our marriage results from a man's—or in this case my own—tendency to be uncreative and allow ourselves to fall into a routine. But there is the real problem of my wife's having put on a lot of weight. I have tried everything to encourage her to diet, go to a gym, and generally take care of herself. I have even suggested we exercise together. She takes offense at each suggestion and kicks me out of the bed, which is okay since I barely fit in anyway. Added to that is the increasing growth of her facial hair, about which she does next to nothing. So on the rare occasions when we make love, I find myself thinking about other women.

Husbands who are married to women who "let themselves go" use it as ample justification for their lackluster sex lives with their wives, or their indulgence in pornography or extramarital affairs. It is a convenient way of passing the buck and blaming the wife for the loss of marriage's most important ingredient: attraction. But before we get all cozy with this notion that wives have decided to indulge their maternal instincts by appearing permanently pregnant and devouring even the wood of the kitchen cupboards, let's delve a little deeper.

First, there is something just a little hypocritical in the argument of husbands that only their wives need to appear sexy—while they themselves can have endless folds of blubber hanging down their stomachs. Sorry, guys, but she does not want to be married to the Pillsbury Dough Boy. You complain that it is challenging making love to the Goodyear Blimp, but having the Michelin Man climb on top of you might not be the most pleasurable experience either. It cuts both ways. If you want her to get rid of her thunder thighs, then perhaps you should consider taking a chain saw to your love handles. Add to this unjust double standard the many husbands who forget just how grossed out wives are with men's peculiar deficiencies in personal hygiene. Eating ear wax may be your idea of a wholesome meal, but it might cause your wife to regurgitate her dinner. And wives *do not* find flatulence as entertaining as their husbands believe. You would not break wind in front of your boss, so maybe you should think twice about letting it rip in front of your wife.

Second, and much more important, is the question of why the size of the average American wife has expanded so much. Some blame childbearing. But that is a spurious argument because there are plenty of women who return to their normal weight, even after having triplets.

Besides, blaming the kids for your wife's bloating is an unfair burden to pass onto your children. Somehow I do not think that telling your kid, "Mommy and I used to have great sex and I was wildly attracted to her until she had you and started to look like a hippo" is going to do wonders for your child's self-esteem.

Still others blame the enormous responsibilities of women who have to balance family and career, leaving them little time for a healthy diet and exercise. No doubt, there is much truth in this assertion. And yet, these same wives who have little time to look after themselves in their marriage suddenly find plenty of time to beautify themselves when and if they decide to have an affair. Studies show that one of the biggest giveaways that a wife is having an affair is when she suddenly begins exercising, dieting, and wearing silk undergarments instead of cotton.

This leads me to the following unassailable conclusion: When wives put on a lot of weight, it is almost always the fault of an inattentive or distracted husband, who *only* notices that his wife has put on weight. He never notices when she gets dressed up or goes to a beautician. He doesn't make her feel attractive, and he will often tell her that she's stupid. When a woman no longer cares about her appearance, it is nearly always because she thinks her husband would never notice anyway.

Women love being attractive. Sure, there are exceptions to the rule, like body-building she-men or tomboys, for whom overalls and armpit odor are heavenly. But, by and large, even brainy career women who want to be appreciated for their minds still long to be physically desirable. What woman doesn't want to be regarded as beautiful? How much more so a married woman who revels in her husband's attention? And so what does it mean when a wife suddenly starts growing a beard and does not go to a beautician, or puts on an extra twenty pounds and does not run to the dietician? She is behaving unnaturally and we have to ask why.

The blame lies with her husband who long ago stopped noticing when she got dressed up, so she concludes: "Why bother? With all the responsibilities I have with the kids, my job, and running the home, why put time into my appearance when he never looks at me anyway."

The healthiest diet for a woman is to feed off of her husband's compliments. When told by the man she loves that she is beautiful, a woman has the incentive to live up to the compliment. Silence and indifference make her bloated. Indeed, marriage runs on what I call the football-fat equation. Every one hour he puts into watching mindless TV equals one extra pound on his wife's backside. Pretty soon, his wife starts looking like a linebacker.

A man from Los Angeles wrote to me about how his wife grew faster horizontally than their two-year-old grew vertically. He told me he was disgusted by her weight, but chose to say nothing because he did not want an argument. "There is no easy way to tell your wife she's fat," he wrote.

"Yes," I agreed. "But there is a very easy way to prevent it from happening in the first place. Did you tell her how beautiful she was when she was thinner? Did you compliment her when she did up her hair? When was the last time you took her to the mall to buy clothes, helped her try them on, and told her what she looks best in?" He admitted that he had not done any of these things in years. Is it a mystery why she gave up? Would a woman who lived alone on a desert island get dressed up every day to please the coconut trees? And if she lives on the solitary island of a lonely marriage, will she not console herself by indulging in the sensual pleasure of food when she is bereft of the sensual pleasure of touch and sex?

While husbandly apathy is the main cause of a wife's weight gain, telling her she is beautiful even when she is overweight is a better weight-loss program than the Atkins, South Beach, and Dr. Phil's diets combined. If your wife has grown too wide, encourage her to trim down—not by telling her she is fat, but by telling her she is gorgeous. Her feeling that you watch her beauty will inspire her to watch her weight. This might sound simplistic—and it is. Simply stated, it works.

Last summer, I bumped into a couple with whom I was friendly more than a decade ago. I remembered the wife as a woman of great beauty and sparkling eyes. But now her body was bloated, her face was shriveled. While she still smiled brightly, she looked different than I remembered. As I subsequently discovered, her husband had gone through a rough financial period. Unable to support his family and falling increasingly into debt, his self-esteem plummeted. He would come home every day feeling depressed and offer his wife monosyllabic responses to her questions. Whereas once he had been attentive, he now came home and got straight onto his computer for hours on end. A week turned into a month, a month into a year, and soon he was barely noticing his wife was alive.

True, he had lost a lot of money, but he still had life's greatest blessing: a young and beautiful wife who loved him. But because he was unable to appreciate her, she became as unhappy as he, and her looks went out the door along with their credit. When I saw her, I told her she looked beautiful. It was not a lie. Her beauty was still there, covered by all her misery. It could still come out, if only her husband would unearth it with laserlike focus. There is a direct correlation between a husband's attention to his wife, and a wife's attention to her looks.

What I have to say to all those uninterested and self-absorbed husbands, who seem to wake up and pay attention only when they want to complain about their wives' growing waistline, is that the next time you notice your wife has added a couple of pounds, perhaps it is you, rather than she, who should be looking in the mirror.

22

∽

FOUR FOUL ARCHETYPES OF WOMEN—FOUR VULGAR ARCHETYPES OF MEN

At the beginning of this book, I discussed the four noble attributes that once characterized women and contrasted them with the four modern archetypes of women that we frequently encounter nowadays. It bears repeating that a woman was once honored as:

1. A creature of superior dignity and grace, interested in love over money, and in a rich inner life rather than a shallow outer life

2. A spiritual intimacy-seeker, unwilling to surrender to a man who is not her soul mate

3. A strongly productive but nonaggressive team player

4. A nurturer and provider, capable of uplifting man to heights of insight, nobility, and pleasure that he would otherwise scarcely comprehend

Through television (especially reality TV), the Internet, and magazines, the popular culture has now reduced women to four essentially crass and degrading archetypes. Let us revisit the four modern female archetypes:

1. *The Greedy Gold Digger:* The woman who loves money more than love and romance and will date and marry practically any guy who's got pockets full of cash

2. *The Publicity-Seeking Prostitute:* The woman who will do anything for publicity, including stripping for the camera and sleeping with strangers

3. *The Brainless Bimbo:* A dunce and an airhead who entertains with her jackass comments

4. *The Backstabbing Bitch:* The woman who will cut the heart out of another woman for social advancement or in a catfight over a guy

Now let us revisit the four vulgar categories of men that are directly inspired by the crassness of women:

1. *The Crotch-Scratcher (aka the Belly-Belcher):* The man utterly devoid of any human refinement

2. *The Harem Gatherer:* The lecherous man who has made it his life's goal to bed as many women as possible

3. *The Selfish Spouse:* The all-too-common uninterested and self-absorbed husband

4. *The Porn Addict:* the guy who is able to relate only to fantasy women

We will examine each of these stereotypes in a moment, but for now let us note that the consequence of a world lacking feminine healing is the emergence of loutish men who regularly two-time women, are addicted to pornography, have huge commitment problems, are inattentive to their wives once they marry, and will not behave like gentlemen.

Men today have no compunction whatsoever about commenting to their girlfriends or wives about women they see on the street. There is no sense of reserve, of acting with decorum in the presence of a lady, since there is so little insistence on or expectation of a woman being a lady any more. Of course, plenty of the blame for this can be shared by the women who sit by, or worse yet, join in their own demoralization. After all, who thinks to censor his dirty jokes in the presence of a woman if she can counter your joke with an even raunchier one?

A man's nature is to be aggressive, to conquer for his own individual glory. One of the hardest things for a man to do is to rein in that natural aggression, to come to believe that he will be better off by being softer, more vulnerable, and gentler. Remember, the caveman idea was that those who were tenderhearted got killed off. Only the thick-skinned and assertive survived. If we revert to a caveman mentality, why should any man develop a gentle underbelly and become more refined? Why should any man feel motivated to give up having multiple sexual partners? After all, it is less fun and less macho to be monogamous. And in business, we have been raised to believe that ruthlessness rather than ethics pays, that nice guys finish last, and that no good deed goes unpunished.

The Four Images of Modern-Day Manhood

Now let's take a closer look at our four modern male archetypes.

The Crotch-Scratcher (aka the Belly-Belcher)

Ah, the crotch-scratcher, that picturesque image of the couch-potato guy, sitting in his apartment wearing a day-old T-shirt with one hand down his pants and the other on the remote. This guy is not the suave charmer who seduces all the ladies he meets with his cool manners and feigned chivalry. Nor is he a homebody who fears real live company. He has friends, he has dates, and he comes home after his dates to brag about them with his friends. During those debriefings, no detail about the woman he has just been out with is too intimate to share with his pals. The crotch-scratcher likes to leer after sexy waitresses. He appreciates a woman who is all too eager to cater to a man's basest nature. He does not look for an equal, but for a woman who can give him what he needs, usually some sleazy women with collagen for lips and silicone for breasts, who can impress his fellow Neanderthals. A trophy girlfriend; and by "trophy" I mean glitzy and gaudy: the shorter the skirt, the deeper the plunging neckline, the better. In all, he is looking for a loose woman who is not above behaving like a tramp.

Luckily for our crotch-scratcher, many women out there fit the bill. Heck, the pool of them gets younger and younger, all being shown the way by idols like Britney Spears and Christina Aguilera. But youth is part of the catch. While the crotch-scratcher seems to have an endless supply of choices for his female companionship, the women are often oblivious that they are boxing themselves into a losing situation. As women who jump into bed to get a man continue to be obliging, time passes on, and they become less appealing. Few forty-year-olds can carry off a belly shirt and pierced navel. And even if they can do so physically, with tremendous cost and exertion, they look ridiculous.

These women have muscled out those with class. They have taught the crotch-scratcher that he can leer after those who show the most skin. He can act crassly and trash women with his friends with nary a consequence. Why should he act dignified? The tarts he goes out with do not object to his juvenile licentious behavior. They do not mind it, that is, until they become too old for him. By then, however, it is too late and there is a younger crop of Britney wannabes waiting in the wings. It is crotch-scratcher's heaven!

A woman with class, decorum, and intelligence can maintain her beauty at any age because it is based on multiple factors. Thus, when age and gravity begin to affect her external looks, she still walks proud and has confidence that radiates through everything she does. And she is beautiful. But, like a finely trained art critic, men must be taught to appreciate the various elements that contribute to a woman's beauty. If they only learn to appreciate a cartoon figure, anything more sophisticated is unpalatable. He just does not know how to read the images before him if they do not include big lunging boobs and a tight butt.

The Harem Gatherer

Unlike the crotch-scratcher, the harem gatherer is a smooth operator. He is not slowing the car down on the corner to allow his date the privilege of hopping in while the vehicle is still in motion. Neither does he release earth-shattering belches in the car on the way to dinner with this date. No, this guy is charming. He shows up at the door with flowers, he is armed with the right compliments, and if he is on a first date, he will probably even remember his date's name and some of her interests. After all, he is a man on a mission, and he is going to dazzle and beguile his prey for as long as it takes to get her. What he does with her after that is another story completely.

The harem gatherer makes a woman feel like a million bucks, but only for as long as it takes to hook her into his collection of devotees. Many women are so unaccustomed to being treated well (even temporarily) that they fall for harem gatherers. But the fairy tale never lasts long. The harem gatherer wants to have many women panting after him. The conquest and compilation are what appeal to him. He bores easily, but he will not, in general, be rude or utterly dismissive. No, our harem gatherer is a charmer and he knows how to dispense just enough attention to keep a lapsing interest intact.

He preys on women who are most desperate to be treated with courtesy, and once he shows an ounce of this, they just don't want to let go, even when they discover that they are one of many women to whom he flashes his alluring smile and attention. Instead of cutting him off at the knees when they discover the truth, many languish in the hopes that they can somehow regain the early attention he once showered on them. Instead of turning on him, the women of his harem turn on one another.

In fact, ABC's *The Bachelor* is a controlled environment that highlights this phenomenon of the harem gatherer and his bevy of babes. The producers of the show have found good-looking successful men who, for the most part, take care of themselves and behave with some gentlemanly qualities. Since this breed of man seems to be dying out, the women quickly turn into cat-fighting witches, trying to snag the "last of the gentlemen." The bachelorettes are, in general, attractive, successful women themselves. Logic would dictate that they would be able to find plenty of decent men who were interested in them. Instead of showcasing their attributes, however, the show makes them look like backstabbing bitches as they compete for the affection of a singular chosen man. This is, literally, modern-day harem gathering at its worst.

In Istanbul, I visited the Topkapi Palace, where the Ottoman Sultans had housed the hundreds of women who made up their harem. The palace and the harem are now a museum. Didn't we all think that condemning women to sexual servitude was a thing of the past, a relic of a bygone misogynistic era? Well, now it's back. But in some ways, it is even worse than the old Ottoman harem. At least there, the women were brought in just one at a time to the sultan. The biblical story of Esther and Achashveirosh conveys much of the same. The Persian king had a huge harem, but even he would not humiliate the women by having more than one of them per night. But on *The Bachelor*, the women actually loiter around watching while the Bachelor chats up one lovely woman after another. And if he grabs a few deep kisses in front of the gang, well, that's just good TV! *Joe Millionaire*, Fox TV's spin on the one-man-dates-multiple-women genre, actually has the ladies standing in two doting lines, facing one another while "Prince Charming" dances with each of them one by one. They stand there dutifully looking on as their competition tries to make a move on the only man in the room. Never mind that the "gentleman" in the room is actually lying to them about his finances, pretending to be a millionaire to test whether his chosen woman is motivated by love or money. That's a whole other issue! In the meantime, all the women are subjected to the indignity of being no better than parts on an assembly line. How dehumanizing. How offensive. How gross.

It can be tough to watch these shows if you consider that desperate women are putting their hearts out on the line and giving in to their most competitive natures for men who are thoroughly unworthy, all for the sake of entertaining you. But it's not only single women who have it rough. It can be even more upsetting to witness married couples, who have managed to get through all the obstacles of the single life and are supposedly committed to each other. But then they will suddenly submit to a show like *WifeSwap* or the truly degrading *Temptation Island*, where they are broken up for a period to amuse the masses. I watched a commercial for *WifeSwap* in which a mother who was transplanted to another family was being yelled at by her new "husband" for some mistake she had made in the household. His face was contorted in rage. Here was the promo of a TV show with a man yelling at the top of his lungs at a woman, and a woman taking his abuse, just to be on television. I really couldn't believe my eyes. Why would anyone subject herself to this? A woman should not allow herself to be yelled at even by her own husband, let alone somebody else's. But it all makes sense when you consider that the show is called Wife*Swap*, not Husband*Swap*. The denigration is always on the side of the woman. It is a man's world.

In everyday life, all too many men simply don't treat women properly. This is the case with our third example of the modern Western man—the dismissive, narcissistic, hurtful husband.

The Selfish Spouse

I do a lot of marital counseling with people who write to me from all over the world. My thinking is that if someone had counseled my parents, maybe I would not have ended up an unhappy child of divorce. From that vantage point, I think that maybe I can turn my pain into something productive by trying to keep these couples together. Still, I am often criticized for taking the woman's side. Many husbands will refuse to come back for further sessions because of what they see as a bias in favor of their wives. Believe me, I am innocent of the charge. I listen very carefully to everything the husband and the wife say, and I ask loads of probing questions before drawing any conclusions. All too often these days, the problems are primarily the husbands' fault. It is as if they have no idea how to be decent husbands. Nobody taught them, they had no role model, and they are averse to learning and compromising.

One husband who accused me of being biased had never spent more than twenty dollars on his wife's birthday or anniversary present—if he remembered at all. He claimed not to have the money, but really he was miserably cheap. Once, he even presented his wife with a $50 gift certificate as a birthday present, but it was a certificate that *she* had gotten from a friend of *hers* the previous year. Yet, when a deal he had been working on for a few years finally went through, he went out and bought himself a new Lexus. He simply had no concept of spending money on his wife or taking her away on a vacation. She worked the same hours that he did, yet did not seek to ease her household burden by hiring a cleaner to come in a few hours a week. When they had a fight that extended over a few weeks, he even had the temerity to take a cruise all by himself. I should mention that this was no bum. He was a well-educated man, a half-decent father, and religiously inclined to boot. But his own father had treated his mother like garbage, and he did the same to his wife. Yet, he accused me of being biased.

The Porn Addict

Unlike our three previous examples of manhood gone awry, the porn addict is often hindered from engaging real women altogether. Instead, this man has embarked on a lifelong quest for the Holy Grail, which to him means the perfect fantasy bimbo. Unlike the crotch-scratcher, he is not hooting after the buxom babes on the street and leering with his buddies at salesgirls clad in short skirts. Unlike the harem gatherer, he is not collecting the affections of hopeful women, only to dash them when he treats them with caddish disdain. The porn addict too often overlaps with the uninterested husband type, who shares a physical proximity with his wife, but exists in a completely different realm. The porn-watcher can hardly relate to breathing, thinking, and feeling women.

A startling *New York* magazine cover story from October 20, 2003, highlighted the plight and persona of the porn-watcher. Quoting Dr. Ursula Ofman, a sex therapist based in Manhattan, the article explained that compulsive viewing of pornography can severely affect relationships in that some men find that they can no longer become aroused by live women. The story went so far as to suggest that there is a crisis in New York of professional young men who would much rather stay home and masturbate to porn than have sex with their girlfriends. I know it sounds crazy, but that is how bad things have become.

Although these New York men have no difficulty being turned on by Internet porn, they become so fixated on the caricatures of women and sex depicted on-screen that they lose the ability or interest in exploring relationships with breathing women. They develop expectations that all women should be beautiful, compliant nymphomaniacs—and when real women do not meet these expectations, they instantly lose interest in the relationship. The expectations these men have about the sexual compliance they should receive from a female partner are thoroughly unrealistic and this disparity often makes them phobic about relationships.

The men interviewed for the article admitted that they used pornography as a substitute for real life. Some even admitted that they saw the pattern described by Dr. Ofman in themselves, and that they had grown more picky when it came to assessing real women. In a follow-up article by Naomi Wolf, she expanded on this idea, postulating that pornography had "deaden[ed the] male libido in relation to real women."

The problem is that these men find fewer and fewer women who can measure up to the perfection they encounter in digitally enhanced pornographic images. Instead of arousing men to lust after women, excessive pornography has become a substitute for real relationships, and in consequence, women have developed even greater insecurities about their sexual appeal. Wolf concludes that we are raising a generation that is unable to have an erotic connection with another human being. The porn-watcher is fixated on his ideal images of the blonde bimbo. He prefers tuning in to watch her instead of putting in the work it takes to establish and maintain a relationship with someone who might challenge him and talk back.

How can real women compete with the digitally airbrushed porn star? How can an exhausted wife measure up to the always-willing cyberbabe? Bottom line, she can't. As long as the porn-watcher requires nothing of himself, refusing to acknowledge the ramifications of his cybersex appetite, he will slip further and further away from any ability to develop serious, interactive intimacy—both physically and emotionally. This is certainly not the image of a man that any self-respecting woman should want to wait for.

23

⚭

BECOMING LESBIANS TO
GET AWAY FROM MEN

If you look around you, I think you will notice that the majority
of women have either become disillusioned with men and relationships or they have actually become masculine themselves. These
women have concluded that being feminine gets them nowhere, so
for the most part, they have abandoned the whole notion.

Women are dumping their husbands in greater numbers than
ever before. According to David Popenoe's *Debunking the Divorce
Myths* (discoveryhealth.com), at least two-thirds of all divorces are
initiated by women. Other statistics cite that women initiate
nearly three-quarters of the divorces in this country. These astonishing numbers are bolstered further by the fact that women rarely
leave their husbands for other men. In most cases, when a wife demands a divorce, she is embarking on a life that she knows she will
be living alone. She would rather be alone then be with her husband, even though he may be the father of her children. The same
is not true of men. The overwhelming majority of men who leave
their wives are doing so because they have fallen in love with
someone else. So whereas men will stay in what is often a loveless
marriage, women are willing to shoulder the financial challenges
of parenting or the aches of being alone, as long as they can be rid
of a man who is unappreciative and indifferent to them.

this, of course, pertains to the women who actually
, because there are tons who will not even do that. Roughly
one-quarter of all American women aged thirty-five and over are
single. (As a related side note, it was Sylvia Ann Hewlett who, in
her book *Creating a Life*, first exposed the shocking fact that between a third and half of all professional women in the United
States do not have children, even though they crave being mothers.) Didn't little girls once want to grow up and marry Prince
Charming? Well, yes. But now that, in their opinion, there are
only frogs to be kissed to no avail. Women today gain far greater
satisfaction from their careers and their friends than they seem
to find with a man. In essence, they are doing what men have
done throughout the ages, finding greater fulfillment in professional achievement than in personal relationships and romantic
commitments.

As marriage—the institution that was once every little girl's
dream—becomes more distant, nightmarish, and unpalatable,
young girls and women no longer envision becoming the wholesome wife and mother figures that used to command our attention. Today, little girls are not watching loving, grounded couples
like the ones on *Ozzie and Harriet* or the *Cosby Show*. There are no
longer examples of wives and husbands partnering together to
share life's joys and tribulations.

I was so taken by the sleeper hit film *Kissing Jessica Stein*, which
came out a couple of years ago, because it spoke to this female dis-
illusionment that I am talking about. While the movie was
charming and witty, it had a poignant and sorrowful message that
treats this issue exactly. In the story, the lovely and accomplished
Jessica is successful professionally and has good friends and a loving—albeit meddlesome—family. She is attractive and funny, and
she just longs to be loved and understood. Having tried and failed
to find love and companionship with different men, she turns to
her last, unchartered territory: women.

We watch as Jessica finds a bright, sexy, self-possessed, caring
woman with whom she can share her innermost self. It's painful to
observe because we know, as does her female lover, that, ultimately,

this is not what Jessica wants or needs. She is not gay, she has simply been so thoroughly disappointed and disillusioned with men that she has looked elsewhere and attempted, desperately, to convince herself that this can be satisfying. "It's not that Jessica has a thing for girls. It's just that she has a thing for Helen," writes Stephen Hunter of the *Washington Post*. After all, Helen takes care of herself, has worthwhile goals and aspirations and, most important, tries to understand who Jessica is and what she needs. For many women, their boyfriends have never behaved this way. Why shouldn't Jessica try to turn herself and her life inside out to find respect and affection from a decent and caring individual?

Most men will see this movie either because their girlfriends drag them there, or because they like seeing two women kiss. The average guy will watch it and insist, "Ha! Cute premise, but it could never happen. Ultimately a straight woman will want a man. She can't just *decide* she would rather be with women . . . right, honey?" Suddenly he notices that his girlfriend, who has been quiet since the movie ended, is now making eyes at the lovely, gamine young woman, sitting with an espresso across the film house café. "Honey?"

Couldn't happen? Don't be so sure.

Jessica's choice of a relationship partner is merely part of the outgrowth of the development that has emerged over the past few decades. Feminism advocated that women descend from their collective pedestal, and while this opened up opportunities in career and lifestyle, the unexpected side effect was that men stopped viewing them as worthy of winning and wooing. Women were there, they were going to be there, they were sexually and emotionally ready at the drop of a hat (or at least an AmEx card). And if one woman required some extra effort or was less than immediately compliant, there were sure to be more damsels to follow. So why make the effort?

And for a while, women were okay with this. They recognized that this was the goal they had fought for, and they made a show of enjoying their newfound sexual freedom. They dated like men, they slept around like men, and poof, the birth of shows like *Sex and the City* portrayed them essentially as men trapped in women's bodies. The underlying message: If you can't beat 'em, join 'em.

At the same time, many women chose to commit to relationships that they thought would get better with time. Such women married inattentive boyfriends in the hopes that time and/or experience would transform them into attentive husbands. When it didn't happen, they found themselves dissatisfied and out of love, and finally declared that a divorce was the answer.

Another response was recently introduced by authors like John Gray in *Men Are from Mars, Women Are from Venus*. Gray argues that women must learn to tolerate men's foibles and flaws, and simply accept that men are prone to inattentiveness and rarely are accessible emotionally. Sure, men need to make an effort to change. But essentially, they are hardwired to go into their caves and not talk about their problems. Women must learn to deal with their own problems because men will continue to fail and disappoint the women who depend on them for their own happiness. It is all about gender difference, honey. I call this the *Science of Gender Neutralization*, the idea being that neither sex has to make significant accommodation, but rather that both male and female must learn to *understand* different gender foibles, so that they don't serve as an impediment to a relationship.

Finally, the last option: Dating women once would have been thought crazy but, amazingly, it is becoming increasingly common. Studies show that over 90 percent of lesbians were once in a heterosexual relationship.

A Conversation with a Reformed Heterosexual Woman

Which brings to mind an interesting conversation I had with Kim, a beautiful young gay woman and doctor who came as a guest to our Friday night Sabbath Salon. Kim had many relationships with men before she began to date women in her mid-twenties. She maintains that while she did have, and indeed still has, an attraction to men, she could never connect with them with as great a degree of emotional depth as she could with women. "I would have preferred to have had a truly intimate relationship with a man," she says, "but I haven't found it with a man. I found it with a woman. While this isn't true for a lot of my lesbian friends, in my case it was a choice to be gay; I made that choice because there was something extremely satisfying about that closeness."

"What makes sex with women much more intimate than with men?" I ask her.

"What made the sex more intimate was talking during sex. I think that talking during sex is taboo and difficult because it's so hard. Men close their eyes and drift into a world of fantasy. Talking makes you vulnerable. It's another thing that people want to close down.

"A lot of times people have canned sex. And that's dirty talk. They do what they're supposed to do. They play out scripted sex. And they use porn as the script for sex. And going outside of that is taboo. You don't know what to do or where it will lead to.

"Straight women can be very boring to sleep with. Compared to lesbians they're much more passive, and less passionate in sex. They're much more expecting that things should be done to them, rather than being an active participant. They're afraid of touching the other woman because they don't know how."

And so Kim stays in a relationship with a woman. She is not, as some people are, solely attracted to members of the same sex by nature. She has made the choice as a response to the emptiness she experienced in her relationships with men. On some level, she had realized that men had long since ceased to make the effort to earn and keep a relationship.

Women are making their own decisions about how to deal with it now, and pretty soon, men will have to make the choice as well. If they want to have a woman in their life—a girlfriend, a wife, someone who will stay with them and be a loving and giving partner—they may, as a man on my radio show suggested, "just allow my wife to be involved with a female relationship on the side! If that'll make her happy, maybe it's worth it." Or else they will wake up and smell the dissatisfaction. They will learn to deepen their relationships with women. They will learn to be emotionally present, to be focused on their partner, to talk, to listen, and to take time. Or else, they may end up alone as the gender divide continues to grow.

Using Men for Sex

While these women, like the fictional Jessica Stein, have gone the ultimate distance and looked for love that thoroughly disassociates them from the disappointments of men, this is an extreme choice. Most women will admit that, sexually speaking, they enjoy and crave men. What these women do, therefore, is use a man for the only thing they absolutely need him for—sexual companionship. But there is no meeting of the minds, hearts, or souls. Instead of making their boyfriends or spouses the center of their universe, they make them a necessary evil. I am not implying that a man should somehow eclipse a woman's universe, not at all. I do believe, however, that in a good relationship, one's partner becomes the bottom line. While we still need friends, family, and professional gratification, we should find our greatest satisfaction and comfort in our spouses. Today, that is far from reality. As a result, most of us do not have the security of a solid emotional foundation that comes from a healthy, enduring relationship. This lack of foundation affects every area of a person's life.

24

∽

RISE OF THE PLATONIC LESBIAN

Because there are so few real men, and so few gentlemen, a new sexual and emotional leaning has developed among the female population. Now, instead of having straight women and gay women, we find straight women who, in all means other than the purely sexual act, have become lesbians. I refer to this as the *platonic lesbian syndrome.* With the ascendance of the crotch-scratcher, the harem gatherer, and their equally disappointing cronies, we find that women have become all but uninterested in the men from whom they have to choose. Soul mates for women, instead of arriving in the form of the man of their dreams, have become other women. For many, their female friends take the place that, once upon a time, would have been occupied by a husband. You can see the platonic lesbians in bars and nightclubs throughout the land. They are the women who go out to together, who trust each other, and who afford one another deep emotional fulfillment in their relationships. Even when they enter into a relationship with a man, they still rely on other women for emotional fulfillment. Their truly trusting relationships are with women rather than men, even as their romantic relationships are with guys rather than girls.

If we look at one of the most popular television series of the past decade, *Sex and the City*, we see this pattern reflected in the show's premise. The women on this show embody the most famous television stereotype of our generation: women who want to be in a relationship but can't find a worthy man. Sure, the four protagonists date men, but seemingly only to complain to each other about the man's inadequacies when they meet the following morning over a latte. *Sex and the City* is really a series about women who are the personification of the platonic lesbian. They are each other's lovers in every respect but the physical. There was even a famous episode—a season-opener—where Carrie and Samantha comfort each other over their inability to find a fulfilling romantic relationship by telling each other that they do not need a soul mate, because *they are each other's soul mates*. In the final analysis, they have sex with men, but they bond with other women and it is that latter relationship that they find most fulfilling. The popularity of the show, especially with women, derives from the warm, sisterly relationship of the four main characters. It is their closeness, rather than the four's foibles with men, that serves as the emotional subtext for viewer loyalty.

In my marriage counseling, I have come across the disciples of the platonic lesbian scenario more times than you can imagine. Janet and Stuart were a couple I counseled once a week for over a year. They were still together, but only because Janet wanted to avoid an ugly custody battle over their son Kevin. Janet had reconciled herself to never enjoying real intimacy with a man. She compensated by becoming increasingly close to her girlfriends and to her son. For the two years that she was happily married before it all went bad, she barely had time for her friends. These days, she saw them several times a week and thoroughly depended on them. "I'd go crazy without them," she told me. "They're the people who keep me sane." Her dependency on her friends was the latest thing that she and Stuart were arguing over. "She's never home. I come home and my wife and my kid are out at her friends' homes," he complained. "What's more, each one of them is single or divorced and they're a terrible influence on Janet. They're jealous, so they egg her on to fight with me." Janet interrupted him, "Did you ever think that I'm not home because I don't want to be home?

Because I hate the miserable atmosphere in the house? That I can talk to them but I can't talk to you? You just don't get it, do you?" What was happening here was that in every sphere but the sexual, Janet was having an affair with her girlfriends. It was they whom she chose to confide in. It was they whom she chose to be intimate with. And just as if these friends were male lovers, her husband was jealous of them.

"He Just Doesn't Get It!"

"He just doesn't get it" was an expression that Janet repeated over and over again during our sessions. It's the expression I hear most from wives who are unhappy in their marriages. They rarely complain about one particular thing. Rather, they say that their husbands "just don't get" the whole idea of marriage and what it means to be a husband.

Stuart was convinced that Janet used the expression because she was too demanding. She credited him with absolutely nothing, he said. "Nothing I do is good enough. Her parents, her brothers and sisters, they all caved in to her, so she expects me to take her crap as well." But truth be told, Stuart really did not get it. Whenever I went to visit them at their home outside of London, he was either exercising on his bike, sitting in front of the television set in his sweats, or, worst of all, nitpicking and criticizing his wife instead of offering praise. Stuart had little idea of how to be a husband. He knew nothing of a woman's deepest nature. An entrepreneur who started his own chain of Laundromats before he met Janet, he got women easily and dated and had sex with "at least thirty" before getting married. He'd never felt any big incentive to discover a woman's innermost needs. His knowledge of women was only skin-deep.

Stuart did not know that a woman wants to be told that she is beautiful, wants to be made to feel desirable and secure, or wants to feel that her husband has subordinated the other interests in his life to her. And because he did not prioritize her, she hung out with her friends, who did. She once told me that the dearth of intimacy in her marriage had led her to contemplate having a real affair. "I get very flattered when men show an interest in me," she said, "but right now I don't feel I need that. I have my friends and they sustain me."

The platonic lesbian fills her life with things other than the traditional feminine accoutrements. Since being a woman has become a role with diminishing returns, many women have hardened themselves—protected themselves, if you will—against even desiring the traditional images. If they have not tried and failed at having a home and family the way Janet did (who was then left with the need to develop her own platonic lesbian relationships outside marriage), then women have utterly replaced these aspirations with goals of having a flashy lifestyle, or a high-power job. In many ways, by yielding to the persona of the platonic lesbian, women have metamorphosed into a replica of the worst kinds of men.

25

∿

THE NEW MANLY WOMAN

Let's return to those four bitingly witty women who captivated America on Sunday nights for the past few years, teaching us more about the modern-day woman and male/female relationships than we might have wanted to know. The sensation of *Sex and the City* lies in that its main characters are women who have become men. They have all the traditional characteristics of men: casual sex, commitment issues, a closer bond with each than they have with anyone of the opposite sex (just like the stereotype of men, who bond much more with each other watching sports and playing cards than talking with their wives). That is exactly why the series is so funny. They are four men trapped in women's bodies. One of the hallmarks of men has always been that they marry women, but remain intimate with their male buddies. Whom do they talk to? Is it to their wives about affairs of the heart, or to their pals about sports, sex, cars, and money? And that is what the *Sex and the City* girls do.

As the women on this show illustrate, today's woman has become manlike. Instead of being the feminine facilitator, strong and soft at the same time, the catalyst for productivity with a conscience, she has become all aggression and manipulation. At the end of the day, women have become as bad as men both in their professional and personal lives.

When First Ladies Are Not Ladies

Moving out of the realm of fictional examples like the *Sex and the City* women, we can choose from plenty of real-life examples of manly women. One of the most obvious models of this scenario is former first lady, and now New York State Senator Hillary Clinton. In many ways, Mrs. Rodham Clinton is the antilady. Yes, she is an astute politician with more than her fair share of professional acumen, and for that she can be admired. She also deserves just praise for being a woman who got ahead completely on her talent and intellect, an important example to all women everywhere. On my radio show, I have long touted Hillary as a partial role model for today's women precisely because she has advanced herself through education as man's intellectual and professional equal.

But for all that, she remains a deeply divisive figure. Hillary maintains that her bouts of unpopularity, the incidents in which she rubbed people the wrong way, came from the fact that she is tough. In truth, the problem Hillary had in garnering national admiration as the first lady was that she was nothing like a lady; she was much more a man. When Mrs. Clinton set out to redo the health care system, she did so with secrecy, stubbornness, and a refusal to take advice from experts. The result was that she alienated even erstwhile allies, and the initiative died a horrible death. Rather than being a consensus builder, her inability to collaborate with others killed her in her first public role. Likewise, when her husband was first accused of an affair with Monica Lewinsky, Hillary became the man in the family and went harshly on the attack, falsely accusing a "vast right-wing conspiracy" of having manufactured the story.

Hillary has a superb mind, an impressive education, and loads of natural ability. She also had the opportunity to be a powerful, ladylike co-president with her husband. But instead of finding the innate security of the female energy to draw on, the spirit that inspires communality and offers the means to be inclusive rather than individualistic, Hillary denounced her femininity. She insulted housewives everywhere when she insensitively repudiated them in the 1992 campaign with the harsh words: "I suppose I could have stayed home and baked cookies and had teas." She yielded to overt partisan behavior rather than opening up and throwing even a scrap to her and her husband's opponents. If she had branched out to include the opposition in some way, she would have been much more popular and successful. When I think of the lost opportunity, it feels almost criminal. Just imagine what could have transpired if Hillary had taken her professionalism and mixed it with the ladylike qualities that Jackie Kennedy possessed. You don't have to choose between them. Orchestrating them together is a powerful mix. The belief that only the ruthless survive is a lie.

Teresa Heinz Kerry, in her husband's unsuccessful bid for the White House, was even worse. She embarrassed herself with her arrogant and insensitive conduct, telling a reporter to "shove it," calling opponents of her husband's health care plan "stupid," and thoughtlessly spouting many other statements that outraged the public. But the big whopper was when she attacked Laura Bush as someone who "never had a real job." She made matters even worse when she offered an apology to Laura Bush, acknowledging that she had forgotten that Laura had worked as a teacher and librarian, thereby implying that her work as a homemaker and mother was still not a "real job." Teresa, known to her detractors as Lady Macbeth, assaulted feminine dignity with her actions and her words.

Money can buy you many things, but it can't make you a lady. Teresa, it seems, doesn't even believe in being a lady, which to her implies a subservient role of weakness. No, she is out to show you that she has elbows just like a man, and watch out because they are sharp. She was out to denigrate her rival Laura as an old-fashioned woman, content to waste her life at home raising kids and playing a subordinate role to a man, while she runs a mega-philanthropy. Teresa knew this would score big points with all the secular feminists in places like New York and San Francisco. Indeed, the magazine *GQ* did a profile of Teresa and Laura in September 2004 that included the memorable line: "If Laura Bush is constipated, then Teresa Heinz Kerry is positively post-coital." Get it? The refined and dignified woman is the one who appears constipated, repressed, buttoned up. But if a woman rejects being a lady, lashes out at others, and insults them, that's cool. It's sexy. It's seductive. Why, it's post-coital.

Women Can Show Men How to Be Powerful without Being Bullies

Thankfully, there are many models of first ladies, from both sides of the aisle, who were actual, true ladies and there are other hints at this model of womanhood, not just in the White House but in other high levels of governance. Eleanor Roosevelt did more to address the needs of the disadvantaged poor and underprivileged than any other American of her day. She was not considered to be a good-looking woman by most; her own mother dismissed her as plain. Nor did she appear particularly feminine in a conventional sense, but none of that mattered. Eleanor tapped into a vast reservoir of feminine, nurturing energy—and used it to serve the public good. Among a long list of phenomenal accomplishments, Eleanor Roosevelt made great strides in bringing dignity and respect to African Americans. Eleanor had several things in common with Hillary, including that she, too, had a husband who was unfaithful. Unlike Mrs. Clinton, however, Mrs. Roosevelt bore the hurt her husband inflicted with dignity. Hillary blamed the whole world when her husband wounded her. Instead of bearing her indignity with private strength and modesty, she sought the spotlight. Amazingly, she wrote about her husband's infidelity as a main selling point of her autobiography. She exploited her pain. Could you imagine Jackie Kennedy or Eleanor Roosevelt behaving this way? Can you contemplate, for even a single moment, Eleanor or Jackie writing about the pain of their husband's unfaithfulness? Lady Bird Johnson's husband cheated on her. Did she get an advance on a book off it? And don't think these women weren't in pain. Indeed, Eleanor Roosevelt was forever alienated from her husband. But she still never stooped to disgracing him to sell a book. She believed in loyalty even when her husband didn't deserve it. I know that many people will say that this is precisely what they like about Hillary. She's a new generation of woman. She is strong and tough. Fair enough. I actually believe women *should* be strong and tough. I raise my daughters to be anything but porcelain dolls. I tell them constantly that my greatest gift to them should be helping them to develop a strong and confident personality. But always with humility and dignity. And it simply is not humble or dignified to share your husband's sexual history and infidelities with the world, no matter how atrociously he has behaved.

This disparity in the behavior of these three women is exactly why the former two went down in history as women who were loved and admired. Hillary, on the other hand, while she has a powerful political career in her own right, and may yet go much further, will always be a polarizing figure. She has her many admirers, but barring major changes in the way she goes about her affairs, she will not be looked on as a woman of great feminine dignity. Lest I be misunderstood, let me make it clear that I am not suggesting for a moment that Hillary allow herself to be stepped on. A woman is not someone who lets people take advantage of her. Eleanor Roosevelt was hardly a shrinking violet. Nor did she lie down and accept her husband's indiscretions with resigned powerlessness. She punished him privately by maintaining a certain distance, but she did it privately and without the grandstanding for the limelight that Hillary seems to crave. Senator Clinton may go far but she will never be admired fully by the nation.

Another potent example of a woman with both power and femininity was Margaret Thatcher, who never had a problem being *Mrs.* Thatcher. Throughout her political career, she embraced her wifely and motherly role, even as she became Europe's "Iron Lady" who stood up to the Soviets and won Mikhail Gorbachev's respect. When Hillary ran for the Senate, on the other hand, all her placards read simply "Hillary"—with her married name either completely absent or so tiny that it was barely noticed.

Feminine Equals Wimp

Obviously, if nobody wants to be feminine anymore, nobody wants to be a lady either. Many young professional women with whom I discussed this book were adamant in their insistence that I was advocating a reversion of women's rights. It seemed to them that I was promoting sending women back to some terrible era in which they were treated as helpless, porcelain dolls. Interesting, isn't it? According to these reactions, it would seem that femininity has become synonymous with subservience and wimpishness. Being feminine implies being passive in a purely negative way, being stepped on, being a doormat, always playing second fiddle.

Taking Strong Women and Making Them Weak

By comparison, to be masculine, well, that means to be promethean, tough, aggressive, successful. For most women, embracing a more masculine image signals that they are real go-getters who know what they want and pursue it. Being masculine means chasing her dreams uncompromisingly and achieving them. I understand and agree with those who do not want to regress to a time when women were considered too fragile to be active.

But their objection is misplaced. In fact, it reminds me of the objection made by Nietzsche to Christianity. According to Nietzsche, the Jews had played a big trick on the world. The Jews were a weak people, lettered in books but not in the art of war. So how could they ensure that they wouldn't get wiped out by the stronger, more warlike nations? Well, they came up with a plan. It was called morality.

The Jews took these huge, hulking, strong Teutonic German knights, who dominated the world with their swords, and preached to them a code of morality. They taught them that forgiveness was greater than revenge, that peace was greater than war. They taught that a really strong man could overlook a slight and get along with others harmoniously. They preached an entire new code of honor, based on morality, and in so doing, they turned the Teutonic knights into wimps. What the Jews did, in essence, was take these ruthless warriors and turn them into people who suddenly believed in love, prayer, and being nice. Nietzsche maintains, therefore, that in giving the world morality, the Jews played the ultimate ruse on the world and ensured their own survival. Hitler and the Nazis agreed with Nietzsche's assessment, and did all they could to reverse and discard the morality preached by the Jews, giving the German nation the SS, a hardened group of fighters who lacked any consideration of justice and compassion.

It would seem that these women, who so strongly object to my advocating the return of the lady, believe the same thing. In their mind, men got rid of competition from women, weakened them and marginalized them, by inventing a fictitious code of honorable conduct for women known as being a lady. By telling women that they should be refined, dignified, feminine, and gentle, men transformed women from highly capable equals into pathetic, malleable subordinates.

To be sure, many women believe this theory. But it is trash.

What the Jews preached to the world was not to be pathetic or spineless. Rather, men were to stand up for themselves, but be just and righteous. They preached that a man could become rich and powerful. But even when he reached that pinnacle, he could still be humble and approachable. He did not have to use his power or his wealth to take advantage of the weak. Indeed, he could use it to protect them. And while ruthlessness might pay off in the short term, it would ultimately backfire because it created so many enemies, as Hitler and his Third Reich discovered when half the world teamed up to destroy them.

The same is true of what women can teach men. Men have always made the mistake of having a deprivation mentality. In their minds, the world is a small place with limited resources. Thus when someone becomes rich, he is actually taking away somebody else's money since there's not enough to go around for both of them. So throughout history, men have pursued their adversary's destruction. Sharp elbows and stepping on others were the keys to success.

But the feminine example was based on a more dignified and moral model. Women seem to inherently understand that success can be obtained without mean-spiritedness. It is for this reason that I equate what the Jews taught the ancient world with what women can teach men. Jews have forever played the role of battered wife in relationship to the nations of the world, urging them to fulfill their latent spiritual potential even as they were beaten and tortured for delivering a moral message.

Sadly, many women have turned against this message, embracing the convoluted masculine belief that toughness is the secret to success. When I encountered the objections women had to my thesis, it seemed to me that these women considered this harsh, masculine personality type to be the only one with any value.

Aggression Equals Success

I write these lines just after the conclusion of what many people consider to have been the nastiest presidential race in living memory—between President George W. Bush and Senator John F. Kerry. Each side has learned that if you don't go on the attack and put the other guy on the defensive, you're going to lose. And I find signs of this attitude in far less significant contests. When I have advertised for a secretary, program director, or assistant, I have received hundreds of résumés. Whether they were from men or women, each sounded pretty much the same and highlighted that the candidate was "aggressive and ambitious." "My strong point is that I aggressively pursue my goals," some wrote in their cover letters. That is the kind of stuff everyone writes, because they assume it is what employers want to hear—and they may be right. Imagine, however, if someone had sent a resume saying, "Young, capable female, ladylike, dignified, and always considerate and cordial." Huh? After the initial shock, my guess is that most employers would keep moving in their search. It is the aggressive stuff that really sells today. I find that sad. I really hunger for a world where we are just as productive, just as successful, without elbowing or stepping on each other.

I, too, can be aggressive. I will passionately go after individuals who I think are egregiously harming our world. But the truth is that that the truly developed men are those who are not afraid to cultivate their feminine side. That doesn't mean you can expect to see me holding a bunch of lilies and wearing ladies' undergarments any time soon. That is not what I mean by a feminine side. I mean the following: Even when I am busy, I try to be much less aggressive and impatient. When I get into a cab, I try to spend a few minutes speaking with the driver, finding out his name and where he lives before I jump on my cell phone to make an important call. I am not patronizing him or her. Rather, I hope that taking those moments will ensure that the driver feels like a human being and not simply the guy created by God to get me from point A to point B. It also means that I believe I have something valuable to learn from the driver's experience. Similarly, when I go out to a business luncheon, in addition to leaving a decent tip, I always try to ask the waiting staff their names and where they live and what they do when they are not waiting tables. Even if it is for a minute, it shows them respect. It shows them that I acknowledge their humanity and that God did not create them to serve me. That they have goals and aspirations of their own. It is all about looking outside the self and noticing the people around you. This kind of awareness is the purview of the feminine energy.

Speaking to cabdrivers was the New Year's resolution that I gave to *Newsweek* when they called me the last week of December 1999 as part of a story they were doing at the turn of the millennium about how few people actually stick to their resolutions. To be honest, it was a lot harder than I thought, precisely because I *am* naturally aggressive and consumed by the goal right ahead of me. This kind of absorption frequently precludes my looking around and noting how many individuals along the way help me to get where I am going, both figuratively and literally. Moreover, being so focused on the prize ahead has often made me forget that people around me also have dreams that they hold dear. But I have really tried hard to change. This includes never forgetting that the nurturing side of me, as a husband and father, is substantially more important than the professional side. It took me a few years to learn to put my family first, but I have largely done it, thank God. I am a wholly involved father who spends a huge amount of time with his children. But this was certainly not always the case, and it took a firm belief in the feminine-passive being superior to the masculine-aggressive to make that switch. It took a redefinition of *success*, a subject that I devoted my book *The Private Adam* to. I decided, based on my principles and values, that success in the personal sphere must always supersede success in the professional sphere.

The reason that most people resist easing up on the aggressive posture is the underlying belief that you cannot be successful and gentle at the same time: that ruthlessness guarantees success, and that taking the time to really appreciate someone else would distract you from crossing your own finish line. Thus, many women feel they cannot be ladies and career professionals at the same time. One must either act bitchy or get stepped on by bastards on their way up to the corner office with a view.

The denigration of the woman along with all things feminine and nurturing has had predictable repercussions. The fact that being feminine is out—and aggressive masculinity is in—has led us to become a colder, darker civilization. On its own, light has no purpose; rather, it gains its purpose by illuminating others. This is the same with the facilitator. The facilitator embodies the belief that we were created not only to be happy, but also to make others happy; not just to succeed and not to be jealous of other people's successes, but to encourage and applaud the success of others; not just to feed ourselves, but to feed the stranger; not just to develop our own potential, but to facilitate the potential of those who surround us. The greatest casualty of today's "me" generation is the death of the feminine. There are no more facilitators. Nobody wants to be a light. Everybody wants to be the man or woman *on whom the light is shining*. We all want to be in the spotlight.

A Belief in Selfishness

Modern-day society places its entire emphasis on the development and promotion of the self. Selfishness is inculcated as a matter of course to today's university students, who are taught that their highest calling is to give *themselves* as a gift to humanity. "Personal growth," "career prospects," and "personal fulfillment" are the catchwords of this generation, and this extends from careers to relationships to all elements of life. Both men and women seem to enter into relationships seeking to receive rather than to give. Moreover, they are quick to discard a relationship that is not endlessly exciting. Many spouses are encouraged to abandon a partner who is indifferent to their needs even before they have seriously explored the possibility of salvaging the marriage. Parenting is affected by this pervasive self-centeredness, as many view having children as a career sacrifice, or something to be pushed off until just before menopause. People are taught to be selfish, to always put themselves first.

The death of the feminine has caused us all to inhabit a meaner world where people do not care deeply about one another. Sure, when Osama bin Laden slaughters us in our buildings, we all run to the Red Cross with our sleeves pulled up to donate blood. The feminine caring and nurturing instinct seems only to be resurrected through tragedy or death. Most of the time, we do not seek to help one another. In fact, we gossip endlessly about each other and derive a degree of satisfaction from others' misfortunes.

But we are capable of reaching higher.

26

~

WOMEN AS HEALERS

When I was the rabbi at Oxford University, my wife was respected by the students even more than I was. Sure, I ran the organization and brought in the big speakers, but they loved Debbie for her character and her caring. A lot of students were away from home for the first time, and my wife provided a home for them that they were sorely missing. It is an amazing thing to be exposed to a feminine woman, and the students gravitated toward her.

This was somewhat surprising to me. After all, this was Oxford University, and you would not expect the female students to look up to a woman who had chosen to have seven children and devote her life to communal activism and mothering. In fact, it is all too common for a woman who has chosen mothering as her life's calling to feel embarrassed when a professional woman inquires as to her career. Ludicrous euphemisms like *homemaker* or the downright ridiculous *domestic engineer* are used to conceal this embarrassment. Rose Kennedy, who died at the age of 104, was never really seen as a role model for American women, despite being the matriarch of the fabled Kennedy dynasty. Many attribute this to the fact that she dropped her career to raise nine children and always stayed in the background. Once when asked in an interview why she dedicated her life to her husband and children, rather than promoting herself, she responded that had she made something showy of her own life, she would have given only one great person to the world. As a mother, she was able to deliver not one, but nine strong personalities who had an extraordinary impact on the world.

I am not, in any way, suggesting that a woman should not have a career. There is nothing I do in my career that does not intimately involve my wife. She is my editor, and I rarely publish an article or a book without her vetting it first. She has better judgment than I; she is wiser and has better taste. The organization I built in the United Kingdom was done with her as an equal partner in all things. And, as the father of five daughters, I ensure that they receive the best education that I can afford. I want them to be successful professionals, but more than that, I want them to be ladies like their mother. My eldest daughter, sixteen at the time of this writing, is a good student, but I was most proud of her when she was asked to serve as a hostess for the school's open house—a time when prospective parents check out the facilities. The principal said that my daughter had been chosen for this job "because she is such a dignified young lady." The school chose her as its representative over others who received better grades because she exuded dignity. It was a proud day for me as a father.

Naturally, I do not imply that academic excellence is not a virtue. Indeed, I believe supremely in the acquisition of knowledge and try to instill a strong yearning to learn within each of my kids. I tell them that to be curious is the soul of existence. Most nights at family dinner, I give my children history and Bible quizzes, for which they can win silly prizes. But in the final analysis, our humanity is not determined by the profundity of our intelligence. If this were so, it would imply that the mentally handicapped are less human than others. It is human dignity that defines our humanity. Animals have no concept of dignity, which is why they need not put on clothes to cover their nakedness. But humans have an invisible aura that is about them always, the aura of dignity, of which we become aware when it is taken away from us in a moment of public or private humiliation. And it is dignity, a recognition of the spark of the divine within us and the infinite worth of every individual, more than anything else, that men can learn from women.

Teachers and Nurturers

The heroic men of the Bible were teachers and nurturers. They were feminine men. The teaching profession is a paradigm of the feminine facilitator. Teaching is about retreating into the background and imparting knowledge and wisdom. It is about empowering others and facilitating *their* success. The nadir of this role is apparent in the current lack of respect accorded to teachers. Being a teacher nowadays ranks just slightly above being a street cleaner. Teachers are paid low salaries and are perceived as leading uneventful lives. In the eleven years I spent at Oxford, I remember only one of the special fellowship students (such as the Rhodes) telling me that his ambition was to teach high school. Most went on to become investment bankers, writers, and politicians. True, many became university professors, but this is still much more glamorous than being an elementary or high school teacher, and the salary is much more generous.

It was not always like this. Once upon a time, being a teacher was seen as the highest and most exalted vocation. In days gone by, being a teacher was far superior to being the man or the woman who captured the headlines. Socrates, Plato, and Aristotle were all teachers. While they may have been celebrated in their own time, their names today are far more famous than the kings and princes of their day. Indeed, Moses and Jesus rank among the most famous men that ever lived, yet both were primarily teachers, thereby uprooting the belief that without being tough and ruthless you can't make a real impact on society. But people today are very shortsighted and live only for the moment. Hence, they degrade the teaching profession. Who today would seriously entertain the possibility that a professor or thinker would be more famous than the president of the United States? I wonder if the average American can name a single famous professor other than Stephen Hawking, who is, in any event, known outside academic circles for achieving remarkable brilliance while in a wheelchair. All of us today want to be *the* man, or *the* woman, and never he or she who helped craft the man or the woman.

Death of the Maternal Instinct

I had the pleasure of hosting Professor Hawking at Oxford, and I can tell you that he loves children. Our daughter Rachel Leah had just been born, and although he can only move one finger on his body, he insisted on holding her for about twenty minutes. His wife wrapped his hands around the baby and we have beautiful pictures of him simply peering into the baby's eyes. I always contrasted his action with the young Oxford women who, with some exceptions, took very little interest in the baby. It was sad to see that the world's greatest scientist had such a strong maternal instinct, while the young women at the university had practically none. Somewhere along the line, it had been purged from them. But it should not surprise us that Stephen Hawking has such a highly developed nurturing instinct. After all, he is a teacher.

When President Bill Clinton visited Oxford in June 1994, I was asked by the *London Sunday Times* to write a story on the reactions from American Rhodes Scholars to his visit. I invited fifteen Rhodes Scholar friends for dinner after they had met privately with President Clinton, a former Rhodes Scholar himself. Around the table, we asked each other if we envied Clinton, or if we too wanted to be president of the United States. After some prodding, everyone answered in the affirmative. When the question finally came to me, I said, "No, in all honesty, I have little ambition, nor any real desire to be the president of the United States. Rather, I would like to be the individual to whom the president comes when he needs answers, when he seeks advice, when he has problems, when he needs to find his way. I want to be a repository of wisdom, a beacon of light." This is the definition of the biblical injunction to become a "Light unto the Nations." It primarily means being a teacher.

Femininity of Light

Light is analogous to the feminine facilitator. It lacks the masculine properties of hardness and rigidity that the objects it illuminates possess. Light has no substance, and it cannot be seized. It lacks the strong qualities of the desk, the intricate and complex nature of the computer, or the beauty and splendid color of the painting on the wall. *But it makes appreciation of all of these things possible.* In fact, without light they might as well not exist. Light is only the facilitator, but, as such, it is the single most important ingredient in our world. Without the sun, the earth would be uninhabitable and existence would be impossible. Blackness and gloom would rule the world.

If you have ever studied the Bible, you may remember that darkness was the ninth plague with which God scourged the Egyptians. Compare darkness with afflictions like frogs, locusts, and lice, and it does not sound too bad. Yet we are taught that aside from the deaths of all Egyptian firstborn children, it was the worst plague. To be in a world of darkness is to live in constant loneliness, pain, and self-doubt. It is to be without happiness or hope.

Many of us lead these lives today because we live in a world with so few ladies, and so little feminine light. We turn on our televisions to escape our loneliness and we go to movies to escape our own lives. But the light of the TV set or the movie screen projector is hardly adequate to lift us out of our dark state.

Even the environment has not escaped our contempt for the feminine facilitator. Like a woman giving birth to life, plants and trees sustain every breath we take. They oxygenate our planet and ensure that we survive and flourish. But there is no spotlight on their contribution, so we take them for granted. We have cut down our rainforests and made them into paper pulp, furniture, and clearings for factories and malls. We seem to be intent on converting every subtle feminine property into hard, raw masculinity. Forget the air. We need lawn furniture. We seek a far more tangible use for the environment, in which our immediate needs are always primary when gauging its direct use and utility for our lives.

When we end up suffocating from a lack of oxygen on a frozen, sterile planet that has been sacrificed in the name of personal achievement and general progress, will we then wake up to what we have done to *Mother* Nature? Perhaps that will happen only after we have degraded the role of the wise men, the teachers, and the thinkers so that these professions attract only mediocrity; then we can suffocate in a dull and facile world shrouded in ignorance and darkness. Will we once again revert to respecting the role of the facilitator, will we ever play the part ourselves?

My kids' favorite Jewish holiday is Chanukah. Kids seem uniquely connected to the light the menorah gives off. Sure, they also love the presents, but I would like to believe that their attraction to "The Festival of Lights" has a lot to do with their innocence. They have not yet been corrupted by a world that will later teach them how to get into the spotlight by nudging someone else out. At their age, they can still simply enjoy.

When my children look into the flames, I give them one of these stodgy speeches about how they, too, should illuminate their surroundings. I tell them that they should be sure that other kids around them are laughing and are happy. I explain that they must never be so overwhelmed by their own difficulties that they are indifferent to the plight of others. By the time I get around to how they should help others maximize their potential, they have already tuned out. But I am lucky. My children have the ideal example of a feminine facilitator in their home because my wife Debbie is the embodiment of the circular spirit. So I trust that the message will get through to them somehow. It has to.

27

LOSING THE HEALING FORCE

In the Louvre's famous painting, *The Sabine Women*, by Jacques-Louis David, the Sabine women are standing between the Romans, their husbands, and the Sabine men, their brothers, to prevent the two from slaughtering each other. Women have often served historically as the main opponents to war. The year 2002 even saw the first "Million Mom March," which gathered at the Washington Mall to protest gun violence in the United States.

After General Douglas MacArthur conquered Japan in 1945 and became its effective ruler, he announced to his staff that one of his first acts would be to grant women the right to vote. "The Japanese men won't like it," one of his aides, Bonner Fellers, said. Indeed, events would later prove that many Japanese men regarded it as "worse than sexual assault." But MacArthur responded, "I don't care. I want to discredit the military. Women don't like war" (William Manchester, *American Caesar* [Boston: Little, Brown, 1978], 440).

Before my parents divorced when I was eight, I remember my father coming home frustrated with professional setbacks. My mother would say to him, "Yoav, you have five healthy children. You have a wife and a warm home to come home to. Isn't that enough?" I have a constant reminder of this childhood memory because my wife regularly says the same thing, only substituting the number five with seven, thank God. In their calming tactics, both of these women saw beyond the immediate obstacles with which their husbands were consumed and assessed the difficult climate from a broader and deeper perspective. They saw the future and the endless potential of their families. This sort of insight is a distinctly feminine gift that we are sorely lacking in today's environment.

When I was about age ten, I liked a girl in our class named Deborah (I must have some cosmic attachment to the name). But there was another boy in the class named Greg who liked her, too. So we fought over her. It was a bit of a suicide mission, given that he was about three feet taller than I. The fight took place right near the buses, in plain sight of all, and I remember the damsel in dispute rushing over and telling us how stupid it was to fight at all, and that she hated both of us for doing it. She stormed off with an air of decorum that I will never forget. This was a common theme in my childhood, as it became a given that the girls had more natural dignity than boys could ever hope to possess. At the time, no one believed that girls were merely conditioned to behave better than boys. Rather, society held that girls naturally and innately had a softer and more refined character than their male counterparts.

There was much evidence to prove that women were innately more dignified and modest than men. Just one case in point comes from the twentieth-century developmental psychologist Bruno Bettelheim. In his book *The Children of the Dream* (1969), he presented his study of children growing up in the socialist kibbutz system of Israel. Part of their upbringing was the intentional dissolution of any gender difference. From the earliest age, the kibbutz system had taken the boys and the girls and had them shower together and sleep in the same beds, to negate what was considered to be artificial gender differences produced by society. But Bettelheim reported something fascinating. As soon as the girls reached or neared puberty, they began to rebel and refused to shower with the boys. They insisted on their modesty, even though it had never been taught them.

Even without the academic studies, the innate dignity of women is a concept that most people accept as fact. Baseball is the national pastime, watched by millions of people each year. But that doesn't stop the guys who play from grabbing their crotch and constantly spitting. They don't think twice about grossing out their fans. Can anyone imagine a team of female players doing this on TV, or even in private? Spitting huge gobs of saliva and grabbing their nether regions constantly? The thought of even the coarsest female athletes behaving that way is unthinkable. Women just know how to behave a lot better than men.

Assumptions about the innate behavioral superiority of girls over boys have come under significant assault. In fact, there is a whole slew of books out now that scrutinize our culture and insist on the opposite conclusion. These books maintain that girls are as mean and as aggressive as boys. No, they are worse than boys. Girls bully in a manner that is far more vindictive than boys and they use their cutting tongues as weapons. They often even beat each other up savagely at school, like the horrendous footage of a female teenager mauling another in a Florida high school in December 2004. I have interviewed many of the bestselling female authors of books on this subject on my radio show, and they are adamant about their findings. In books like *Queen Bees and Wannabes*, *Odd Girl Out*, and *Fast Girls*, girls are portrayed as hostile combatants. Female bullies use social manipulation to inflict pain on their victims. They invoke rumors, exclusion tactics, and backstabbing to exact the greatest psychological pain from their adversary. This kind of bullying is assessed to be worse than the black eyes and concussions aggressive boys inflict on one another. The scars from girl bullies are harder to treat, since according to these studies they often go undetected.

To all those who say that the myth of female refinement has been shattered by modern research, I would argue that these studies contradict serious historical research of the way women *used to be*. To study women as they currently are is to study women who have become significantly masculinized. Women today lack dignity because they have been recreated in the image of men. Women are seemingly doing everything possible to repress their natural instincts and nurturing qualities, and today's studies of female refinement reflect this transformation.

Throughout history, violence has been mainly the domain of men. History also supports the undeniable fact that women have an innate mothering instinct that must be developed in men. The purpose of books that portray girls as nasty and cruel is to destroy any and all ideas of difference. Modern-day liberalism has promoted the idea that equality means sameness. Hence, egalitarian thinking seeks to obliterate all gender difference, even when it is to the detriment of women. What all the books ignore is that girls are exuding such mean-spirited behavior because they are learning to ape the boys. The gradual masculinization of women has become the societal norm. Women, therefore, are becoming meaner as they slowly prove to men that they can be just as bad.

Men have screwed up the world for thousands of years with senseless wars, horrifying persecution, and blind discrimination. We need women to help save us. But if the women copy the men and exhibit the same flaws, then we are destined to inhabit an un-refined sewer. Without any curb on male vulgarity and lewdness, our culture will sink into the abyss.

Increasingly, people believe just that. In fact, the *New York Times* magazine ran a cover story back in 2000 that described how America's religious Christians once sought to make mainstream society more moral. The article revealed that these same moralists have now given up, and instead, have chosen to create "their own private America." They home-school their kids and cut themselves off in every which way from the nefarious influences of modern American popular culture. Many religious Jews and Muslims in the United States have come to the same conclusion. They have retreated from the popular culture, put their kids in private parochial schools, thrown the television out of the house, and cho-sen religious videos for their kids rather than the usual fare from Blockbuster. But this is, at its best, a temporary solution. It will not be long before the dam bursts and the culture begins to seep in, as many of my religious friends are discovering. They cannot shield their kids forever, especially in our media-saturated society.

If we cannot hunker down and block out the world as a means of protection, the solution has got to be that we labor to make things "out there" better. There are several ways to accomplish this—you could run for public office, for example—but there is no more efficient means to enact change than to understand that it is woman who rescues man, to cherish the women in our society as providers of a needed counteractive energy, and to nurture that same energy within ourselves, regardless of gender.

28

∽

GAY MEN AS THE WORLD'S LAST NURTURERS

With the ubiquity of the four degrading archetypes of today's women and the masculinization of womankind, gay men are beginning to supplant women in the popular consciousness as the world's nurturers. Since there are no longer female role models to undertake the task of being the feminine facilitation, gay men have taken their place. As the latest successful reality TV show, *Queer Eye for the Straight Guy*, highlights, feminine women have been thrown out of the picture. Women are not women anymore—they are manly. The task of facilitating men to be better now falls to other men who have abandoned the brutish masculine world completely. That is the idea behind *Queer Eye*, and it is a smash hit.

My radio producer once recommended me as a subject for *Queer Eye*. Even more startling, the producers of the show sent around a team to interview me because they were interested. This is not at all flattering when you consider that the purpose of the show is to rescue straight men from the throes of Philistinism. Their enthusiasm for me can only mean that they consider me to be a backward, unsophisticated Neanderthal who needs to be redeemed by the charitable impulses of the Fab Five.

My producer volunteered me because he thought it would be good promotion for my radio show. And although I should have dismissed it out of hand—after all, who wants to be exposed on national television as an unprocessed hillbilly—I was intrigued by the idea that gay men have become the straight man's savior.

Remember back in school when the gay guys (yeah, they denied being gay, but it was undeniable) were beaten up for their lunch money? Remember how they retreated deep into the closet because everyone picked on them for having whiny voices, dressing too smartly, hugging everyone when greeting them, and generally being wimps?

Well, how times have changed. Those same gay guys who you gave wedgies to in high school have now evolved to the top of the pecking order, while the straight guys—sweaty and smelly—have devolved into apes. The success of *Queer Eye for the Straight Guy* is based on the premise that today's heterosexual men are coarse, smelly savages with no manners. They are hairy orangutans who need their chest and back hair shaved. They are bad-mannered brutes who need a lesson in civility, and their apartments look like a crater in the middle of Baghdad. Basically, these heterosexual clods are thoroughly unlettered in stylishness and unschooled in being gentlemen. They need the Fab Five to rescue them from their abysmal boorishness. Amazingly, few who watch the show disagree.

I watched one episode where the Fab Five poured into the apartment of a quiet cowboy with two brain cells and one eyebrow. His apartment was sparsely decorated with furniture that looked as if he had scrounged them from a junkyard. His five o'clock shadow made him look like the twin of Uday Hussein. The show revolved around the poor derelict's plans to propose to his live-in girlfriend, but the Fab Five made it clear that in his current primate state only a she-wolf in heat would agree to marry him. So they spruced him up, plucked his eyebrow (and from one there came two), and taught him how to make chocolate mousse. They even instructed him how to say "I love you" in his girlfriend's native Armenian. Presto. "And on the sixth day the Fab Five created man." When they finished, the marriage proposal worked. Adam got Eve. And from them, a new world was born.

But as I watched this clueless cowboy being taught how to dress, how to clean up after himself, how to decorate his home so that it did not look or smell like a stable, and how to talk romantically to a woman rather than his horse, it suddenly struck me that this is exactly what *women* in my life did for me. My mother taught me how to tuck my shirt in and how to keep my room tidy. And if I used foul language, she would wash my mouth out with soap. My wife took over from there, teaching me how to act like a gentleman, especially in the presence of a woman. If I ate with my mouth open she subtly rebuked me. (Often she just gagged and I took the cue to stop.) Before I would go out to give a speech, she would straighten my tie and take the lint off my jacket. If I was unappreciative of the people who worked for me, she would remind me that kindness, rather than ruthlessness, was a virtue. When we first started dating, she taught me all about chivalry. She got upset when I ran into a restaurant ahead of her and let the door slam in her face (the broken nose went unappreciated as well). And by her eyes lighting up whenever I bought her flowers, she taught me the power of the romantic gesture.

So why do men today need the Fab Five? Simple. These days, women teach men none of these things. How could they, when they need these lessons themselves? Raised in a world where the best way to get male attention is to flash a thong strap rather than a kind smile, and brought up in a workplace where masculine aggression earns respect over feminine grace, there are precious few ladies left.

Women once taught men that true stature results from dignity. But honestly, what can a woman who flashes her breasts for the *Girls Gone Wild* teach a man about civility? What can a woman who prances around in her underwear on the Victoria's Secret Fashion Show teach a man about regal bearing? I mean, come on. If you were a guy, would you listen to these women as they lectured you about not belching in public? Even if they do not admit it, most men no longer believe that women have class. And while they are prepared to date them and bed them, there is a fat chance that they are going to be open to learning from them.

In a world of such rampant misogyny, where women have become complicit in their own degradation, women can have little influence over men. It has therefore fallen to what is perceived to be the last feminine, nurturing spirits in our society—gay men— to teach the straight men the basics of class and refinement.

Gay Men Are the Only Ones Who Want to Get Married These Days

Amazingly, gay men are even teaching straight men about the importance of marriage. The heterosexual man is so bad and clueless at being a husband that most don't even want to get married. They date a woman for five years, move in with her, and then never pop the question. When the woman mentions the word marriage, the guy breaks out into hives. He gets all sweaty. He is covered with a rash. Gay men are the antithesis of the heterosexual commitment-phobe. Not only are they excited about getting married, they are positively fighting for it. They are consulting their lawyers, they are pushing the courts, they are lobbying their congressman. The straight guys are also consulting their lawyers about marriage—but their primary concern is how to get the tightest possible prenup.

The ascendance of the gay man is directly related to the fall of the straight man, and indicates how, in the popular culture, the gentleman who knows how to treat a woman, with rare exceptions, is dead and buried. I have long said that society would be perfect if only gay men would be attracted to women, marry them, and raise boys and girls who are similarly domesticated and nurturing. And I would not be surprised if there were plenty of women who would be ready and willing if any of the Fab Five declared themselves opting for heterosexuality and fatherhood. I can see it now: "Straight Tie (as in the tie of marriage) for the Queer Guy?"

29

CHIVALRY: AN ACKNOWLEDGMENT OF THE SANCTITY OF WOMAN

When I first learned about *Queer Eye for the Straight Guy*, it seemed to me that popular culture had acknowledged and confirmed the downfall of the heterosexual. Suddenly, it was the more feminine, more refined, more graceful gay man—the nurturing man—who was the last hope for malekind. Ten years ago, who would have predicted that not only would gay men be in vogue, but that they would also emerge as the heterosexual man's rescuer? We are reaching a point at which we are going to need the Fab Five to teach women how to be feminine again.

Awe and Wonder

In June 2002, I happily accepted an invitation to a book festival in Asti, Italy, because I am in love with Italy and have even given myself an Italian name, *Massimiliano* (it was the longest one I could find, thereby allowing me to use plenty of hand gestures when I pronounce it, as would any good Italian). While there, I made a point of going to Rome to see Pope John Paul II deliver his regular Angelus on Sunday. St. Peter's Square was crowded with about fifty thousand people. Many were American tourists. Men were shirtless against the strong Italian summer heat, and most of the women wore tank tops and shorts. It was hard to tell whether any of the people there were religious. But then, precisely at noon, the pope appeared at his palace window high atop the square. In an instant, everything changed. I saw bare-chested men feeling naked and suddenly covering up. I saw women putting shawls on, or even using plastic shopping bags, to cover their cleavage.

It was remarkable. The feeling that a holy man had entered the throng was almost palpable, and people had to change the way they were speaking and dressing in accordance with the holy presence. Most of the people did not appear, in any way, religious. They covered up as an innate, almost intuitive response to being in the presence of something holy, lofty, and awe-inspiring. This idea of physically showing respect for a spiritual superior has many precedents. In the famous narrative of the burning bush, when Moses first encounters God in the desert, he is commanded by God to take off his shoes lest he trample on holy ground.

Chivalry, too, was once predicated on the idea that men had to mind their manners in the presence of creatures that reflected the divine spirit, and women were always assessed as beings that reflected the grandeur and greatness of God. Everything from their beauty to their sublime dignity was a reflection of God's majesty. They were his mirrors on earth. When a woman entered a room, it was akin to the entrance of the divine spirit, or the pope appearing at his palace window. It was expected that men would get up to greet the divine presence. The big difference between the rabbis and the pope on the one hand, and women on the other, is that the rabbis and the pope had to work on becoming holy. Women are born that way. Their higher spirituality is innate.

When something or someone displays this innate sacredness, it is deserving of special treatment. Even today, on the Sabbath we dress differently and act differently. An obvious reminder of this is the familiar story of Eric Liddell, the hero of the film *Chariots of Fire*. Liddell refused to run on the Sabbath and gave up an almost certain gold medal because he would not compromise on the seriousness of respecting and prioritizing that which is holy. Observant Jews do not transact business or even use electricity on the

Sabbath. In Christian families, children and parents put on their Sunday finery and go to church. In both faiths, loved ones gather together to consecrate the day. By altering our behavior through the conscious modifications we make in how we dress, speak, and act, we elevate the Sabbath above the rest of the days of the week.

The Death of Chivalry

Once upon a time, men reined in their natural inclinations and behaved like gentlemen around women. Just as they would not swear in church, they would not swear around women. Just as they dressed their best in synagogue, they were always careful to be well groomed, trim, and proper in female company. Just as they would hide their bad manners in an audience with the pope, so too, they would curb their bad behavior—burping, breaking wind, yelling—in front of their wives. There was a sense of reverence for a woman, and chivalry was the actualization of that reverence into a daily practice. Chivalry arose spontaneously from a man when in the presence of a woman because he felt he was standing before something sacred and lofty. Such was the sense of awe that a lady awakened in a man, and such was the sense of reverence that she evoked within him.

Today, chivalry is all but dead. Men behave in the most abominable manner around women. They will pick their noses, laugh about breaking wind, and empty their bowels. When I was the rabbi at Oxford University, I would regularly see the male students urinating in front of their dates—I kid you not—at the big celebration balls at the end of the year. It was disgusting and unbelievable, especially at the world's most prestigious university. There is no concept of men according women any special treatment, and it seems that women want it that way. In this age of equality, they find chivalry patronizing at best, degrading at worst.

This is all based on a false and superficial understanding of chivalry. The popular conception of chivalry relates to the actions that medieval knights undertook in protecting damsels. According to this comprehension, the purpose of chivalry was to seek honor by defending the weak and the innocent. In his book *From Chivalry to Terrorism*, author Leo Braudy (Knopf 2003) compares the chivalry of the solitary knight to the samurai swordsman and the wandering cowboy in Western movies. His argument is that masculinity has certain characteristics that reappear in history. Masculinity always wants and needs to be asserted before a crowd. Thus, for men, chivalry is an act of sacrifice against one's own self-interest through which one attains honor. That is why so much chivalric behavior has played itself out in the art of war, the most renowned example being the war over Helen of Troy. The classical definition of chivalric duty requires a great warrior to flourish his militaristic aptitude, thereby earning a woman's appreciation and becoming the object of her fawning attention. Endless fairy tales, replete with fair maidens and shining knights, convey the same idea.

This traditional misunderstanding of chivalry is the reason for its demise. Edmund Burke lamented the death of chivalry that he believed he saw in the imprisonment of Marie Antoinette: "But the age of chivalry is gone." Burke wrote, "That of sophistors, economists and calculators has succeeded; and the glory of Europe is extinguished forever." Now from what I have read about Marie Antoinette (and that includes the modern revisionist biographies like that of Antonia Fraser that seek to portray the French queen in a favorable light), I am no great fan so her imprisonment does not offend my sensibilities. She was everything I decry in this book, a mean-spirited, deeply materialistic, power-hungry woman who, for all her fancy clothes, could hardly be called a lady.

Nevertheless, Burke's lament about the death of chivalry is inspired. To his mind, chivalry died because gallantry had lost out to the pursuit of money. Materialism and economics replaced honor and nobility. Men were no longer judged by their valor but by their wealth. But most men repudiated the chivalric code because they understood it as an old-fashioned and outdated obligation to protect the weaker sex. Modern women were rightly revolted at being labeled men's inferior. As Harvey Mansfied argues in his *New York Times* review of Braudy's book, "Protecting the weaker sex is not now endangered by calculators so much as by those who, like Dr. Braudy, deny that there is a weaker sex. These people have created the sensitive male with the intent of replacing the chivalrous male in our new gender-neutral society. Women today have no more momentous personal choice than whether to look for a sensitive male or a chivalrous one."

What chivalry really should be, far from being the honor received by a knight in shining armor for defending a poor and helpless creature (or even a code that governed conduct between knights themselves), is a code of conduct adhered to by a gentleman in the presence of a woman. It is the realization by men that when they stand in the presence of women, they are showing respect to lofty, spiritual creatures. It is an acknowledgment that in this holy presence they must behave accordingly.

If you visit Israel and go to Jerusalem to see the Western Wall, the last remnant of the Holy Temple and Judaism's holiest site, you will, no doubt, notice that many men and women who come to pray there have the custom not to turn their back on the wall. They walk backward as they leave the wall's promenade. In similar fashion, I have met men who also have the custom of never turning their back to a woman. Real chivalry emanates not from a desire to protect or coddle women, but from a sense of awe that a man experiences when in the *presence* of a woman.

Encountering Awe

If you do not know what I mean by experiencing awe that ultimately compels you to modify your behavior, let me offer an example. In the summer of 2003, I traveled to Northern Ireland to broadcast a few radio shows and see the Catholic/Protestant conflict for myself. I stayed on the north coast of the island at a world heritage site called the "Giant's Causeway." I spent an entire day walking along the coastal trail atop cliffs that look down hundreds of feet into the ocean. On my right side, thousands of sheep were chewing the greenest grass. On my left side were the blue waters of the Irish Sea. Because the trail is frequented by tourists, there was also the occasional paper cup and piece of paper scattered about. Although none who know me would accuse me of being particularly tidy, I found myself gathering pieces of garbage and throwing them into the wastebaskets. To me, everything about my surroundings was majestic, and I felt inspired to a degree that I had experienced only a few times before in my life. The reverence I felt for the place was simply incompatible with the garbage on the ground, and that reverence prompted my unexpected drive to clean up.

The four new offensive archetypes of women utterly fail to inspire men with a sense of awe, wonder, or reverence. And so a heartbreaking scenario is created: With no feminine women, there are no men to live up to the chivalric ethos; the self-feeding cycle will perpetuate, and we all—men and women alike—will inhabit a darker, harsher, less romantic society.

RESTORING WOMEN TO AN HONORED PLACE

30

∾

BROADENING THE PEDESTAL: LEARNING TO BE SUCCESSFUL WITHOUT BEING RUTHLESS

I have spent a good many words developing an argument against the shocking degradation of modern women into empty fleshpots, and I have tried to show the pernicious effect such degradation has on our culture and society. Respect for women and respect for feminine attributes, though a must for their own sake, are a crucial panacea for healing our world. If women had a voice in Arab countries, there would be a natural foil to the call for violence. Real feminine influence in the West would refine an increasingly crass and aggressive culture. And if men learned how to respect and please women, we would not have a 50 percent divorce rate, our families would be stronger, our children would be gentler, and they would grow up with greater stability and security.

Now that we have evaluated the extensive damage to our society and our world, it is time to think seriously about what we must do to remedy the situation. Women were once seen as men's superior in the important areas of natural dignity, personal refinement, innate spirituality, and a congenital ability to determine what is important in life and get along with other people. But women began to resent their place on the pedestal because they felt it was disempowering. So, with feminism, they decided to get off the pedestal and essentially become like men. They could work as hard as men, be as aggressive as men, sleep around like men, and succeed like men. All true. But the success could have come about without aping men, without the vulgar crassness that has so degraded the fairer sex. Women could have achieved those ends in a noble manner that would have helped the world realize the incredible healing that comes from following a feminine example. In sum, women could have expanded the pedestal and invited men atop with them. They could have learned to succeed in all ways that men fail to do—not only without compromising their femininity, but by influencing men to be more refined and compassionate in the pursuit of their success as well.

When women were deemed to reside atop a pedestal, the notion that these sainted creatures would want to sully their hands in the business world or in the political arena was ludicrous. Certainly, this misnomer needed to be thwarted because women obviously have extraordinary abilities in all these areas. However, rather than merely jumping off the pedestal to join men in the muck below, women should have focused on expanding their platform, on making it wide enough to allow men to join them on the podium. The motto should not have been that women, *too*, can fill a business suite impressively, but rather that a feminine nobility could and should infuse Washington and Wall Street.

The objective now must be to teach men how to be successful without being ruthless, how to be productive without being envious of another's success. A lady, after all, is capable of accomplishing anything a man can do but bests him by accomplishing it with a positive, feminine style. She is seldom driven by envy or a desire to thwart her competition. In fact, she has a nurturing instinct and therefore tries to help others to realize success as well. She does not believe that ruthlessness facilitates her success, because, unlike men, she knows that there is room for more than one victor at the top of the ladder of success. She stems not from the finite God of the line, but from the infinite God of the circle. She has all around the presence of the eternal and suffers no mental deprivation as a result.

A true lady who embodies the circular spirit never makes the mistake of evaluating professional success over personal success. She considers her relationships to be her real accomplishments, no matter how much acclaim and success she finds in other arenas. These are the priorities that women need to impart to men, and this is the sort of influence they should seek to have in society.

Feminism, however, went in the direction of chasing masculine goals. In the process, it lost its responsibility as a watchdog for women's needs because it focused completely on political and professional gains. At present, when a man hits it big and is successful in the professional realm, this triumph is usually accompanied by diminished success in his personal life. Suddenly, he begins to have affairs, divorce looms, and all too often, if he has stuck around long enough to have children, he winds up watching them wander through life like ghosts, destined to repeat the same harsh, cold cycle. We know that women, more and more, are beginning to follow the same patterns instead of weaning men from them.

A Kinder, Gentler World

The sixteenth-century Jewish scholar Rabbi Isaac Luria (known as the Ari), who was the most influential Kabbalist of all time, wrote that the Messiah would not come, and the perfection of the world would not be achieved, until men started to listen to their wives and women started demanding their rightful role in the world. This was the concept behind God's insistence that Abraham follow the opinions of his wife Sarah because she had a more developed and mature assessment of things. Her judgment—and the judgment of women in general—was wiser and more substantial. We must heed this lesson and recognize that the world will not achieve perfection until the feminine trumps the masculine, love trumps honor, wisdom trumps savvy, compassion trumps ruthlessness, and decent, considerate husbands trump womanizers like Trump.

For this to happen, women must reclaim their self-respect and the role in society that they are meant to have. All too many women stroke their insecurities rather than cultivate their strengths. The struggle for civil rights has ultimately left women in a subordinate position, more disempowered than ever. Although the earlier goals to achieve women's suffrage and equal pay were necessary, political disempowerment was only one kind of subordination. Yet it eventually subsumed all other missions. The ultimate form of disempowerment, however, is personal disempowerment, which can make women feel that they have to *do* in order to *be*. When women buy into the notion that they have to look a certain way or fit a particular stereotype to be a success, they assume the essence of degradation. Can anyone seriously say that today's women (and men) do not subscribe to this sort of thinking? In truth, as a society we may have achieved political freedom, but we are more shackled than ever.

One of the cornerstones of the women's liberation movement was the fight for women's sexual liberation. The notion that a woman only engaged in sex for procreation or out of a duty to her husband had enabled a culture to develop in which women became mere physical entities to be used in creating alliances between families, tribes, or nations, or in producing heirs. The feminist movement rightly insisted that women had desires and needed fulfillment. But rather than teaching men to see physical intimacy as a foundation for spiritual and emotional growth, women instead claimed that they could be as self-serving and unemotional in sexual matters as men. They too could have sex without attachment, without emotional intimacy. How did this ever become a desirable or even acceptable end? Rather than destroying the antiseptic and unrealistic ideal of female sexuality, the movement essentially created a new model for female sexuality that spawned the crotch-scratcher. Meaningless sex came into vogue.

A Return to Innocence

It used to be a lot simpler. Remember the whole "boy meets girl" equation? A guy and a girl would meet at college or at a dance, and they would just feel attracted to each other, without all the complications. She didn't feel self-conscious about fending off his advances or judging his intentions, and he didn't plot what to say to get her back to his room for sex. She could go out on a date and not feel defensive, and he could go on a date and not feel he had to be manipulative. Why? Because men were gentleman and maneuvering a woman into bed was against their personal code of honor. And even if they would have suggested it, women who were ladies would never have accepted it. Since "getting something off her" was off the table, they could just speak and laugh and truly get to know one another. There was no need to be cautious or uptight. A woman could let herself go without the fear of someone taking advantage. The date was not a means to an end, it was an end in itself. But all that changed. Dating went from allowing a man and a woman to get to know each other to allowing a man and a woman to use each other. He would use her for sex, and she would use him to make her feel special and desirable. That is, until he got bored, or felt she was too demanding, which happened nine times out of ten.

This boredom sets in for a simple reason. Men are not meant to be experts in women. There is meant to be an air of mystery and detachment. A man is supposed to spend his life getting to know a woman. Men are seekers, and they love the mystery of a woman they do not yet know mentally, emotionally, and especially physically.

But in an age where women have allowed themselves to be made into the walking fulfillment of a man's hormonal needs, both by having sex without commitment and by taking off their clothes in TV advertisements, men have become "experts" in women. They know what a "good" set of boobs look like, and how to evaluate a woman's behind. They know what weight a woman "should" be. And they know when a woman is good in bed, and when she's just average.

Imagine a man buying his wife a diamond for their anniversary. Now imagine that she is a diamond dealer by profession. Rather than just being impressed at the sparkle of the diamond, she'll first look at it, scrutinize it, and determine whether it's a valuable present—because she has the knowledge. Experts are people who can spot flaws. And that is what has happened with men today. They have all become diamond dealers. Virtually all are clinical, discerning experts of a woman's physical appearance. They can tell you if a woman is a perfect ten, or just a plain old five. And that's the way they actually think and talk to each other. They'll sit having a beer together, rating every woman who passes by. They have all become diamond dealers—but like so many diamond dealers, they mostly spot imperfections. I truly bemoan that men have become so expert in assessing women that a woman needs to be a perfect diamond (read "supermodel") to elicit male attention.

31

A CASUAL SEX FREEZE-OUT

As we discuss the essential, innate spirituality of women, we are acknowledging their wondrous natural ability to elevate the most mundane occurrences to something more significant and spiritually satisfying. Reinfusing society with a greater appreciation for the feminine will have repercussions on many of our daily activities and general ideals. The world is hungering to rediscover the lost sacred feminine, the underlying theme behind bestselling blockbusters such as *The Da Vinci Code* and all its many copycats. I do not, however, want to ignore that while we are talking about male and female energies, we are also talking about humans—sexual beings who relate to one another in the most primal, physical sense. Society is vitally in need of embracing the feminine spirit, because if we are to restore an appreciation for the sacred female energy, there must be a moratorium on casual sex. Random sexual encounters take what can be the most spiritual human instinct that two people can share and degrade it to nothing more than the most basic human physical exertion, devoid of any deeper connective or transformative capacity.

Unlike the manipulative ideas behind *The Rules*, or the feminist distortion of intimacy as merely a physical pleasure, women should embrace that sex is a prized closeness that fuses people together. During adolescence, young ladies should be inculcated with the idea that sex is a shared personal experience that should only be offered to a man who has earned it. When I use the verb "earn," I do not mean it in a calculating or controlling sense. I am thoroughly opposed to the idea of using sex as a weapon or a bargaining chip. I mean that a man must earn his access to a woman by committing himself to her, by elevating himself to her lofty heights. No single factor has led to the greater debasement of women than the widespread availability of casual sex. If a man can get a woman without having to earn her, what incentive does he have to try to become a gentleman? And men want sex more than anything else. He'll take the easiest path to get it if that is what is offered to him.

This whole idea is worth reviewing for a moment. What incentive is there for a man to move away from his natural aggressive and self-absorbed streak and become a gentleman? Is it making money? Of course not. On the contrary, ruthlessness in business is rewarded. Screwing your competitors is what is going to make you money. And do you need to be a gentleman if you want to succeed in politics? Forget it. Politics is about viciously attacking your opponent. That is what usually makes you successful. What about earning the respect of your peers? Do you need to be a gentleman for that? Absolutely not. Your friends, in this shallow culture, are going to respect you for being rich, famous, or influential. And if you achieve those things you are going to be top dog in your community. If you do not believe me, just look at Donald Trump, an inveterate womanizer and braggart, who is known for his selfish and gaudy lifestyle rather than for any kind of philanthropy. Trump remains an American icon simply because he has money and is an expert at getting attention.

So the question comes back: What incentive does the male species have to refine his character, to pull himself up from the level of animal and become a man? And the traditional answer to that question had always been that the pursuit of a woman would elevate him—the one object of male desire that could not be won through ruthlessness. Women wanted romantic and loving men who knew how to dress, how to behave, and how to treat a woman softly and devotedly. Aggressive men with crass manners were highly unattractive to them. On the contrary, it was the knight in shining armor for which they dreamed. Women were refined creatures who could not be wooed by vulgar suitors. So a man simply had to ennoble his character, soften his touch, and become a romantic if he wished to have a woman. Then, along came the sexual revolution of the 1960s and all that changed. Men discovered that in this new climate of feminine liberation—which in reality turned out to be *masculine* liberation because it liberated men from having to be gentlemen—they could act like complete pigs and still get women. Even Stokely Carmichael, the initiator of "Black Power," contributed to the prejudice against women in the midst of his efforts on behalf of liberty. At the same time that Stokely was fighting for black civil rights, he was asked what the proper position for women was in the SNCC (Student Nonviolent Coordinating Committee). In reply, Stokely famously offered a one-word response: "prone." It seems astonishing that even at that time, when blacks and whites were fighting together for black civil rights, such efforts could be accompanied by such utter contempt for women. The objective may have been to achieve a kind of color blindness but gender bias was alive and well!

Still, since at the core we are talking about physical beings, the key to elevating our essential selves is to acknowledge our physical components and seek to refine them. Therefore, if we want men to raise themselves up, as in the medieval days when courtly love prevailed and men had to better their character to be worthy of women, the formula is straightforward and simple: Women should not have sex with men who have not married them. Period. If women collectively implemented this policy, it would change men overnight. Not only would men begin courting women again and look forward to marrying them, but they would also return to the idea of sex as a spiritual act that sews and fuses together two individuals into one flesh. Gone would be all the horrible misogyny we hear about in rap songs with women being described as bitches and "hoes." We would cease to hear mention of men "doing women" (one of the most horrible euphemisms for sex ever invented) thrown about in casual conversation. Likewise, we would no longer have to endure the college term of two coeds "hooking up," which seems better suited to describe the interaction between a station wagon and a U-Haul than between a man and a woman in love.

And speaking of hooking up, no one summed up just how casual and unfulfilling sex has become, in an era where women give it away to complete strangers, better than Tom Wolfe in his noted 2001 essay by that name:

> Hooking up was a term known in the year 2000 to almost every American child over the age of nine, but only to a relatively small percentage of their parents, who, even if they heard it, thought it was used in the old sense of "meeting" someone. . . . Back in the twentieth century, American girls had used baseball terminology. "First base" referred to embracing and kissing; "second base" referred to groping and fondling; "third base" referred to fellatio, usually known in polite conversation by the ambiguous term "oral sex"; and "home plate" meant conception-mode intercourse, known familiarly as "going all the way." In the year 2000, in the era of hooking up, "first base" meant deep kissing, groping and fondling; "second base" meant oral sex; "third base" meant going all the way; and "home plate" meant learning each other's names. (Tom Wolfe, *Hooking Up* [New York: Picador USA, 2001], 1)

Women Must Move Forward as a Collective Entity

In 2000, I appeared alongside New York radio host Richard Bey in a debate against the women who penned *The Rules*. While I disagreed with much of what the authors said, mostly because a good relationship should not be manipulative, nor contrived as the book recommends, I certainly agree that women who sleep with men early on in a relationship have undermined the future potential of the relationship. Richard, who is in his forties and still a bachelor, got up and said, "That's ridiculous. Sure, I agree that men who push a woman to have sex with them almost immediately are rarely serious about that woman, but if she were to say no, there are thousands of women that he can move on to. She's always going to lose out because, while she might insist on having some dignity, thousands of others won't. So why should a guy hang around and date a woman who won't sleep with him?"

Richard's right. None of this can happen in isolation. It is like a union that agrees to strike against low wages or unfair working conditions. The only way the strike is going to succeed is if all the workers agree to not cross the picket line. The moment management can undermine the strike, by getting some workers to cross over, the strike becomes ineffective. If women as a whole made it clear that they demanded dignity, that they want parts in movies that do not require undressing, that they want to be like male recording artists who do not have to strip to get an album, that they want to be like male news anchors who do not have to get plastic surgery to read the news, only then can it succeed. This is not going to happen unless there is a concerted campaign, waged by the country's women, against the wholesale degradation of their gender. That is why I am arguing for feminist leaders to emerge from their protracted silence and cry out against the misogyny in the culture. Cry out for women to take back their dignity from men who have trampled on it.

Marriage, Not Cohabitation

Part of this revolution includes the rejection of casual sex and the reclaiming of greater righteousness and spirituality. With a broader embrace of the moral and spiritual self, women will remember to see the sexual act as a spiritual act and thereby share this vision with men. And they will expect them to commit to the relationship in the same spiritual, profound way. This means marriage, not cohabitation. Moving in together has become a bandage for commitment-phobes. In essence, it is the appearance of commitment—without the actual act of committing. True commitment is a sign of depth and maturity that only comes about with one's willingness to form a permanent union with another human being.

When I give lectures on relationships, audience members often ask me what my explanation is for the repeated statistics that show approximately 70 percent of couples who live together before they get married end up breaking up or divorcing. The answer is simple: Commitment brings out the best in us. The Talmud says that a human being, like an olive or a grape, needs to be pressed to produce his or her best oil and wine. When commitment is absent from a relationship, when a man and woman move in together to "see how it goes," there is no incentive for them to dig deep and find their best self. They end up getting less of each other, and it usually shows in the poor quality of their relationship. Besides, to move in with a man without the permanency of the marriage bond is to "cross the picket line." It breaks ranks with all other women who are sick and tired of men's juvenile and manipulative behavior by delivering to them a woman that they have not elevated themselves to deserve.

SUGGESTION #1:   Women should stop sleeping with unworthy men. It is time to bring back the dignified and time-honored value that a man should never be granted entry to a woman's body until he has married her. Courting a woman should replace dating her.

The first step, therefore, is for women to stop sleeping with men until the men have made serious commitments to them. And what better gauge for a serious commitment than a ring on the finger?

Of course, we cannot start with the symptom of a problem in the hopes of ameliorating it. Instead, we have to tackle the heart and soul of the issue. We have to step back and first address the maturation of girls before they fall into the same low self-esteem traps currently plaguing women.

32

THE TWENTY-FIRST CENTURY LADY: A FULL BRAIN VERSUS A WELL-POISED CRANIUM

By the time today's young woman has entered the workforce and is living on her own as an independent adult, she has absorbed a culture filled with disparaging female images. She has soaked up the images of womanhood presented by pop culture and has developed a skewed view of what it can or should mean to be a woman. It is essential that she recover some of the dignity that women aspired to in days past. Love and discipline will help girls become independent thinkers with moral character rather than spineless followers inclined to the whims of the crowd.

Girls should be raised as ladies with a sense of their own dignity and modesty. In searching for a school for my daughters, this ethos of imbuing dignity is always what I've looked for most. Sure, I want a school with high academic standards, but equally important, I want a school that raises girls to be ladies: a school that insists on modest standards of dress and imparts to a girl a sense of her feminine value. This is radically different from the shallow finishing schools that used to be popular and eventually became the butt of jokes. I do not need my daughters to balance a book on their head. I prefer a full brain to a well-poised cranium, but this

ctual pursuit must come with a sense of their own value as
n beings. Unlike men who must be taught dignity, women
have an innate sense of it. It is the role of both school and parents
to work toward preserving and cultivating that dignity.

In addition to possessing a more innate sense of dignity, girls
also have a greater affinity for a natural sense of modesty. I emphasize modesty because the way a woman dresses is the fastest external revelation to her own inner self-esteem. Women who dress
immodestly are nearly always insecure about their ability to attract male attention with anything other than their bodies. And
they do attract attention—unfortunately it is from womanizers.
As mentioned, the developmental psychologist Bruno Bettelheim
showed in his book, *The Children of the Dream*, that modesty came
innately to little girls. Women's sense of modesty is congenital and
inborn, and they must start listening to these instincts again—
rather than complying with what lascivious men want to see.

SUGGESTION #2: Modest dress codes should be reinsti-
tuted in schools. Girls, from elementary school to college,
should be required to wear dignified and unrevealing
clothing, immediately conveying to men that they see their
principal contribution as something other than the sexual.

Yes, I know that coercion invites rebellion. I also realize that
women need to internalize a sense of their own feminine honor
rather than having it foisted on them. But these are extreme times,
and they demand forceful responses. If you consider this suggestion
too prudish, I ask you, isn't there a code of dress for teachers? If a
female teacher came into school wearing the tightest jeans, with
the straps of her thong showing above those jeans, and a giant view
of cleavage to boot, would she not be reprimanded? And if teachers
have to dress in a dignified way, why shouldn't the students?

Girls, dressed modestly, also send a powerful message to boys:
Girls are not designed to give you a thrill. They are to be respected.

The Jewish religion argues that every woman is a princess, the
daughter of the King of Kings. Traditionally, Jewish girls have

been raised by their parents in accordance with this high ideal of being royalty. This has devolved to conjure the image of the "Jewish American Princess," a synonym for a spoiled diva, but that is not what the idea is really about. Instead, being a Jewish princess has always been about expecting women to live up to their true nature, which would have them carry themselves and act like members of royal blood. In the ancient world, it was a widely held belief that women, possessed of the unique capacity to create and bear life, were goddesses whose sense of refinement was infinitely higher than a man's.

One of my daughter's teachers chided a group of her students one day when she noticed them being a bit rowdy on the street. "Girls," she said, "would the Queen of England scream across the street to get her friend's attention? Would she cackle and call jokes out loudly or sit like a truck driver? Well you girls are as noble as she, and I expect no less from your own behavior." Dignified behavior befits not only queens, but all women. Now, the Queen of England is dismissed as stuffy and aloof, and I am not advocating that today's women reinstitute unnecessarily rigid and old-fashioned ideas of feminine propriety. But while superficial propriety need not be reembraced, self-respect and inner dignity should be.

Dressing for Yourself as Opposed to Dressing for Others

Before anyone tosses her scepter at me, let me preempt any criticism that I might be advocating a return to the time when women wore opera gloves and glass slippers. That antiquated showiness was a false and external portrayal of refinement, and it is not at all what I am talking about. We live in a far more casual and authentic world than the one inhabited by European royalty, and I thank God for that. But while we need not go to the stiff blue-blooded extreme, we certainly do not have to yield to the opposite end—girls in thongs with their straps showing and their midriffs exposed. While Princess Grace of Monaco may have overdone the whole female dignity thing, Courtney Love has grossly underdone it. Certainly, finding a happy medium is the healthiest option.

When a woman wears colorful, attractive, form-fitting, and yet unrevealing clothing, she sends the message that she understands her own innate attractiveness and has the confidence to put herself forward in the most favorable light. Alternatively, when she wears clothes that are no longer fitted, but downright suffocating and tight, she sends the message that in her own estimation she has more form than substance. *She is no longer dressing for herself but for others.* Ultimately, she must live with the consequences, which usually includes dealing with men who assume that she thinks of herself as their object of play.

I discuss this subject with my daughters all the time. To be sure, they are raised as religious Jewish girls and therefore they dress modestly as it accords with what both their parents and their school require. But even with these safeguards, there are things about how they dress that bug me. For example, I dislike the jean skirts that are so popular. They look as if they are built for workmen, and they are anything but elegant. I tell my daughters that my greatest wish as a father of girls is to see them grow up to be intelligent, motivated, and dignified ladies, and that the first sign of a lady is modest dress. Of course, I want my daughters to grow up to be successful professionals, highly educated and accomplished. Dainty women who hang out in the kitchen have little appeal for me, not to mention that this is a silly, shallow, and outdated stereotype. Likewise, the suburbanite women who drop their kids off at private schools and then spend the rest of the day at the hairstylist or shopping are equally nauseating. I believe that my daughters can still be all the things that men are, and do all the things that men do, while remaining ladies. Look at the American secretary of state, Condoleezza Rice. She is a woman of obvious refinement, grace, and intelligence. And none of that stopped her—indeed it propelled her—to one of the highest positions in the land.

Spring Break Debauchery

If there are other parents out there who feel as I do, they are for the most part staying silent. They are not prevailing on or influencing their daughters to be ladies. Look at the spring break phenomenon. Every year, hundreds of thousands of college students travel down to Miami Beach, where I grew up and where my mother and siblings live, for the requisite debauchery. It is a time of raucous behavior, a time to blow off steam with the knowledge that the long school year is nearly finished. In the midst of this merrymaking, however, it is pitiful to see the way some of these young women frolic around town. The skimpy way they dress and promiscuous way they conduct themselves is saddening. From her early childhood years playing with Bratz dolls, to purchasing thong underwear from the dELiA's catalog, to the college coed on her own over spring break, each phase of a girl's journey into womanhood has become dominated by the need to hone her appeal to men—lowly men at that.

One March, when I was visiting with my family in Miami, I went with my nephews to play football at the beach. It was high season for spring break and the beach was packed. A young woman, about nineteen years old, walked over to my sixteen-year-old nephew, who was wearing a Texas Longhorn T-shirt, and asked him if he was from Texas. My nephew said, curtly, that it was just a shirt. Still, she lingered, openly and shamelessly flirting with him in front of all of us. She explained that she was down in Florida with two other female friends from their college back in Texas. Finally she extended an invitation to my nephews that it would be great if they decided they wanted to join her and her friends for a drink.

Within moments of her eye-batting at my nephews, she sauntered back to her beach towel and lay down next to a young man who proceeded to hug and caress her on every part of her body. Was that her boyfriend? It sure looked like it. But if that was the case, why in the world was she flirting with another man only moments earlier? This seemed so odd to me that I thought about it for a few minutes until it hit me. Why had she been so anxious to thrust herself on these strange men? Simple, she was playing a role. Many young women today, especially on college campuses have been subtly conditioned to serve as male entertainment. Their first persona is one of flirtatiousness and they simply can't shut it down. It has become second nature. It is part of the whole *Girls Gone Wild* mentality. In the same way that a waitress who works in a restaurant understands that her job is to wait on tables, women today seem to have concluded that their job is to dress and act in a way that is pleasing to men.

33

∞

WHERE IS DAD?

As I watched these saddening girls on spring break, all so intent on being a boy's little toy, I could not help but think about the first men in their lives: their fathers. Where were they in all this? Had they given their daughters self-esteem? Had they made their daughters feel like they mattered to their father infinitely and unconditionally? I could not imagine that this was the case, because if it were, they would not be so desperate for male attention—any and all the male attention they could possibly garner, without any discernment. All too many fathers today fail their daughters in the most basic ways. They neglect them, and without that foundation of healthy male admiration, without the sense from the first man in their lives that they are special and dignified, so many daughters run directly into the arms of men who are beneath them, simply wanting to use them.

A cover story in the *New York Times* reported on high school teenagers and sex. The article told the story of a fifteen-year-old girl who refused to have sex with her sixteen-year-old boyfriend. He said he understood but quickly began cheating with another fifteen-year-old who *would* have sex with him. When his girlfriend found out, she, understandably, became very angry. But listen to how she responded to his cheating: The young woman went to her boyfriend at school and suggested that they both cut class and go back to her house and have sex. When the reporter asked her why she would do such a thing, she replied with tears in her eyes, "To keep him." Astonishing, is it not? A woman gets cheated on by her low-life boyfriend but instead of being indignant at the betrayal, she decides that she is prepared to compromise herself in order not to lose him to some bimbo. Most startling of all, the girl is still a kid—just fifteen years old. As I read, I found the same question echoing through my head again and again: Where is her father? Where is her father's shotgun, for that matter. Had her father made her feel valuable, she would not need to cheapen herself to have a boy like her. She would not be so desperate for male attention that she would nullify her own self-esteem. Had her father been a strong male presence in her life, she would not have been so desperate for the affection of a scoundrel.

The Alan Guttmacher Institute released a study in 2001 showing that 80 percent of American eighteen-year-old girls are not virgins (in 1959 it was only 23 percent), with 7,700 American teenagers losing their virginity every day, a shocking and astonishing statistic that painfully demonstrates the loss of innocence among our youth. And lest you think these girls have sex as a matter of choice, 89 percent of these same girls said that they were having sex because of pressure from boys.

And to give you an idea of how acceptable it has become among high school girls for their boyfriends to cheat, a related study by the Kaiser Family Foundation and *Seventeen* magazine (December 2002) found that 42 percent of teenage girls fifteen to seventeen years old believed that it was acceptable for boys to have multiple sexual partners. The American Academy of Pediatrics (January 2001) also reports that 21 percent of high school seniors have actually had four or more sexual partners.

The promiscuity of American high school girls is so advanced that 55 percent of sexually active fifteen- to seventeen-year-old girls have had two or more sexual partners, while a truly staggering 13 percent have had six or more sexual partners (The Alan Guttmacher Institute). Of course, 2,800 American females under age twenty become pregnant every day.

Try and Get Past My Bushmaster

Let me make it absolutely clear and declare, unambiguously and in writing, that if any man or boy gets near my sixteen-year-old daughter for any sexual purpose, I am going to get my Bushmaster rifle and blow him away. That's right. If you read in the newspapers that some pimply, horny, sixteen-year-old kid was found dead with his pants down near our New Jersey home, you will know that I did it. I will readily confess ahead of time and will proudly serve my time (assuming, of course, that I don't get sent to the chair).

Of course, I realize that my grievance is not actually with some horny youth. As a father, my focus is on my own daughters. The moment those adolescent boys have swaying power over them, it means I have failed them in my duty as their father. To make sure that I never have to cock that rifle, I take the much more civil, and ultimately most effective, approach. I simply remain so close to my daughter—so available, so loving, and so understanding—that she will never need to have some vulgar youth to tell her that she is beautiful. No doubt, when she is slightly older and a really worthy guy comes along, his words to her about her beauty will be far more meaningful than mine, and then, and only then, will it be time to loosen the umbilical chord. But even after she, God willing, marries and has children of her own, my work with my daughter will not be complete and my attachment will never be severed. Fatherhood is a lifelong commitment.

Fathers and Daughters: The Forgotten American Relationship

In our society, we have it all backward. Too much is made of the father-son relationship at the expense of the father-daughter one. The image of a boy being taught by his dad to catch a baseball or throw a football is commonplace, while the only mainstream image of a father interacting with his teenage daughter is telling her not to come home too late when she goes out with her boyfriend. Pop tarts like Britney Spears and Paris Hilton, who use partial nudity to advance their careers, are often close to their mothers, who may even serve as their managers, while their dads are nowhere to be seen. The newspapers have made much of how Britney and Paris are strongly influenced, and in Britney's case managed, by their mothers.

Where you *do* read about a father's central involvement in his daughter's career, it usually leads to respectable and self-confident women like Steffi Graf, who resisted the offers for provocative photo spreads even after she became famous as a tennis star. This is not because mothers don't love their daughters, but because men are much more successful at protecting their daughters from other men. And when a daughter receives strong masculine validation from a loving and caring father, she is usually not desperate for sexual attention from manipulative and hormonal Neanderthals.

When I go to a Yankees game, I don't leave my daughters at home. I take them along with my older son. True, they often don't know the names of the players or even the score, but they know their father loves them and hates being separated from them. Daughters have a special connection with their fathers that even a mother cannot replicate, which grants young women a startling immunity from compromising themselves with jerks later in life.

When a daughter is close to her father and respects him as a man and a dad, she begins to judge other men by that same high standard. When she dates men, she will not judge them by their smooth talk but by the depth of their commitment because her own father was not a talker but a doer. She will not jump into bed with a man just to please him. She has high self-esteem, and she expects the men in her life to make an effort to please her rather than the reverse. Her idea of a relationship is not going down to the guy's level, but raising him up to hers.

This is why it is so important for a father to remain the most important man in his daughter's life until she is at least twenty. I always lament witnessing the deterioration of the homes of my friends whose teenage daughters are always out, either with girl-friends or boyfriends. My daughters will not date until they are of marriageable age—in our community this begins at the age of nineteen or twenty. Up until that time, my own love for them will sustain their need for male attention. They will not be forced at too early an age to worry whether they are pretty enough, smart enough, sexy enough, or attractive enough. To their father, they are just perfect. And they will internalize that message in their most vulnerable years so they can grow into confident and robust women who attract men out of strength rather than weakness.

I am thoroughly convinced that the primary blame for the seemingly collective agreement of so many women to become utterly willing to compromise their dignity lies first and foremost with their fathers. By nature, they crave male attention and affection, and when they do not get it from a healthy source, they will settle for an unhealthy one.

A specific case in point is the actress Angelina Jolie, who is talented, beautiful, and articulate. But then why did she marry a notorious womanizer like Billy Bob Thornton who was on his fifth marriage? Could she not foresee the painful and bizarre union she was destined to have, eventually leaving him when she could no longer tolerate his indiscretions? Where was her self-respect? When I heard about this, I could not help but wonder if her perplexing behavior had anything to do with her being publicly estranged from her father Jon Voight. Voight is an acquaintance of mine whom I hosted at Oxford University as a speaker in the early 1990s. I know him to be a committed humanitarian and a man of deep humility and spirituality. But he was not always like that. By his own admission, Jon says that he was once an uninvolved parent. Might that contribute to the reasons why someone as bright and beautiful as Angelina would have chosen to marry a great actor who is anything but a gentleman?

In my counseling experience, I have often worked with women married to significantly older men. Usually, these husbands turn out to be men who had previously been married and divorced. Many of these "May–December" marriages are horrendous. A recurring theme in my counseling with women in this situation was that nearly all of them were not close to their own fathers and ended up looking for father figures as substitutes. The role of a husband, however, is completely different from that of a father. When a woman has a loving father, she receives the confidence in herself to know when it is time to leap, to release her firm grasp on paternal dependence and begin a loving relationship with a man whom she can trust to be her partner. A successful partnership is a vulnerable relationship, because it means granting another person complete access to one's heart, body, and soul. A woman who has been given a solid foundation to trust her judgment and her intrinsic worth will not fear showing and embracing her vulnerability. This foundation is formed by her father showing her that the world can be trusted. If, on the other hand, she feels betrayed by her father, she may often find herself running to men as a bandage for her pain rather than as a means to find love.

As for the criticism that too close a relationship with your daughter will impede her ability to later form close connections with romantic partners, exactly the opposite is true. A young woman with an involved and loving father receives the confidence in herself to sever the umbilical chord from her father and begin a loving relationship with a man *precisely because she has learned to trust men.* She has no fear of being vulnerable, a prerequisite for romantic love (they don't call it "*falling* in love" for nothing), because her father has shown her an example of a man who can be trusted and relied on. But if she feels betrayed by her own father, she will often run to another man more to escape pain than to find love.

SUGGESTION #3:   Renew the father-daughter covenant. Make the father-daughter bond even stronger than the mother-daughter one. Fathers should be the principal men in their daughters' lives until at least the age of nineteen.

34

∞

EDUCATION EDIFICATION—TAKING THE SEX OUT OF SCHOOLING

A significant aid in raising young girls to be both successful ladies, and ladies who are a success, would be to make single-sex education much more widespread. For a host of reasons, I would never, in a million years, contemplate sending my daughters to school with boys. First, the purpose of schooling is to get an education. The social aspect to one's academic career, while important, must always remain subordinate. Having members of the opposite sex share a classroom, not to mention a school yard, raises the social element to a degree at which it truly can conflict with learning. Don't believe me? Well just look at the topics emphasized in adolescent entertainment. In nearly every teen movie, high school students are portrayed as being totally absorbed by the mayhem of their relationships while concerns about their grades or their futures are seen as remote issues—if they are featured at all. I saw this firsthand in my eleven years as rabbi at Oxford. Here, at the world's most prestigious university, more than half the students' time—at a minimum—seemed to be taken up with the vicissitudes of their relationships and dating; and the counseling they sought from me pertained to romantic issues more than any other (which is one of the main reasons I began writing books on relationships).

Second, and much more important, why should girls, before they have developed the self-confidence of a solidly formed personality, be subjected to the anxiety of wondering how popular they are among the boys? Isn't that a recipe for insecurity? And why rob young girls of that feeling of naturalness, of being able to just be themselves, which is the greatest gift of childhood, by placing them in an environment where they are made to feel self-conscious before their characters have had an opportunity to form?

My purpose as a father is to make my daughters feel that they matter intrinsically. My objective is to make them feel beautiful, loved, worthy, and righteous, and those efforts can be easily subverted the moment they are held up for approval by insensitive, self-obsessed male peers. Likely, teenage boys will compare them with all the other girls around and will choose to lavish attention on those who might stand out, for reasons that could cause a father to cringe.

I am amazed that there still seems to be a debate as to whether coed education is better than single-sex education. Anyone who went to coed schools will remember feeling profoundly self-conscious, and often anxious, around members of the opposite sex. If I was having trouble understanding something in junior high school and wanted to ask my teacher a question, I felt uncomfortable because I feared that my question might be dumb and that would make me look bad in front of the girls. Often, as a result, I simply did not ask.

The whole popularity game was something that I hated as well. Through my thirteenth year, I attended a coed Jewish day school. I vividly remember being more interested in deciding how I would dress the following day than in doing my homework. The presence of the girls was inescapable and made all of us boys that much more self-aware, in an unhealthy rather than a healthy way. We were concerned about the image we projected rather than the people we were beneath the external layers. Not until the age of fourteen, when I dumped all that nonsense to go to an all-boys' yeshiva and begin my rabbinical training, did I discover the liberation that comes from being immersed in an environment that is devoted solely to study. Some argue that single-sex education impedes a child's later ability to get along with the opposite sex, but that is ridiculous. Sexual attraction is innate and does fine if allowed to unfold gradually rather than being forced. If anything, the very opposite is true. Too early an exposure to the opposite sex can easily cause a girl to feel profoundly insecure about her value and rank in the boys' estimation. At any rate, the insanely high divorce rate that has come about since coeducation became the norm, and the ensuing sexual revolution would seem to prove that, if anything, men and women cannot sustain a lifelong commitment, now that they are overexposed to one another from the earliest possible age.

Attending single-sex schools, in which boys do not have instant access to girls, has sound benefits for the boys as well. It teaches them not to take girls for granted. After this educational experience, instead of being bored by all but the prettiest girls in the class, who usually garner all of the male attention, they are enamored by womankind instead of just a particular *kind* of woman. Women in general hold a mysterious attraction for them.

But even if parents are going to disagree with me on the issue of single-sex education, I hope they will agree that girls should not be dating until they have a strong foundation for their character and a solid sense of self. The modern-day insistence on propelling boys and girls into relationships at an early age has effectively eliminated the period of childhood innocence—a time during which these distinctly sexual pairings of males and females should never enter into young consciousness. The penchant for formal dances and the attending coupling off for dates propels young girls into adolescent mind-sets long before they need to be grappling with these issues. Is there really something wrong with being a kid? Are we shortsighted enough to condone our children's natural desires to grow up well before their time? Isn't it our job as parents to keep them as kids and let them develop naturally and organically, rather than allowing them to skip critical stages in their development so that they become like rickety buildings without a solid foundation? I believe that any kind of formal dating should be postponed until at least eighteen, with the most serious forms of relationships reserved until the age of nineteen and on. At that age, it can be hoped that a young woman will have been nurtured and strengthened by a healthy relationship with her father, and is strong and grounded enough to allow other men to enter her life.

SUGGESTION #4: Go back to single-sex education, where women can develop a strong identity that is impervious to popularity with the boys.

35

∞

A MORE MYSTERIOUS SOCIETY

What I am arguing for, above all else, is a softer, subtler society that embraces the influence of femininity—rather than one that corrupts and neutralizes it. To be sure, there are some strong feminine currents in society even now. While the male energy is focused on the tangible, material world and solid, obvious objectives, the female energy is often pointed inward and upward. It embraces a sense of purposefulness, of the inner person and his and her place in the larger scheme of the universe. The penchant these days for therapists and self-help books is very much in line with such thinking as scores of individuals try to uncover their dormant, inner potential. This exploration includes not only a journey into one's psyche but also into one's spiritual essence. More and more people seem to want to reclaim a sense of transcendence, to give their lives greater meaning. The trend of New Age and Eastern religions that is slowly creeping into mainstream Western thought is indicative of a more feminine, contemplative, and meditative society: a world where the coarseness of aggressive action is better balanced by reflection and introspection.

Compared with the tidal wave of negative images and attitudes that hits us through popular culture, the increased awareness of Eastern philosophy is still coming in at a trickle. But there are other hints of feminine influences as well, such as the public clamoring for a more civil political discourse. Other feminine streams include the increasing presumption that husbands should take on greater domestic responsibility, and be more involved with child-rearing and the home. There are also growing expectations that sporting heroes and celebrities should take an active part in charities, and that those who are recognizable to the public should serve as nurturing role models to kids.

But while all these feminine trends should be applauded, they have little value if we corrupt our women. A renewed reverence for women among men is essential if we are to cultivate a kinder and gentler world. The female energy is much more mystical and spiritual than the male energy, and therefore, it is in a woman's nature to be more innately pious and nurturing. The spirituality of society is fundamentally dependent on learning to respect women.

We're not doing this yet. Even in many religious and traditionally minded homes, religious training for boys is prioritized over training for girls, a terrible error with serious consequences. This has got to change. In many orthodox Jewish homes, the father takes his sons to synagogue while his daughters stay at home. This is especially true of synagogue on Friday and Saturday nights, as opposed to Saturday morning where for the most part the girls attend. But I never go to synagogue without taking my girls, and my daughters receive the same rigorous religious training as my sons. My daughters are different from my sons. But for me, the words "different but equal" are a credo that I live by. I will never treat my daughters as if they are any less than my sons, and religious communities need to begin to live by this idea. This does not mean that I believe that women have to become priests in Catholicism, rabbis in Judaism, or imams in Islam. I fully recognize that many religions—orthodox Judaism included—do not accord women the public ritualistic functions of men, the rationale for which I addressed at length in my book *Judaism for Everyone* (Basic Books). But even if a woman cannot be the rabbi of a synagogue, she can surely be its president; she can give learned lectures on the Torah, as well as occupy a position of lay leadership and scholarship in the Catholic or Islamic communities without contravening the ritual laws of those religions.

SUGGESTION #5:   Parents should place special emphasis on offering their daughters religious training or some significant spiritual component in their upbringing. All too often, religious training, especially in traditional households, is emphasized for boys and is not seen as of vital importance for girls.

36

~

CAN MEN RESPECT WOMEN IN THE OFFICE IF THEY ARE CONDITIONED TO BE PERVERTS OUTSIDE IT?

The greatest push must also be made to begin portraying women in a dignified and refined light in our culture, whether it be on television, in films, or in magazines. If we don't do so, it may soon be impossible for men and women even to work together without one group accusing the other of harassment. In a culture that sexualizes women constantly, the line between watercooler chat and harassment is increasingly thin.

In late 2004, Bill O'Reilly, the popular television and radio talk show host, was sued for sexual harassment by his former producer, Andrea Mackriss. She alleged that on many occasions, both in person and over the phone, O'Reilly engaged in lewd conversation against her will. Many believed that Mackriss was simply out to get O'Reilly and the Fox News Channel, and indeed her lawsuit seemed to gratuitously mention Fox chief Roger Ailes. In my own interactions with O'Reilly, he has always been the consummate gentleman, considerate and gracious, and I was therefore saddened to see him viciously and perhaps unfairly attacked. But whatever the truth of the allegation, which was quietly settled out of court, the story brought to the fore much of what is wrong with our increasingly perverse culture. The question that the growing phenomenon of sexual harassment in the workplace raises is this: Can we really expect to have a healthy office environment, where men treat women as colleagues and intellectual equals, when everywhere else in the culture women are being completely sexualized? Is it realistic to ask men to separate what they see on TV and in magazines from their interactions with women in the boardroom? When men are being deluged in virtually every electronic medium with the message that women want to be recognized for their bodies rather than their brains, is it reasonable to expect that men will suddenly think differently the moment a woman dons a business suit?

Never in history have women been as sexually exploited as they are today. College girls expose their breasts in exchange for a T-shirt on the *Girls Gone Wild* videos. MTV has transformed the women's music industry away from vocals to an emphasis on cleavage. Posters of Victoria's Secret models dressed in thongs and highly revealing lingerie line our main thoroughfares, billboards, and buses. So are men really expected to shut all this off the moment they stand in front of a copy machine? Can we really expect a pure office environment to emerge from a degenerate culture? And will men willingly submit to such arbitrary demands of compartmentalization?

In an environment where everything from the Internet to sporting events is sexualized, it becomes difficult to determine what exactly constitutes harassment in the workplace. If a man watches *Sex and the City* and, knowing that his female colleagues love the show, mentions at the watercooler how much he enjoyed the previous night's episode which, say, featured Samantha giving a stranger oral sex, is it harassment? Or is it small talk?

And let's say a boss comes into the office after watching the Super Bowl and asks his secretary if she saw Janet Jackson's breast pop out during the half-time show. Is he making lewd and inappropriate comments? What if a guy watches *Titanic* on DVD and comments to his female coworkers the next morning about how sexy he thought Kate Winslet was in her nude love scene, is that harassment? And if it is, can we at least recognize that we have made a huge portion of American culture off limits in the workplace, because of how perversely sexualized it has become?

My purpose here is not to let men off the hook for boorish, and possibly illegal, behavior. On the contrary, I wish that all men were gentlemen, behaving in a dignified and refined manner, especially around ladies. And I also wish that it didn't take the threat of legal action to get them to behave as gentlemen. Lewd comments from lecherous men is the last thing that women should have to tolerate.

But let's acknowledge the incredibly mixed, contradictory, and unfair signals that are being given to men. In life outside the office, men's lechery is encouraged in order to persuade them to watch TV or part with their cash. Near-naked twins sell them beer, women in thongs advertise the Miss America pageant, and Britney Spears and Christina Aguilera simulate masturbation in coming attractions for their shows on HBO and Showtime.

After being fed the idea in every corner of culture that women primarily desire sexual attention, are these men supposed to believe that women are going to be insulted, rather than complimented, by uncouth comments about their bodies?

What complicates the question of harassment is that women are being subtly conditioned to use their sexuality to get ahead in the office. Even the marketing genius Donald Trump advised women on *The Apprentice* to play up their sexuality to gain a competitive advantage over men. And many women fall for this degrading advice, coming to the office dressed like streetwalkers. Dress codes today are considered outmoded and draconian, and fashion dictates that many women wear blouses cut very low and skirts cut very high. Yet men are expected not to notice. A woman's breasts can be spilling out of her blouse at a board meeting, and men are expected to see her intelligence.

On my radio show, one man called in to say that a woman who works right across from his cubicle wears see-through blouses nearly every day. "She's essentially wearing only a bra in the office, and I often have to put my hand in front of my face to block her out to stop myself from staring."

I am not blaming the victims or insinuating that women are inviting harassment. Far from it. No matter what men are exposed to and no matter how women dress, men must be in control of themselves and treat women as dignified and intellectual equals. I have never, and will never, excuse boorish behavior. But that does not change the fact that sexual harassment in the workplace is being vastly increased by a culture that fosters the idea that women are primarily sexual objects and that puts too little emphasis on men and women dressing modestly and professionally.

And you can be sure that until the sexual exploitation of women is reversed, and women reclaim their dignity by refusing to be portrayed on television and on the Internet as a lecherous man's playthings, the number of women who have to suffer male crudity is only going to increase.

SUGGESTION #6: Sexual innuendo must be totally banned from the office, and modest dress codes should be reinstated in the American workplace. A woman deserves to feel like a cherished equal at the office. But just as men are obligated to treat women with respect, women, too, should show men that they desire respect by dressing respectfully and behaving professionally.

37

∽

YOUNG GIRLS SHOULD HAVE
HEALTHIER OUTLETS THAN SHOPPING

From their earliest age, women should be encouraged to embrace their innately transcendent nature instead of being offered an heirloom of impulse purchases and material indulgence. Thus women should be steered away from the shallow consumer culture of acquisition and status seeking. I feel a special responsibility to encourage my daughters to avoid the shopping culture that seems rampant among today's teens. I give them a religious education and religious values. I take them to the great historical places and museums of the United States. I engage them in conversations about the deeper things in life. I try to inspire them to read a lot of books, form an opinion on current events, and develop an appreciation for the wonders of nature and the beautiful outdoors.

Once, when we were at the National Museum of American History in Washington, D.C., I wanted to go to the exhibit entitled "Freedom's Sacrifices," which was about the history of American military efforts and the men and women who have given their lives to safeguard liberty throughout our history. The girls asked if they could go to the exhibition on First Ladies' Inaugural Gowns. That just said to me that I had to make the far more important exhibit about soldiers' sacrifices for their country more interesting to them. I mean, gowns are nice, but the feminist dream was that women would contribute to society in ways other than fashion, right? So, rather than just take them through the exhibit about military sacrifice, I tried to explain every important exhibit, often with personal anecdotes and insights. I understood that it was incumbent upon me, rather than the museum, to interest my daughters in something higher. I didn't mind that they also went to the Gowns exhibition. But ultimately, it is a parent's responsibility to raise his or her daughter's interests to something more than clothes, even when the clothes are historical.

I completely understand that men and women might naturally have different interests and pursuits. But what I reject is the belief that a woman's interests are naturally more shallow than a man's. It is a parent's job to elevate a daughter's interests. And women need to hear constantly that they are the intellectual equals of men, capable of doing everything a man can do. When Larry Summers, the otherwise brilliant president of Harvard, created a stir in January 2005 by insinuating that gender difference might account for the smaller number of women in the sciences and mathematics, I thought his words, for which he apologized (and ought to be forgiven) were terribly misguided. Women have to hear the exact opposite: anything men can do in the intellectual realm, they can do just as well or better.

Parents must begin weaning their daughters away from a shopping mall culture by offering engaging activities that channel their girls toward productive and purposeful goals. A young woman's potential dare not be snuffed out in the suffocating confines of a shopping mall. Young women must be taught to thrill to something other than the impulse purchase. It is fine to be a tough disciplinarian, but recognize that imposing restrictions without offering engaging alternatives is unjust as well as ineffective.

I believe that friendships are important for children, but I am adamant that too great an emphasis on friends is ultimately detrimental to a daughter's connection with siblings and parents. I have witnessed far too many examples of a girl's frenzied attachment to friends leading to a decentralized and dysfunctional family. I always feel for parents when they tell me that they barely see their teenage daughters because they are always out with their friends, and I wonder why they allow it. More important, why did they allow such a stagnant atmosphere to develop in the home, leading their daughters to always want to be out? Parents have got to make the good things exciting, so that their daughters don't have to turn to bad things to escape boredom.

For all its benefits, friendships open daughters to values and behavior that may be inimical to a parent's standards. But I recognize that I cannot curb my daughters' dependence on friendship without offering them a better alternative. I can only restrict them from hanging out with friends if I think that hanging out with me is going to be more exciting.

Being no expert in the cultural arts, I have not bequeathed to my daughters a legacy of music or dance. Less so have I imparted to them an appreciation for classical opera or ballet. Aside from the most obvious virtue—a love for God and godly action—I *have* sought to hand down an appreciation for three virtues that, if absorbed, would ensure that they would not have to turn to shopping or talking about clothes to entertain themselves: The first is a love for reading. The second is a love for history. And the third is a love for nature and the great outdoors.

I have taught my daughters that anything humans can make, God can make more beautifully. Neither Rome with the marvels of the Pantheon nor Athens with the grandeur of the Parthenon can equal the sheer awe-inspiring beauty of Niagara Falls or the Grand Tetons. A shopping mall seems dull when compared with colorful fall foliage.

We are a camping family with an RV and tents, and we try to go on most summer weekends to campgrounds. We take pride in being a Jewish redneck family, more comfortable in a trailer camp than in Manhattan with its ritzy Fifth Avenue shops. On Sundays, I try to take my kids hiking, swimming, or bike riding, and in the winters, skiing at a local New Jersey mountain.

Once upon a time, kids were filled with energy. Today, they seem lifeless and listless. Go to any home and look closely at the teenage kids when their parents introduce you. You'll see that what they most want to do is be left alone, to head back to their rooms so that they can watch TV, get online, or listen to music. And they all seem so depressed. According to Columbia University, 500,000 American teenagers attempt suicide every year, with the fastest-growing age group for attempted/completed suicide being ten- to fourteen-year-olds (American Association of Suicidology).

Our children are divorced from nature, the source of life. They are surrounded by artifice, and it is sucking the joy out of them. Almost everything about growing up these days, from video games to iPods, to hanging out at the malls, to fast food is artificial and unnatural. Kids today have lost an appreciation for the serenity of a clear blue lake and the power of a flowing, whitewater river. They would rather go to a film than a mountain range, would rather be in a mosh pit than on a boat in an august sea.

The American idea of the great outdoors has been reduced to a manicured lawn and a gas-fired barbecue. The great French philosopher Jean-Jacques Rousseau argued convincingly that man is corrupted when he is separated from nature. Cement and concrete harden hearts. But tall grass and flowing water dissolve pretense and bring out authenticity. This is especially true of girls and women, with their natural connection to *Mother* Nature.

Better to take your daughters hiking, to a museum, or to a bookstore on Sundays than to clothing stores. Even without you, they will discover the clothing stores soon enough. When my daughters *need* clothes, my wife takes them to get what they need. But shopping is treated as a necessity rather than as a form of entertainment. I consider shopping one of life's most wasteful activities, and I'm trying to get my daughters to hate it as much as I do. Okay, perhaps hate is too strong a word. But I want them to treat it as a necessity rather than a pleasure. Walking around some silly store and seeing the latest fashions would be a colossal waste of our family's time, and would send a message of complicit approval that I do not wish to give them. They know that their spiritual lives are much more valid and fulfilling then their material lives. Every Friday and Saturday we go to synagogue together, and several times a week, I study some books of the Bible with them at home.

I know that encouraging my girls to develop and flourish in their spiritual lives will help them stay in touch with their essential selves and allow them to remain centered from an early age.

In certain Jewish communities, every month, in celebration of the new moon (with its cyclical connection to women) female study groups meet for a social and educational gathering that focuses on perpetuating constant spiritual growth. These events encourage an appreciation for the feminine energy, and they are both empowering and enriching. Implementing practices such as this will foster women who have a deeper sense of their intrinsic spirituality, and that is something both men and women need to encourage. For the spirituality of our women is not limited to them alone—the very health of our society depends on it.

SUGGESTION #7: Girls and women should be weaned off a materialistic culture of shopping, fashion, and beauty and inspired to internalize more wholesome and rewarding pursuits.

38

∽

MARRIAGE IS NOT "SEX ON TAP"
OR LEGALIZED PROSTITUTION

A new vision of marriage must also be created. The negative stereotypes of marriage as either legalized prostitution or a "ball and chain" must be countered aggressively. How I wish that prominent personalities and popular celebrities would speak out in favor of marriage. I guess one of the reasons is how few have managed to stay married. But there are some noteworthies who have long, stable relationships and genuinely seem to enjoy their married existence. Some of them include Billy Crystal, Tom Hanks, Steven Spielberg, and, of course, Paul Newman. They should speak up and be a beacon to others.

On an individual basis, wives must hold their husbands to high standards at all times. A man has to know that his wife is his partner, and therefore he must live up to her expectations. A husband who does not help out at home is being disrespectful, and a man who does not pay attention to foreplay should not be rewarded with sex. In the Jewish religion, sex is not lawful, even in marriage, until a husband has "seduced" his wife. A husband should at least be required to make some authentic romantic effort.

I would even go so far as to advocate crisis strategies to stave off a fallout. If necessary, withholding sex to reach a more solid union can be a last resort. To be sure, none of this is meant as a war tactic in which sex is a weapon, but rather it is a means to elevate man and woman into a mutually fulfilling and bonding relationship. Far from being a weapon to hurt or blackmail someone, sex is the ultimate intimate cohesion. Given the weightiness of its impact, sex dare not be diluted so that it fails to bring a husband and wife closer together or, more frighteningly, so that it further alienates a wife from her husband.

SUGGESTION #8:   The sacredness of marriage must be restored, with husbands being encouraged to learn how to please, pleasure, and protect a lady. Husbands should receive sex from their wives when they have earned it with affection and foreplay. Husbands should never allow their wives to become, or feel like, their cleaners.

Throw Your Husband's Porn Collection in the Trash Can

In addition to demanding romantic efforts from their husbands, wives need to insist on being the recipient of all of their husbands' sexual energy. This means that they ought to object vehemently when their husbands look at porn. I know it is out of fashion, but wives *should* police their husbands. I cannot tell you how many wives have told me in counseling sessions that they have no problem with their husbands looking at pornography. Many even bought their husbands a subscription to *Playboy* as a birthday gift. And let's not forget about my friend whose fiancée had no *serious* objection about him bringing his huge collection of porn DVDs into their new home. These women are nuts. Aside from what should be the obvious insult of their husbands not finding them sufficiently erotic and needing to look at strangers to get excited, do these women know just how destructive pornography is to a relationship? Do they realize how men who consume huge amounts of porn come to objectify women, compare them, and hone in on their imperfections? Do they know that pornography leads men to fantasize about other women while making love to their wives? Do they know that porn makes men think that the strangers they are drooling over on the Internet or in girlie magazines are genetic "stars," while they consider their own wives to be "ordinary?"

Wives must become watchdogs, policing their husbands and shielding their marriages from the dangerous effects of pornography and adultery. Hillary Clinton suffered enough through her husband's public infidelity. But without blaming the victim, a legitimate question is whether she should have been keeping a far more watchful eye on a husband whom she knew to have a roving eye, especially when she says in her autobiography that he told her that he was growing close to an intern, but only for the purpose of guiding her life.

The idea of policing your husband, of calling him to account for his, shall we say, less than gentlemanly behavior, might feel antiquated or petty, but it is valid, in fact, critical. When I have asked wives how they feel about their husbands looking at pornographic material, I have heard the gamut of answers. There are those who are overzealous in asserting how "cool" they are with it and even claim to join in the viewing. And there are those who are utterly horrified but feel it is not their place to object. Wake up ladies, you have a right to put your foot down and if you don't think you need to, you have even greater problems with your relationship than you know.

Many wives may not realize this, but an act of infidelity, when it occurs, is not what ultimately kills a relationship. Infidelity is the most overt sign that a marriage is languishing, but the cause of its illness is starvation from a lack of attention and effort. The hurtfulness that a husband causes his wife by being unfaithful is not, in itself, the deal breaker in their marriage. The wives whom I have counseled through a husband's infidelity are prepared to forgive him if they love him. The real deal breaker is that he has lost focus. His wife is no longer the focal point of his sexual and romantic energies. A marriage is like a stomach. It needs to be fed regularly. And when you give the food away to someone else, the marriage experiences the pangs of hunger. When husbands and wives are not wholly focused on one another as the means of finding erotic excitement, they begin to drift apart. This is where policing becomes essential because, initially, men believe that a little peek at another woman's nudity is a harmless means of generating excitement and certainly not as significant as an actual act of infidelity. But I warn you, these "harmless" leers are the first symptoms of neglect.

Let me explain just why pornography is so nefarious. Far from being a healthy outlet for raging hormones, pornography is a cancerous proclivity that slowly undermines healthy relationships. On a basic level, excessive viewing exposure to nude, female bodies contributes to the penchant of men to think about other women while making love to their wives. In fact, 84 percent of men admit to doing just that (and they're dumb enough to believe that their wives don't notice). We can even go so far as to say that once you bring another woman into your bed, even if only mentally, you are practicing a form of mental decapitation and merely using your wife's body for friction, replacing her head, her essence, with the images of another woman. The Torah, which is very concerned with fostering the mental and emotional intimacy that physical intimacy is meant to promote, actually calls men to task by deeming it a prohibition to fantasize about other women while being with one's wife. So the husbands have to learn that they can't be making love to their wives in bed, while in their heads doing a guest appearance on Desperate Housewives.

Women today are so cow-towed into being manly and tough that few will admit to being pained that their significant other dreams of another woman during their intimate moments. But replacing one's wife with "Miss February" is a degrading act. It indicates that one's wife is not worthy enough, or thrilling enough on her own. Most men tell me that it is unrealistic to expect husbands not to sometimes think about other women during sex with their wife. Perhaps that is so. But that is no excuse not to resist it.

Pornography, even the now-mundane and tame nudity seen in R-rated films, is impairing our ability to be satisfied with our spouse. This is one of the basic problems with explicit material.

When men are constantly barraged with airbrushed images of the perfect female body, it is impossible for them to remain naive and spellbound by the female form.

It is certainly safe to say that by the time a boy in the United States hits the age of fourteen, he probably thinks he knows exactly what a naked woman should look like—the emphasis being on the word *should*. Magazines and movies have long touted the svelte, busty combination of the supermodel. But what pornography does is take us even further away from an ability to appreciate women. Once the clothing is removed, there is no mystery left and husbands are well trained at what they think they should be seeing during an intimate moment with their wives. Speak to any photographer and you will hear that even the perfect bodies that are trotted out for viewing pleasure on the pages of *Playboy* rarely look like that in real life. But we have become so accustomed to this image of airbrushed perfection that our expert eyes are impossible to satisfy.

When a man sees his wife naked, the trained eye that he has cultivated will be immediately drawn to her flaws rather than her beauty. Not only does this degrade his wife, but it also hinders his ability to find satisfaction. With a single standard of beauty, it is nearly impossible to be content with the varied body types that exist in the real world. Unable to find true contentment with their partners, many men look elsewhere. Moreover, men who are used to looking at pornography are rarely contented with a single image of perfection. Notice how a playmate is never repeated in multiple issues. Even "Miss June's" seemingly flawless form is not good enough to win her the "Miss July" or "Miss August" spot. Once she has been seen and digested, she is no longer captivating enough to be seen again.

The bottom line is that pornography desensitizes men. Instead of being automatically drawn to a woman as he should be, today's man is too much of a connoisseur to ever lose himself completely. Erotic attraction, which should bring men and women together, has been compromised and neither is above evaluating the other according to the most stringent of scales. More than simply providing the measure by which all *real* women are judged, pornography hinders a man's attachment to a single woman because it impairs his ability to build deep relationships. Sexual intimacy is meant to bring a couple together on emotional and mental levels. Once a man feels removed enough to judge his wife by external comparisons, he loses some of his excitement for her, and mistakenly believes that a more perfectly formed woman would provide him with the physical titillation he craves.

Becoming Addicted to Porn

In reality, pornography is intensely boring. It is boring precisely because viewing is a one-dimensional experience. There is no mutual interaction between the viewer and the viewed and, therefore, excitement has to be generated constantly with an ever-changing visual image. It becomes an addiction, in which the viewer needs more and more stimulation to achieve the same level of excitement that he once experienced. This effect is perfectly illustrated by studies showing the range of pornographic viewing on the Internet. While most men will start looking at adult websites for an average of fifteen minutes, within months they are online for hours. At the beginning, like a drug, it only takes a short "hit" to achieve the desired effect, but with time, these quick glances are no longer enough. Again, like a drug, the dosage has to be increased. The irony is that a real woman is infinitely more exciting than the manufactured images that attract the consumers of pornography. Rather than being a one-dimensional experience, interacting with and allowing oneself to be aroused by a live partner—despite her apparent physical flaws—is ever changing and therefore consistently exciting. Ultimately then, pornography deadens a man's attraction for his partner, which in turn deadens his ability to have healthy and sustained passionate relationships.

And don't be misguided into believing that the answer to this is the "Don Juan syndrome," in which some enviable man manages to become the ultimate womanizer and enjoy a variety of real women. In fact, it is well known that womanizers are second-rate lovers. Even JFK's mistresses admitted that the female-loving president was less than expert in bed. If a man is focused on his wife and making her happy, he is forced to expand his repertoire and develop new and exciting means of pleasing her rather then simply repeating the same tired moves on many different women.

While love can only be shared between two equals, and the act of love is all about sharing, once pornography enters into a relationship, women become subordinate because they have been objectified and commoditized. In the world of pornography, women are portrayed in only three ways, as the mindless playmate, the insatiable nymphomaniac, or as one who craves pain. All are deeply destructive images that erode male respect for women.

As an equal partner, a woman's approval and respect used to imbue a man with a sense of worthiness. Once women lose their equal footing, men find themselves looking for validation in bragging rights by boasting to their friends about their conquests of multiple women. It is understood, of course, that the success of this boasting is measured by the desirability of the women involved, and in this we are again faced with this single image of beauty and perfection that pornography devises. Hugh Hefner wouldn't be nearly as enviable if he were seen flanked by Mrs. Johnson, the cleaning lady. No, no! Hugh is envied because he gets it on with the hourglass-shaped, busty women that men are trained to desire.

The truly unfortunate element in the prevalence of pornography is the acceptance that so many women silently or overtly provide by refusing to demand that their husbands and boyfriends turn off the computer and turn them on instead! Once upon a time, women were seen as and treated as man's superior. They were placed on a pedestal and garnered the natural respect they commanded. Today, women have leaped off their elevated platform to say that they are equal to men. This has been a disaster for both men and women. For women, because they are no longer a prize to be acquired by men who make themselves worthy of them; for men, because the thrill of the chase is gone once women are so easily had.

We cannot deny that a defeminization of women has occurred when we hear about them accompanying their partners to strip clubs. You cannot convince me that a woman actually enjoys watching the array of bras and G-strings while swigging back beers with the boys. Indeed, I remember the sad story of one woman whose husband pushed her to come with him to a strip club. When I asked her in a counseling session how she had felt, she answered tragically, "I felt like a man."

In her efforts to get closer to man, woman has lost her own uniquely female attributes, at a great cost to both genders. What happened to being a gentleman? Why doesn't the party line maintain that a man doesn't look at another woman because he doesn't need to and has too much respect for his wife to ever degrade her by making such a comparison? Why not? Simply put, because women today no longer require their men to be gentlemen.

When I've asked women about policing their husbands, about insisting that they get off the computer or throw out the dirty magazines, the resounding answers I receive fall along two basic lines. The first is that many women believe that they have no right to determine what their husbands do, see, or think. The second is a desire not to appear insecure, petty, or nagging. Let's deal with the second issue first. In essence, when a wife tells me that she doesn't want to show her vulnerability and admit that she is wounded by her husband's fascination with other women's bodies, she is demonstrating a priori the modern masculinization of women. What is wrong with being emotional, or showing your hurt? It is only when women believe that they must be strong and stoic that they hesitate to reveal their softer vulnerability. But ladies, are you not worthy of respect, do you not have a right to demand that your husband be with you and you alone when you are in bed together? This takes us straight into the second excuse about not having a right to monitor one's husband.

What wives tell me is that marriage is supposed to be about trust and respect. Supposedly, respecting your husband's space and trusting that he won't take his mental and visual infidelity further is all that a wife has a right to hope for. How far we have sunk in our expectations of marriage and commitment! Once upon a time, it was not politically incorrect to think of a husband and wife as *belonging* to one another. Today, we are conditioned to think that independence is the be-all and end-all and that no person is possessed or should be possessed by another. The staggering divorce rate is a symptom of this unfortunate conditioning. If you belong to one another, you have a right to make demands, to freely express that an action or behavior hurts you, and to expect that your spouse, whose number one concern is your happiness, will amend the hurtful behavior. We are very protective of what is ours and when two people belong to one another, there is nothing they won't do to protect that bond.

Too many of us have bought into the notion that marriage is about the coming together of separate, independent beings who will preserve that separateness and individuality throughout the marriage. If a husband and wife are these independent parties, then it is problematic to make demands. You might say, "I prefer that you don't look at pornography but I cannot dictate what you can and cannot do." In Judaism, we are taught that everything belongs to God. It is not degrading to be so possessed and, in fact, the kippah worn by men is a reminder and a symbol of that bond and belonging. We are taught that our money, our children, our possessions—our very being—all belong to God, and to think otherwise is sheer human arrogance. God even says in the Bible that He is a jealous God, because He wishes to be loved by humanity. Thus God makes demands of us and we, in our attachment to him, ask for what we need. It is a reciprocal relationship. It is only when we feel unworthy that we hesitate to insist that our needs be met, and a husband and wife should never be made to feel unworthy in this manner. Remember, you are not only married in body, but in mind, heart, and soul.

So get your whistle out, Mrs. Jones; stake your claim, Mrs. Black. Tell your husband that he needs to be a real man—help him be the man worthy of you, not "Miss May" and her playmates. It is time that wives start asserting their self-respect. They need to make it abundantly clear to their husbands that they are not willing to stand for this regressive and adolescent behavior. Many women who fashion themselves to be modern, progressive wives believe that they are merely changing with the times by allowing their husbands to persist in degrading and dismissive behavior. In reality, the psychological effects of this conduct wear away at their personal esteem. Ultimately, many women build up a stockpile of unreleased resentment until it reaches a boiling point. As mentioned, 74 percent of all divorces are initiated by wives—a number that would no doubt be lower if the women refused to permit behavior that was destructive to their self-esteem or the marriage, and objected to it well before the marriage is in crisis.

SUGGESTION #9: No woman should ever tolerate her husband or boyfriend's use of pornography. Period.

39

∾

YOUNGER WOMEN SHOULD
REFRAIN FROM DATING
MUCH OLDER MEN

Not long ago, I gave a lecture in Boca Raton, Florida, to a group
of singles over forty. It was advertised to both men and women,
but as so often happens with singles events for this age-group, the
vast majority of those who turned up were women, and the majority were age fifty or over. Most of them bemoaned that they were
alone and vehemently lamented the lack of unmarried, eligible
men today. The common refrain was that no worthy men were to
be found. I told them that that did not surprise me in the least. For
starters, a lot of the single men their age were conditioned to pursue much younger women. "What can we do about it?" they asked.
"How can we get men to act their age and be mature?" I told them
that this overhaul of the male population could only occur if all
women were to act in unison.

   Imagine if society shunned men who insist on only dating
much younger women, the way it shuns (or at least used to shun)
men who are adulterers. The eventual result would be that those
same men would come to take pride in dating women in their own
age group. The problem is that our society does nothing of the
sort. Instead, we pat the old guy on the back and consider him a

"stud" for robbing the cradle. If women started to function as a proud, harmonious group, younger women, feeling an affinity with older women, might conclude that by dating older men, they were robbing the older members of their society of potential husbands. They would understand that they are consigning so many fine, more mature, women to a life of loneliness. With a cultivated empathy, they might recoil from such behavior and look to connect with their own age group. Not only would this offer more options to older women, but it would, in general, allow more authentic love to develop between peers. By doing so we deal a blow to the runaway culture of deifying youth over experience. But again, this cannot happen in isolation. Women have to band together, and that means creating a sisterhood through which they look out for one another's best interests.

SUGGESTION #10:   Younger women should show solidarity with older women, who are unfairly treated as unattractive, by not dating men who are, at most, more than fifteen years their senior.

40

WOMEN SHOULD FROWN ON
SHALLOW EXHIBITIONISTS—
NOT DEFEND THEM

Once when I was visiting my family in Miami Beach, we saw a
topless girl on the beach who could not have been more than sixteen years old. My brothers and sisters and I were amazed. It starts
that young? A girl that young felt she had to bare her body to get
noticed? Don't you think it would be constructive if society became more judgmental about this kind of exhibitionism and other
women gave that girl a disapproving look until she covered up? A
young girl who behaves like that should be made to reconsider her
choices in a different light. But let's back up a step. Instead of
merely treating the symptom—her trashy dressing (or lack
thereof) as a teenager—let's cure the disease. From birth, this girl
should have been brought up with the ethos that such actions
harm the entire sisterhood to which she belongs.

This has to start with the role models presented for mass
consumption. What should happen is this: Every time an actress
agrees to appear nude in a male entertainment magazine, or
seminude in one of the lad magazines, female leaders should call
for an embargo of the performer's movies, TV shows, CDs, and
other professional outlets. The statement should be, "You have

just undermined other women who want to get a recording contract for their talent rather than their body. You're making it impossible for a woman to get a role in a movie on the basis of her skill rather than her décolletage. You've pulled us all down, and we refuse to support those who pull us down."

Martin Luther King Jr. said that individual blacks could not end racism because if even one yielded to the pressures of bigotry, the foundation for change would crumble. The same is true for the feminine revolution. Only a united whole can effect change. A picket line is only successful if no one in the union crosses it. It works through collective bargaining. We need a generation of women who collectively reclaim their dignity. Any program to end misogyny must call on every woman to subscribe to the higher ideal, to look into their own depth and reclaim their elevated feminine energy.

This hold on dignity is severely lacking, as demonstrated on a recent episode of the *Oprah Winfrey Show* featuring the cast of the Julia Roberts' movie *Mona Lisa Smile*. The film is about the early days of the second wave of feminism as it affected a group of Wellesley College women. The audience was made up of vocal, spirited women regaling one another with issues about female pride and power. During the question-and-answer segment, one audience member rose to voice her concern about the lack of sisterhood among today's women. As she put it, there is a fractured line between women, some of whom want to be smart and dignified, and others who hanker to appear in *Girls Gone Wild*. When I heard her insightful, eloquent comment, initially I was overjoyed. Finally, I cheered, someone was saying the obvious.

To my chagrin, however, no one in the studio audience agreed with her. Indeed, one outspoken woman seated a few rows below the speaker proclaimed that, by making this statement, the woman was assuming that the *Girls Gone Wild* participants were not smart. In fact, continued the second woman, feminism allows women to do what they want, to make any choice that they want, and that includes the right to thrust their bare breasts out at a bunch of slovenly men. To my horror, the majority of the audience concurred. Not one other person pointed out that intelligence was not the crux of the issue here. It was not a matter of whether these breast bearers were mental midgets or giants but rather that their behavior was crass and immodest. While we cherish and even lay down our lives to preserve our freedoms, should there not be some standard for decency and accountability? And rather than argue about the standard, can we not simply agree that an unacceptable standard is any time a woman allows herself to be portrayed nude to stimulate, excite, or titillate men, especially for a commercial purpose? Moreover, is there no sense that perverse, degrading actions harm not only those who are subjected to it, but also those who perpetrate such behavior?

Women have fallen prey so completely to the icon of womanhood that has been concocted in the popular culture that they are hardly cognizant of how manipulated they have been. With a thoroughly misguided sense of pride in the *right* to indulge in degrading behavior, women are forgetting the importance of dignity. As long as there is no standard of behavior and catering to the basest of instincts is somehow a statement of empowerment, there will never be progress. The rift between women who hold to standards and those who yield to the lascivious desires of the crotch-scratcher continues to grow. And as long as there are women willing to put up with it, more and more men will join the ranks of the Neanderthals, and more women will feel deeply dissatisfied.

The truly proud ladies who are unwilling to compromise and require men to be gentlemen cannot compete with crasser, less noble women. The only elixir for this maddening spiral is to educate all women, instilling within them the urgent message that they can, and should, demand more. They must become sisters and join the revolution.

Boycott Brain and Behavior Rot

To succeed, women must collectively shut out those among them who embrace the stereotype of the brainless bimbo. This kind of persona must be attacked vigorously until no self-respecting woman can imagine playing that part. Women should be encouraging one another, above all else, to develop their minds even more than their bodies. In that vein, they should boycott pop culture offerings like *Joe Millionaire, The Swan,* and myriad similar reality television shows that promote harmful mores and dangerous stereotypes.

Women need to organize to oppose the misogyny in our present culture. Just as the NAACP organizes boycotts against companies that discriminate against African Americans, outstanding female leaders must lead groups in opposition to television networks and recording labels that move product by exploiting women. For that to happen, new female leaders must emerge who are gutsy, principled, and, most of all, have well-chosen priorities. Even without such leadership, individual women should decide that they are not going to buy clothes from misogynistic offenders like Abercrombie & Fitch or watch TV shows that degrade women. Let's do away with trivial protests over women not being allowed into elite country clubs or other old boy networks. Who cares! Let's not stand by and idly play the fiddle while Rome is burning. Let the guys play golf by themselves. This is not really a bad thing, as long as they come home as refined gentleman who know how to be committed husbands, and as long as they date women honorably instead of putting all their energies into simply getting women into bed.

We are desperate for a new generation of feminist leaders who will organize huge rallies outside the television networks that seem to be competing to find new ways of degrading women. If millions of women voiced a protest and declared that they were removing the garbage spewed by the major television networks from their homes, there would be a change overnight. And when this goal is achieved, the next rung must be climbed. Government must be lobbied, indictments must be issued, and our culture must be held accountable for the hate crimes it incites. Websites that even remotely incite sexual violence against women must be prosecuted according to the full letter of the law.

Pornography, nudity, women being portrayed as stupid, greedy, and only interested in money—this incendiary material has become the fiber of modern popular culture. It is time for women to put on their fighting gloves and demand full-scale change. Where are the female Martin Luther Kings? Where are the female Gandhis? The Elie Wiesels in female form who thunder against the injustice? Why have so many feminist leaders and politicians been so utterly silent?

SUGGESTION #11: Women should organize to collectively boycott organizations that exploit women sexually and portray them in a degrading light. From pornography, to the beauty pageants, to the misogynistic reality TV shows, to the soft-porn female recording industry, to the TV dramas that depict women as pure sleaze, companies that degrade and exploit women should be subject to a powerful economic boycott by women who represent an incredibly powerful market. And legislation must be passed to label as incendiary hate mail all spam e-mail that refers to women as "bitches" and "sluts."

It All Depends on *You!*

Rather than lament the deafening silence, I prefer to encourage you, yes *you*, to fill the void. If you are a woman, choose today to be the authentic feminine voice that once brought the world so much redemption. If you are a man, be careful not to tread on sacred ground. Treat women with respect. Look at women as an end, rather than a means. Raise your daughters to be ladies. Make your wife feel like a queen. Date your girlfriend in a way that says to her, "I want to know you, rather than ever use you."

Together, men and women working can usher in a golden age of feminine awe and magic. Together, we can create a softer, gentler, and brighter world illuminated with the light and warmth of the nurturer.

ACKNOWLEDGMENTS

∽

For almost five years, I have wanted to write a book about the shockingly negative portrayal of women in Western culture. Indeed, I have devoted many columns to the subject. But this project was given greater impetus through my conversations with my friend and publisher, Judith Regan, who has passionately shared my viewpoint of widespread cultural misogyny and the negative portrayal of women as sleazy, slutty, and stupid everywhere we look. This book is meant to combat that deplorable state of affairs, and I want to thank Judith for her constant encouragement throughout its development. Judith is a strong woman, and many argue that it is her toughness that has propelled her to the top of American publishing. I disagree. I know that underneath that formidable exterior, which many successful women develop as a means of competing in a man's world, is an unbelievably warm feminine softness that has so endeared her to authors like me, who look to her as a warm and caring friend. This is my third book for Judith, and I look forward, God willing, to many more.

This book is dedicated to my five daughters and they are the real impetus behind its ideas. I love my two beautiful sons as much as my daughters, of course. But for a father, there is nothing like a daddy's girl. I have written this book so that my daughters, whom I as a father must always protect, will grow into a world that appreciates their minds and nurturing spirit much more than their packaging. If I cannot help create the kind of environment that respects them as women, then I have failed them as a father.

My foremost model of feminine refinement and grace is always my wife Debbie. Living with her has taught me about the superiority of the feminine to the masculine, something I extol throughout the book. Sharing life with my wife is an eternally humbling experience.

My mother is the courageous lioness who raised me and my four siblings practically by herself. A woman of incomparable heart, my mother exemplifies the unbridled compassion that is unique to womankind. She is my hero.

My Rebbe and teacher, Rabbi Menachem M. Schneerson, passed away more than ten years ago. But I feel that he is with me always. He was the trusted shepherd of Israel—a maternal, nuturing light, who facilitated development of the potential of millions, myself included.

Most of all, I would like to thank God Almighty, for giving the world that feminine, nurturing spirit in the form of woman, who brings to the world elegance and poise, wisdom and softness, gentility and warmth. I hope that this book will deal a mighty blow to the corruption of that lofty ideal.

Shmuley Boteach
Englewood, New Jersey
Spring 2005

INDEX

∾

ABC, 8–9, 101, 115, 118, 175, 201–2
Abercrombie & Fitch, 20–21, 37,
    159–61, 168, 308
Abraham, 45, 58, 253
acquisition and status seeking, culture
    of, 287
Adam and Eve, 53–54, 87–93, 172, 240
adolescence:
    accelerated, 166–67
    dELiA's catalog of pornography for
        teens, 168–70, 267
    friendships versus family, 288–89
    innate modesty in girls, 236
    lingerie, 129–30, 168–70
    plastic surgery, 38
    rape, 6
    sex and sexuality, 6, 257–58, 269–70
    spring break debauchery, 267–68
    suicide attempts, 290
    see also girlhood/young girls
affirmative action, 160
Afghanistan, Miss, 6–7
Afghani Taliban, United States' war
    against (versus war against Iraq),
    139
African Americans:
    American Rhodes Scholar, 112
    concern with appearance, 38, 160
    immorality of slavery, 99
    movies with negative images of, 35
    oldest black radio station in the United
        States, 157
    slave mentality without great black
        leaders, 37
    South, old segregated, 18, 187
    symbolism/stereotypical thinking, 13,
        35, 101
    see also King, Martin Luther, Jr.
Agassi, Andre, 188–89
Agca, Mehmet Ali, 44

age differences:
    father-figure substitutes, May-
        December marriage, 273–74
    younger women refraining from dating
        older men, 303–4
aggression, 67, 224–27
Aguilera, Christina:
    Axis of Evil, Musical, 109, 111
    Britney on, 116
    image/influence, 32, 200
    Madonna and, 113
    nude/semi-nude magazine pictorials,
        123–24
    simulating masturbation, 285
Ailes, Roger, 283
airline flight attendants, 18–20
Alan Guttmacher Institute poll, 270
Alexander the Great, 58, 74
Alley, Kirstie, 164
al-Masawabi, Bashir, 144
American cultural landscape:
    pop stars as soft porn, see Axis of Evil,
        Musical
    reality television, see television shows
    truck-stop metaphor, 55–59
American Idol, 51
Anderson, Pamela, 106
animal nakedness, 230–31
anorexia, 175
Anthony, Susan B., 17
Anti-Defamation League (ADL),
    35
appearance, see physical appearance
Applegate, Christina, 123
Apprentice, The, 51, 85–86, 285
    see also Trump, Donald
Arab countries:
    ancient, 137
    lack of women's voice in, 57, 251
    martyrs, 32

Arab countries *(Continued)*
    mothers of suicide bombers, 32, 57,
        144
    world terrorism, 52
    see also Islam
Arafat, Suha, 144–45
Arafat, Yassir, 144
archetypes, foul/vulgar, 197–206
    men, 31, 198, 212
        Crotch-Scratcher (aka the Belly-
            Belcher), 31, 198, 199–201
        Harem Gatherer, 31, 198, 201–3,
            212
        Porn Addict, 31, 49, 198, 204–6,
            298–302
        Selfish Spouse, 31, 198, 203–4
    women, 29–34, 198, 239, 248
        Backstabbing Bitch, 30, 198
        Brainless Bimbo archetype, 30, 198,
            307–8
        Greedy Gold Digger, 30, 86, 101–2,
            198
        Publicity-Seeking Prostitute, 30,
            198
Are You Hot?, 8–9
aristocracy of the beautiful, 153
    see also physical appearance
Around, Miriam, 14
Art of Courtly Love, The (Capellanus),
    30–31
Attila, 74
Augusta National golf course, ban on
    women, 25
Average Joe, 102
awe/reverence for women:
    Boteach's first date, 89–90
    lost, 26–27, 177–80, 183
    students at Beis Yaakov (young
        women's seminary in Jerusalem),
        42–43
Axis of Evil, Musical, 109–19, 166
    see also Aguilera, Christina; Madonna;
        Spears, Britney

Bacall, Lauren, 4
Bachelor, The, 101, 201–2
Backstabbing Bitch archetype, 30,
    198
Baird, Jeffrey B., 185
Barash, Susan Shapiro, 97
Barayev, Movsar, 142
Barton, Clara, 17
baseball players, 236–37
Beatles, 113

beauty:
    aristocracy of the beautiful, 153
    enhancing (versus concealing ugliness),
        129–31
    see also physical appearance
Beis Yaakov (young women's seminary in
    Jerusalem), 42–43
Belly-Belcher archetype (aka Crotch-
    Scratcher), 31, 198, 199–200, 254
Bernard of Ventadour, 46
Berry, Halle, 124
Bettelheim, Bruno (*The Children of the
    Dream*), 236, 264
Bey, Richard, 260–61
Beyonce, 116
Bible:
    Abraham, 45, 58, 253
    Adam and Eve, 53–54, 87–93, 99, 172,
        240
    chronology of God in, 73
    darkness as ninth plague, God
        scourging the Egyptians, 233
    designations for creator, 62, 63
    Esther and Achashveirosh, 202
    Isaiah, 58, 59
    King David, 58
    King of Kings, 62, 264
    Moses, 47, 58, 89, 231, 244
    see also Christianity; Judaism
"bitch," 4, 36, 48, 93, 186
Black Widows (Chechen female
    terrorists), 142–43, 149
Blake, Patricia, 70
Bloomingdale's, French version of;
    strippers in, 127–29
Bolero lingerie ad campaign, 130
Bonzai restaurant, 100
Booker, Cory, 112
Borgata Babes (Atlantic City casino
    resort), 162
Boteach, Shmuley:
    awe on first date, 89–90
    cabdrivers, speaking to, 225–26
    criticized for taking woman's side in
        marriage counseling, 203
    as father, 5, 36, 226, 230, 266, 276
        camping trips, 55–56, 289
        dating edicts, 272–73, 277
        legacy of love for reading/history/
            nature, 289
        protecting daughters ("try and get
            past my Bushmaster rifle"), 271
        spending time with daughters, 272
    fight over girl, 235–36

letters to, 81, 85–86
mother, 36, 41, 80
parents' divorce, 203, 235
rabbi at Oxford, *see* Oxford University
student rabbi in Australia, 89
wife, 89–90, 229–30
women nurterers, 241
yeshiva in Jerusalem, 4, 42–43
Bowlen, Pat, 10–11
boycotts, organizing, 307–9
Brainless Bimbo archetype, 30, 198, 307–8
Bratz dolls, 13–14, 267
Braudy, Leo (*From Chivalry to Terrorism*), 246–47
Braun, Eva, 70, 149
broadcast journalism, 25, 37, 134, 153, 155–57, 164, 261
Brokaw, Tom, 25
Brown, Aaron, 134
Buddhism, 64–65
Burke, Edmund, 246
Bush, George H. W., 32
Bush, George W., 3, 57, 176, 224
Bush, Laura, 3, 27, 178, 219

cabdrivers, speaking to, 225–26
Caesar, 74
Caine, Michael, 181–82
camping trips, 55–56, 289
Capellanus, Andreas (*The Art of Courtly Love*), 30–31
Carmichael, Stokely, 259
Carter, Jimmy, 175
Casablanca (movie), 35
Castiglione, Baldesar (*The Book of the Courtier*), 82–83
Catholicism, 113, 280
cult of Mary, 44–45
Pope John Paul II, 44, 243–44
Cayabyab, Cherry, 100
CBS:
canceling Miss America pageant (2004), 15
cheerleader shots, network rejoin, 134
Super Bowl broadcast with Janet Jackson, 9, 110–11, 123, 284
Victoria's Secret Fashion Show, 125–27
celebrity endorsements, 150
Chamberlain, Wilt, 56
Chanukah, festival of, 58, 234
Chariots of Fire (movie), 244–45

Chastain, Brandi, 134–35
Chechnya, 142–43
checks and balances, women as nature's, 147–50
cheerleading, 133–34
Cher, 25
childbearing, and weight, 193
child pornography, 168
children:
as career sacrifice, 227
neglect, 95
weight-loss efforts in, 175
Chinese (yin-yang), 45
chivalry, 47, 177, 245–47
Christianity:
conquerors' invasion of Muslim-controlled Spain, 137
families observing Sabbath, 245
feminine side of Jesus, 44, 58
medieval scholar, 64
Nietzsche's objection to, 222, 223
Churchill, Clementine, 149
Churchill, Winston, 71–72, 149
circle/line (feminine/masculine energies), 53, 61–76, 234, 252
circle enveloping the line, 68–70
circle men, 74
feminine facilitator, death of the, 74–76
goal orientation versus means orientation, 66–68
God of the Circle, 61, 62–63, 252
God of the Line, 61, 62, 67, 252
men (line), 65–66, 72
natural osmosis from masculine to feminine, 73–74
sexual and sensual, 71–73
universality of masculine and feminine, 64–65
women (circle), 65–66, 72, 234
civil rights movement, 18, 187
see also King, Martin Luther, Jr.
cleaning-woman mentality, 181–89
Clinton, Bill, 156, 175–76, 232
Clinton, Hillary Rodham, 218–21, 295
CNN, 134, 155, 162, 168
Cochran, Steve, 182
college cheerleading, 133–34
Comedy Central's *South Park*, 26
commitment:
diminished, 33–34, 177, 261–62
of fatherhood, 271
maturity and, 261–62
competitiveness of men, 67

Continental Airlines, 19
Corman, Cis, 112
Cosmopolitan magazine, 96–97, 155
courting versus dating, 87, 89, 262
  see also dating
courtly love and the unattainable woman,
  45–46
Cowell, Simon, 51
creation, 53, 54–55
crime, *see* violence/crime
criticism, preempting, 16, 17, 48
Crotch-Scratcher archetype (aka the
  Belly-Belcher), 31, 198, 199–200,
  254
Crystal, Billy, 293
Cyrano de Bergarac, 49

Dante (*The Divine Comedy*), 46
Darcos, Xavier, 130
darkness/light, 233–34
Dateline NBC, 122
dating:
  Boteach's daughters, 272–73, 277
  Boteach's sense of awe on his first date,
    89–90
  changes in dynamic of, 32, 88–89,
    254–55
  courting versus, 87, 89, 262
  suggestion that younger women refrain
    from dating much older men,
    303–4
David, Jacques-Louis (*The Sabine Women*
  painting), 235
Da Vinci Code, 257
defeminization of women, 95–97,
  217–27, 237–38, 251–53, 300
Delaoutre, Paul, 128–29
dELiA's catalog of pornography for
  teens, 168–70, 267
Delta Airlines, 18–19
de Sade, Marquis, 17
Desperate Housewives, 9, 186, 296
diamond dealer analogy, 255–56
Diary of a Flight Attendant, 20
DiCaprio, Leonardo, 167
dignity:
  forgetting importance of, 307
  human (versus nakedness of animals),
    230
  masculine; feminism inspiring, 47–49
  Queen of England, 265
disinterested husband syndrome,
  191–96
Disney Corporation, 10, 11

divorce:
  initiated by women, 34, 207, 302
  pattern of, 253
  rate, 52, 301
  women remarrying or entering into
    other relationships after, 4, 34
Doherty, Shannen, 123
"doing" women, 259
dolls, 13–14, 267
Don Juan syndrome, 298–99
Dowd, Maureen, 25–26
Down with Love (movie), 97
dress codes:
  office, 285–86
  school, 264
dressing for yourself (versus others),
  265–66

Eastern oppression versus Western
  degradation, 7–11
Eastern philosophy, increased awareness
  of, 279
Ebadi, Shirin, 145
Eden, *see* Adam and Eve
education:
  religious training for girls as well as
    boys, 280–81
  single-sex, 275–78
Edwards, Elizabeth, 163
Edwards, John, 162, 163
Edward VIII, 47
Egyptians, plague of darkness, 233
Ehrlich, Kendel, 116
Eisner, Michael, 10, 13
Eleanor of Aquitaine, 45
Electra, Carmen, 124
Elimidate, 188
Elokim (masculine name for God), 63
energy, feminine, 52–55
  versus male energy, 279
  see also circle/line (feminine/masculine
    energies)
English football (soccer) matches,
  135–36
Enron (*Playboy* magazine's "Women of
  Enron"), 7
equality of sexes, misleading notion of,
  26–27, 69, 79–86
Errico, Melissa, 110, 113
ESPN (*Playmakers*), 10–11
Esquire magazine cover, 117–18
Eve, *see* Adam and Eve
exhibitionists, frowning on (versus
  defending), 305–9

Extreme Makeover, 154
Eye Candy, 168, 169

Facenda, Michael, 162
facilitators, death of, 74–76, 226–27
"falling" in love, 274
Farrell, Warren, 66
Fast Girls, 84, 237
father-figure substitutes, May-December
    marriage, 273–74
fatherhood, 96, 269–74
    see also Boteach, Shmuley, as father
fat/ugly women, assault on, 153–70
    see also physical appearance
Fear Factor, 51–52
feminine energy, 52–55
    see also circle/line (feminine/masculine
    energies)
feminine facilitator, death of the,
    74–76
femininity:
    innate dignity and modesty, 236
    innate spirituality, 244
    inspiring masculine dignity, 47–49
    light of, 233–34
    as panacea for solving world's ills, 56
    as subservience and wimpishness,
        222
    superiority of women, 80, 220–21,
        223–24
    trends, 279–80
feminism:
    fall of the dream, 3–14
    fall of Eve, 87–93
    negative aspects of, 24–25, 27, 253,
        254
    positive accomplishments, 23–24, 84
    unequal equality, 79–86
    unmet potential of, 83–84
    women behaving like men, 95–97,
        217–27, 237–38, 251–53, 300
Fey, Tina (*Mean Girls* movie), 84
FHM (For Him Magazine), 124
FIFA Women's World Cup
    Championship, 134
fighting negative images, 35–38
fight over girl, 235–36
fin' amour, 45–46
first date, personal sense of awe on,
    89–90
First Ladies:
    Inaugural Gowns exhibition,
        287–88
    and "lady" ideal, 218–20

Fitzgerald, Ella, 111
football:
    cheerleaders, ~~133, 134~~
    English (soccer matches), 135–36
    marriage and the football-fat equation,
        194
    Monday Night Football, disgusting
        intro to, 9
    NFL protesting ESPN drama
        Playmakers, 10–11
    Super Bowl broadcast with Janet
        Jackson, 9, 110–11, 123, 284
    violence at games, 135–36
For Love or Money, 4, 102
Fountains of Wayne ("Stacey's Mom"),
    169
Fox television network:
    Joe Millionaire, 7–8, 101, 202, 308
    O'Reilly, 283
    Simple Life, The, 105
    Van Susteren (plastic surgery), 37
France:
    Galeries Lafayette, strippers in,
        127–29
    public school battle against Muslim
        girls who want to wear head
        scarves, 130–31
Fraser, Antonia, 246
freedom:
    perception of, versus reality, 5–6,
        162
    sex and, 97, 177
Freud, Sigmund, 99
friendships, adolescent, 288–89

Galeries Lafayette, 127–29
Gallagher, Justine, 175
Gandhi, 74, 309
gay men:
    desire for marriage, 242
    Queer Eye for the Straight Guy, 239–42,
        243
    as world's last nurturers, 239–42
gay women:
    past heterosexual relationships, 210
    platonic lesbian syndrome, 213–16
    women becoming lesbians to get away
        from men, 207–12
gentlemen, 29, 49, 81, 188
Gibson, Mel, 35
girlhood/young girls:
    aggressiveness, versus boys, 237
    dating, age for, 272–73, 277
    innate modesty of, 236

girlhood/young girls (Continued)
   lingerie, 129–30, 166–67
   loss of reverence for women and,
      165–70
   religious training for, 280–81
   shopping mall culture and, 287–91
   single-sex education, 275–78
   see also adolescence
Girls Gone Wild videos, 5, 143, 241, 268,
   284, 306–7
Girl with the Pearl Earring, The (movie),
   124
God:
   chronology of, 73
   of the Circle (creation), 61, 62–63, 66,
      252
   of the Line (history/justice), 61, 62,
      67, 252
   see also Bible
Godhead metaphor, 61, 62
Goebbels, Joseph, 149
Goebbels, Magda, 149
gold diggers, female, 30, 86, 101–2,
   198
golden age for women, 48, 83
Golden Age of Hollywood, memorable
   ladies of the silver screen, 4
Gone With the Wind, 35
Gorbachev, Mikhail, 221
Graf, Steffi, 272
Gray, John (Men Are from Mars, Women
   Are from Venus), 210
Greedy Gold Digger archetype, 30, 86,
   101–2, 198
Green River killer, 184–87, 188
groupies, rock stars, 56–57

Hamas, 144
Hanks, Tom, 293
Hannibal, 74
Harem Gatherer archetype, 31, 198,
   201–3, 212
Harvard, 288
Hassan, Nasra, 144
Hawking, Stephen, 231–32
healers, women as, 229–34
healing force, losing, 235–38
Hefner, Hugh, 122, 123, 299
   see also Playboy
Hegel, G.W.F., 53
Helen of Troy, 246
Hepburn, Katharine, 4
He's Just Not That into You, 33
Hewlett, Sylvia Ann (Creating a Life),
   208

Hillel, 38
Hilton, Paris:
   Comedy Central's South Park, 26
   dearth of brains, 114, 164
   Fox TV's The Simple Life, 105, 106,
      107
   parents, 271–72
   pop cultural image/icon, 4, 47, 106
Hindu, 45
Hite, Shere, 97
Hitler, 67, 70, 149, 223
   see also Nazi Germany
Hoffman, Dustin (and Mrs. Robinson in
   The Graduate), 170
Hollywood's Golden Age, memorable
   ladies of the silver screen, 4
Hunter, Stephen, 209
husbands:
   cleaning-woman mentality, 181–89
   disinterested husband syndrome,
      191–96
   expecting sex on demand, 179–80
   football-fat equation, 194
   gifts, 204
   lost awe/reverence for wives, 177–80,
      183
   see also marriage
Hussein, Saddam, 67, 74, 118

ideology, 24, 48
independence in marriage, 301
infidelity, 96–97, 216, 295
innocence, a return to, 254–56
intellectual pursuits, twenty-first
   century lady, and, 263–68
Internet:
   dating firm, Alaska voyage, 158–59
   pornography, 11–12, 26, 49, 92–93,
      184, 205, 299
Iran earthquake, 140
Iraq, United States' war against (versus
   war against Afghani Taliban), 139
Ireland, Giant's Causeway, 247–48
Isaiah, 58, 59
Islam, 137–45
   Chechnya, 142
   cry of humiliation as wounded male
      pride, 140–41
   debasing of, 139
   female influence in, 280
   female suicide bombers, 141–45
   French public schools, battle against
      Muslim girls who want to wear
      head scarves, 130–31
   Miss Afghanistan, 6–7

Nigerian court, 139
terrorist attack in Russian city of
    Beslan, 143
Israel:
    Beis Yaakov (young women's seminary
        in Jerusalem), 42–43
    kibbutz system, 236
    modern, 58
    rejected offer of help to Iran, 140
    Western Wall, 247
    yeshivas in Jerusalem, 4, 42–43
Istanbul, Topkapi Palace, 202
Italy, 243

Jackson, Janet, 9, 110–11, 123, 284
Jackson, Michael, 114
Japan, Princess Sayako of, 75–76
Jaradat, Hanadi Tayseer, 141–42
Jennie Craig, 164
Jewish faith, see Judaism
job discrimination, 23–24
    see also workplace
Joe Millionaire, 4, 7–8, 101, 202, 308
Johansson, Scarlett, 124
Johnson, Lady Bird, 220
Johnson, Magic, 56
Jolie, Angelina, 273
Jones, Norah, 110
Jones, Paula, 176
Jones, Starr, 164
Judaism:
    ancient world and, 57, 222–24
    anti-Semitism in Passion of the Christ,
        35
    creation, 53
    everything belonging to God, 301
    feminine/masculine balance, 57
    festival of Chanukah, 58, 234
    holiest site (Western Wall), 247
    Jewish American Princess, 265
    orthodox education:
        religious training priority for boys
            not girls, 280
        sexes strictly segregated, 42
    reality TV shows (hypothetical
        examples showing absurdity of),
        7–8, 107
    Sabbath observance, 244–45
    sages/scholars of, 38, 74, 253
    and Teutonic German knights,
        222–24
    women and, 4, 44, 45, 109, 264–65,
        290–91
    see also Israel
Judaism for Everyone, 280

Kabbalah, 57, 61, 62, 63, 64, 68, 74, 114,
    118
Kant, Emmanuel, 99
Kelly, Grace (Princess Grace of
    Monaco), 4, 266
Kennedy, Jackie, 219, 220
Kennedy, John F., 176, 299
Kennedy, Rose, 229–30
Kerry, John F., 57, 162, 163, 224
Kerry, Teresa Heinz, 27, 163, 219–20
kibbutz system, 236
"kinder, gentler" nation/world, 32,
    253–54
King, Coretta Scott, 18
King, Martin Luther, Jr., 37, 74, 306,
    309
Kirkwood, Tim (The Flight Attendant Job
    Finder and Career Guide), 20
Kissinger, Henry, 65
Kissing Jessica Stein (movie), 208–9
Koran, Sura 55 (72 wide-eyed virgins for
    martyrs), 143
Kosher Adultery: Seduce and Sin with Your
    Spouse, 159, 183, 191
Kosher Sex, 129, 183

lady, ideal of the:
    circular spirit, embodiment of, 252–53
    diminished influence of, 55
    feminism, and loss of, 26–27, 49, 223,
        307
    First Ladies and, 218–20
    inspiring men to be gentlemen, 29–38,
        49, 178
    raising young girls as, 263–64
    of the twenty-first century (full brain
        versus well-poised cranium),
        263–68
La Ferla, Ruth, 13–14
La Meute, 128
Lebensborn programs (Nazi Germany),
    149
Lee, Tommy, 106
Left Behind series, 58
Lennox, Tom, 160
lesbians:
    past heterosexual relationships, 210
    platonic, 213–16
    women becoming, to get away from
        men, 207–12
Lewinsky, Monica, 176, 218
Liddell, Eric, 244–45
light/darkness, 233–34
Lil' Kim, 124
Lincoln, Abraham, 37

320   Index

line, *see* circle/line (feminine/masculine energies)
lingerie:
Bolero lingerie ad campaign, 130
dELiA's catalog of pornography for teens, 168–70, 267
high school, 129–30
little girls, 166–67
thongs, 15, 129, 166–67, 169
Victoria's Secret, 13, 168, 169, 186, 241
live-in boyfriends that won't commit to marriage, 33–34
Lopez, Jennifer, 25
Lost in Translation (movie), 124
love:
courtly (and the unattainable woman), 45–46
"falling" in, 274
making, *see* sex/sexuality
only by equals, 299
Love, Courtney, 266
Loveline, 174
Luhrmann, Baz, 155
Luria, Isaac (the Ari), 74, 253
Lurie, Jeff, 11

Mackriss, Andrea, 281
Madison, James, 147
Madonna, 109–19
books by:
for children, based on Kabbalah, 118
Sex, 112
children, 118, 119
chutzpa, 118
copycats, 111
criticizing television, 118–19
Kabbalah, 112–13, 118
kissing Britney, 113, 124
movie *Swept Away*, 113
"Musical Axis of Evil," 109, 110–11, 166
Newsweek about, 114
nudity, 123
popularity of, 170
simulating masturbation, 25
vulgarity of, 25, 110–11, 118–19
Malcolm X (movie), 38
males, *see* men
Mandela, Nelson, 74
Mansfield, Harvey, 246–47
Maples, Marla, 85
Marie Antoinette, 246

marriage:
ancient cultures, 47
cohabitation versus, 261–62
commitment of, 261–62
football-fat equation, 194
gay men wanting, 242
housework and, 179
husbands have lost awe and reverence for their wives, 177–80
independence versus "belonging" to one another, 301
May-December, 273–74
men's shallow criteria for selecting spouse, 76
Middle Ages, 23
new vision of, 293–302
sex and:
not "sex on tap" or legalized prostitution, 293–302
sex on demand, 179–80
see also sex/sexuality
turning your wife into the cleaner, 181–89
weight and, 162–65, 175, 191–96
Western importance of, 65
wives holding husbands to high standards, 293–94, 300
women delaying, 34
see also husbands
martyrs, 143
see also suicide bombers
Mary, cult of, 44–45
masculine characteristics, *see* men
masculine energy, *see* circle/line (feminine/masculine energies)
masculinization of women, 80, 95–97, 217–27, 237–38, 251–53, 300
Matsumoto, Yuko, 75
Mattel (Flava dolls), 14
McCay, Bruce, 156
McEnroe, Patrick, 110
men:
aggression/violence, 67, 96, 238
archetypes, modern, 31, 198, 212
Crotch-Scratcher (aka the Belly-Belcher), 31, 198, 199–201
Harem Gatherer, 31, 198, 201–3, 212
Porn Addict, 31, 198, 204–6
Selfish Spouse, 31, 198, 203–4
bringing passion/zeal to women, 72
creativity only realized through feminine expansion, 54
crisis in manhood, 171–76

sensual versus the sexual, 173–76
womankind versus individuals, 171
disappointing women, 34
infidelity, 48
liberation of (feminine liberation as),
259
not vulnerable (when portrayed as
stupid), 108
philosophy about women, changing, 84
protecting daughters from other men,
271, 272
see also fatherhood; gentlemen;
husbands
Messiah, 58–59, 74
Miami Beach, 267–68, 305
Middle Ages, 23, 46
Miller Lite commercial ("Catfight"), 100
Million Mom March, 57, 235
Milosevic, Slobodan, 74
misogyny:
analogy about old segregated South, 18
growing, 4
past mistreatment of women versus
current, 48
in rap songs, 259–60
wake-up call about, 15–27
see also prostitute, woman as
Miss Afghanistan, 6–7
Miss America pageant, 15, 284
Mona Lisa Smile (movie), 306
Monroe, Marilyn, 154
Montesquieu (The Spirit of the Laws),
147–48
Montreynaud, Florence, 128
Moore, Demi, 124
Moore, Michael, 164
morality:
defining characteristics of, 6, 99
women's traditional dominance, 96
Morehouse College, 17–18
moron-man as TV stereotype, 107–8
Moscow theater, 142
Moss, Kate, 165
motherhood:
death of maternal instinct, 232
demands of, 27, 96
as honorable profession, 27
pride in, 84
professional women, 208
single mothers, 36, 80
"Mother" Nature, 63, 72, 234, 290
mothers of suicide bombers, 32, 57, 144
MTV, 106, 114, 127, 284
Mya, 124

mysterious society, 279–81
mystery of a woman, 255

NAACP:
fighting negative images, 35
organizing boycotts, 308
Naked Gun, The (movie), 108
naked women, see nudity/partial nudity
Napoleon and Josephine ("don't bathe"),
173
National Airlines, 19
National Museum of American History,
Washington, D.C., 287
Nazi Germany, 8, 148–49, 223
see also Hitler
NBA brawl (2004) Detroit Pistons and
Indiana Pacers, 56, 136
NBC, 25, 102, 122
Nemitz, Cheresa, 101
Newell, Waller (What Is a Man?), 83
Newlyweds, 106, 114
Newman, Paul, 293
news, broadcast, 25, 37, 134, 153,
155–57, 164, 261
Nicholas of Cusa, 64
Nicholson, Jack (in As Good As It Gets),
178
Nietzsche, 222, 223
Nineteenth Amendment (women's
suffrage), 17, 23
Nixon, Richard, 175
Noel, Peter, 157
Noonan, Peggy, 32
Norville, Deborah, 37
Norway, 150
nudity/partial nudity:
becoming famous by becoming naked,
121–32
career development, 124–25, 271–72
celebrity nude photo spread, 123–24
Girls Gone Wild videos and other
standard fare, 121–22
Victoria's Secret Fashion Show on
CBS, 125–27
Caine on difference in genders, 181–82
embargo against, 305–9
human dignity, versus nakedness of
animals, 230
men's seeing flaws in wives, 297
Miami Beach, 15–16, 306
shock factor, 123
teenage, 305
what's wrong with doing it for money,
182

nudity/partial nudity (Continued)
    why is taking off your clothes for
        money an act of liberation, 17–22
    "Women of Enron," 7

Odd Girl Out, 84, 237
office dress codes, 285–86
Ofman, Ursula, 205
oppression, Eastern (versus Western
    degradation), 7–11
Oprah Winfrey Show, 306–7
O'Reilly, Bill, 283
Osbourne, Sharon, 156
Ottoman harem, 202
overweight women, 18, 162–65, 175,
    191–96
    see also physical appearance
OxBow Incident, The (movie), 35
Oxford University, 22, 90–91, 112,
    229–32, 245, 275

panty-raiders, 91
Paradise Hotel, 102
parochial schools, 238
Passion of the Christ, The (movie), 35
passivity, man rescuing woman from, 73
pedestal (glorification of women):
    broadening, 251–56
    critics of, 43–44, 81, 84–85
    Judaism, and, 47–49
    men looking up to women without
        patronizing them, 22–26
physical appearance, 153–70
    Abercrombie & Fitch not hiring "ugly
        people," 159–61
    airline flight attendants, 18–20
    aristocracy of the beautiful, 153
    beauty, enhancing (versus concealing
        ugliness), 129–31
    disenfranchisement of non-bombshell,
        157–59
    loss of reverence for women causing
        loss of girlhood, 165–70
    adolescence, accelerated, 166–67
    dELiA's catalog of pornography for
        teens, 168–70
    overweight women, 18, 162–65, 175,
        191–96
    erotic life of marriage, thinness
        decimating, 165
    hatred for fat women, 162–65
    husbands to blame for, 191–96
    single versus married women (fridge
        joke), 175

plastic surgery, 37–38, 261
professional marketplace, 20,
    153–54
    Borgata casino (firing women for
        gaining weight), 162
    broadcast journalism, 25, 37, 134,
        153, 155–57, 164, 261
    Wall Street, beautiful female
        assistants, 20
    thinness synonymous with beauty,
        165
    women's freedom, and being judged
        by, 6
Pinsky, Drew, 167
plastic surgery, 37–38, 261
Playboy, 17, 122, 167, 294
    see also Hefner, Hugh
Pope John Paul II, 44, 243–44
Popenoe, David (Debunking the Divorce
    Myths), 207
pornography:
    addiction to, 31, 49, 298–302
    archetype of Porn Addict, 31, 198,
        204–6
    boring nature of, 298
    career development, 124–25
    child, 12
    defense of, based on choice, 182
    dollar amount spent on, 6, 80
    as exception in Boteach's advice for
        spicing up sex life, 129
    focus on male climax, 184
    Internet, 11–12, 49, 92–93, 205, 299
    negative impact on relationships, 205,
        295, 296, 297–98
    Wolf's "The Porn Myth," 124
    women tolerating, 92, 294–98
Portman, Natalie, 167
power as aphrodisiac, 65
prenuptial agreements, 84
Princess Grace of Monaco, 4, 266
Princess Sayako of Japan, 75–76
Private Adam, The, 226
professional athletes and rock stars, 56
professional marketplace, see workplace
prostitute, woman as:
    archetype (Publicity-Seeking
        Prostitute), 30, 198
    cultural portrayal of, 9, 26, 75, 128
prostitution:
    defense of, as "honest job," 12–13
    marriage as legalized, 293–302
Publicity-Seeking Prostitute archetype,
    30, 198

Qaddafi, Muammar, 118
Queen Bees and Wannabes,, 84, 237
Queen of England, 265
Queer Eye for the Straight Guy, 239–42, 243

Raider games, violence at, 136
rape, 6
Raubel, Geli, 149
Reagan, Ronald, 71
Real Cancun, The (movie/documentary), 122
Reynolds, Joey, 109–10
Rhodes Scholars, 112, 232
Rice, Condoleezza, 157, 158, 266
Ridgway, Gary L. (Green River killings), 184–87, 188
Riefenstahl, Leni, 148–49
riot, Detroit Pistons and Indiana Pacers (November 2004), 56, 136
Ritchie, Nicole, 105, 106, 107, 114
Roberts, Julia (*Mona Lisa Smile*), 306
Roosevelt, Eleanor, 71, 149, 220–21
Roosevelt, Franklin, 71, 149
Roosevelt, Theodore, 70
Rosenthal, Ellen, 14
Rousseau, Jean-Jacques, 5, 162, 290
Rubens, 174
Rubenstein, Richard (*Aristotle's Children*), 137–38
Rules, The, 257, 260
Russert, Tim, 182
Russian troops, 142–43

Sabbath, 54, 244–45
Saudi Arabia, 139, 141
Savage, Anthony, 185
Sayako, Princess (of Japan), 75–76
Scandinavia, 150
scent of a woman, 173
Schellenberg, Gary, 136
science of gender neutralization, 210
Seattle restaurant using women as plates, 100–3
secular feminists, 219
selfishness, belief in, 227
Selfish Spouse archetype, 31, 198, 203–4
Selznick, David O., 35
Senegal, 38, 172
sensuality:
    Clinton, 175–76
    pleasure from five senses, 111–13
    sense of smell, 173–74
    sense of touch, 174
    sex and, 71–73

September 11, effect of, 137–38, 139
Serrano, Antonio, 160
Sex and the City, 33, 107, 209–10, 213–14, 217, 218, 284
sex/sexuality:
    adolescents, 6, 257–58, 269–70
    bases (first/second/third base), old/new definitions, 260
    canned sex, 211
    capriciousness of both genders, 97
    casual sex moratorium, 257–62
    circle/line metaphor, 68–69, 72–73
    cleaning-woman mentality in men, 182, 183
    climax:
        ancient biblical proscription on woman first, 183
        percentages in marital sex, 183
        in pornography, 184
        portrayal of women as walking male orgasm, 99–103
    euphemisms:
        doing women, 259
        hooking up, 260
    freedom and, 97, 177
    husbands' complaints about wives not initiating, 165
    innate attraction, and single-sex education, 277
    as internal (versus external) undertaking, for women, 26
    intimacy of talking during sex, 211
    marriage as "sex on tap," 293–302
    sensuality and, 71–73
    "sex on demand," 179
    spicing up, 129–30
    weight and, 165, 191–93
    women using men for sex, 212
sexual harassment, 6, 283–86
Sheridan, Nicolette, 9
shopping mall culture, 287–91
Showtime, 115
Simonetti, Ellen (*Diary of a Flight Attendant*), 18–19, 20
Simpson, Jessica, 106, 114
single motherhood, 36, 80
single-sex education, 275–78
single women in America (statistics), 208
slavery:
    immorality of, 99
    slave mentality until great black leaders came along, 37
SNCC (Student Nonviolent Coordinating Committee), 259

Solomon, King ("Ode to a Woman of
    Valor"), 4
South, old segregated, 18, 187
South Park, 26
Soviet Union, 70
Spanish tennis tournament, 189
Spears, Britney, 109–19
    Axis of Evil, Musical, 109, 110, 111,
        166
    Boteach meeting, 114
    crude behavior, 25, 114–17, 178, 285
    cultural icon, 4, 116, 164, 166, 200
    family, 116, 271–72
    ignorance, 114
    In the Zone album, 115
    kissing Madonna, 113, 124
    Madonna's influence on, 114, 118
    narcissism, 116
    Newsweek interview, 116
    nudity/partial nudity, 115, 117–18,
        123, 271–72
    personal life, 115–16
    simulating masturbation on prime
        time television concerts, 25,
        114–15, 285
Speer, Albert (*Inside the Third Reich*), 70
Spellman College, 18
Spielberg, Steven, 293
sports, 133–36
    see also football
Sports Illustrated Swimsuit Edition, 134
spouse selection criteria, 76
    see also marriage
spring break debauchery, 267–68
Sri Lanka, 141, 150
Stalin, Joseph, 70
Starbucks coffee chain in Riyadh, 141
Stefani, Gwen, 124
Stein, Jessica, 212
Stephanopoulos, George, 156
stereotypes, *see* archetypes, foul/vulgar
Stiles, Julia, 167
Streisand, Barbra, 111–12, 124
suffrage, women's, 17, 23
suggestions:
    #1 women not sleeping with unworthy
        men, 262
    #2 modest dress codes in schools,
        264
    #3 renewing father-daughter covenant,
        274
    #4 single-sex education, 278
    #5 religious training for daughters,

#6 banning sexual innuendo from the
        office, installing modest dress
        codes, 286
    #7 weaning girls/women from
        materialistic culture of shopping,
        fashion, and beauty, 291
    #8 restoring sacredness of marriage,
        294
    #9 wives not tolerating pornography,
        302
    #10 younger women not dating older
        men, 304
    #11 boycotting organizations, 309
suicide:
    gender and, 80
    teenagers, 290
suicide bombers:
    female, 141–45
    mothers of, 32, 57
Summers, Larry, 288
Super Bowl broadcast with Janet Jackson,
    9, 110–11, 123, 284
supermodels, sad, 165
Swan, The, 308

Tagliabue, Paul, 10
Tantric masters, 45
teachers/nurturers, 231–32
teenagers, *see* adolescence
television:
    ABC, 8–9, 101, 115, 118, 175, 201–2
    CBS, 15, 125–27, 134
        see also Super Bowl broadcast with
            Janet Jackson
    cheerleader shots, network rejoin,
        134
    CNN, 134, 155, 162, 168
    grounded couples *Ozzie and Harriet*
        and *Cosby Show*, 208
    hypothetical Jewish examples showing
        absurdity of reality shows, 7–8,
        107
    Madonna criticizing, 118–19
    Miss America pageant (2004), 15
    moronic men getting shows, 106–8
    MTV, 106, 114, 127, 284
    NBC, 25, 102, 122
    news, 25, 37, 134, 153, 155–57, 164,
        261
    protest rallies against, 308
    reality shows, hypothetical examples
        showing absurdity of, 7–8, 107
    Super Bowl broadcast with Janet
        Jackson, 9, 110–11, 123, 284